Python for Excel Users

Introduction: Elevate Your Analytics with Python

In today's data-driven world, the ability to efficiently analyze and interpret information is more crucial than ever, especially in the business sector. *Python for Excel Users: A Beginner's Guide* is tailored for business students and professionals who are proficient in Microsoft Excel but are ready to embark on their Python journey. As a powerful and versatile programming language, Python has become indispensable in data analysis. This book bridges the gap between Excel and Python by providing parallel exercises that demonstrate how Python can amplify business analytics tasks with unmatched efficiency and flexibility.

Through its side-by-side comparisons, interactive Python exercises, and a "teachable moment" approach, this guide offers a unique and intuitive learning experience. By translating familiar Excel tasks into Python's dynamic and versatile ecosystem, you'll not only enhance your data analysis skills but also gain confidence in programming.

Why Python?

Did you know that Python powers cutting-edge technologies like ChatGPT? Indeed, Python forms the foundation of many machine learning algorithms, including large language models (LLMs). Python is more than a programming language; it's a tool for understanding and shaping the digital world. Despite its advanced capabilities, Python's simple, readable syntax makes it accessible to everyone – from professional software developers to citizen developers like you. Dubbed the "language of the people", Python is revolutionizing how we approach problem-solving and automation in the modern world.

Becoming Tomorrow's Tech-Savvy Leaders

The leaders of tomorrow are not just visionaries – they are innovators who harness the power of technology to drive change and inspire others. This book guides you through different scenarios to help you understand the connections between business questions and analytics steps we are taking.

As business students embracing Python, you're positioning yourselves as future-ready leaders equipped to navigate and excel in the complexities of modern business.

Welcome to a journey that will elevate your analytics, expand your technological fluency, and transform you into a tech-savvy leader of the future.

Python for Excel Users

A Beginner's Guide

Chi-Chun Chou and David Wang

CRC Press is an imprint of the
Taylor & Francis Group, an **informa** business

A CHAPMAN & HALL BOOK

Designed cover image: Shutterstock ID: 2217716843

First edition published 2026
by CRC Press
4 Park Square, Milton Park, Abingdon, Oxon, OX14 4RN

and by CRC Press
2385 NW Executive Center Drive, Suite 320, Boca Raton FL 33431

CRC Press is an imprint of Informa UK Limited

British Library Cataloguing-in-Publication Data
A catalogue record for this book is available from the British Library

ISBN: 9781032936765 (hbk)
ISBN: 9781032936758 (pbk)
ISBN: 9781003567103 (ebk)

DOI: 10.1201/9781003567103

Typeset in Minion
by Newgen Publishing UK

Access the Support Material: www.routledge.com/9781032936758

Contents

Introduction

IN TODAY'S DATA-DRIVEN WORLD, the ability to quickly and effectively analyze information is crucial, particularly in the business sector. *Python for Excel Users: A Beginner's Guide* is specifically designed for business students and practitioners who are well-acquainted with Microsoft Excel but are taking their first steps in Python, a powerful and versatile programming language that has become indispensable in data analysis. It serves as a bridge for business students and professionals looking to transition from Excel to Python through parallel exercises in both platforms. You will learn how Python can elevate business analytics tasks with efficiency and power. The book's side-by-side comparison, interactive Python environment, and "teachable moment" approach offer a unique and intuitive learning experience. By transforming familiar Excel-based tasks into Python's versatile domain, this methodology enhances your data analysis skills and builds your confidence in programming with ease.

• Why Python?
Before we outline some reasons, do you know ChatGPT is built on Python? Yes, Python is the foundation of most machine learning algorithms, including the state-of-the-art large language models (LLMs).

DOI: 10.1201/9781003567103-1

Nevertheless, its simple and readable syntax has made it accessible to everyone, from professional software developers to citizen developers like yourselves. It is also known as "the language of citizen developers" or the "language of the people" in the world of coding. By using Python alongside Excel examples, you will quickly see the parallels and power of programming in solving real-world problems. Your existing skills in data manipulation and analysis will only be magnified, opening doors to new possibilities. Below are some advantages for business-major students to learn Python:

1. **Integrating Python with Business Acumen**: As business students, you possess a unique understanding of market trends, consumer behavior, and organizational dynamics. Learning Python adds a remarkable tool to your toolkit, allowing you to apply computational techniques to these business concepts. From automating repetitive tasks to predicting future trends using machine learning, Python equips you with the skills to make data-driven decisions that can propel your career and your organization to new heights.

2. **From Excel to Python: A Seamless Transition**: Many of you have known Excel, a powerful tool in the world of business analytics. Now, imagine taking those skills and amplifying them with the power of programming. Python's Pandas library, coupled with your Excel knowledge, will allow you to manipulate, analyze, and visualize data on a whole new level. This synergy between Excel and Python Pandas is your gateway to becoming not just proficient in data analysis but truly exceptional.

3. **The Age of Automation and the Role of Python**: In today's fast-paced business environment, efficiency is key. Automation is no longer a futuristic concept but a daily necessity. By learning Python, you are stepping into a world where mundane tasks are automated, complex data is deciphered with ease, and business strategies are optimized with precision. Python's versatility and compatibility with various technologies such as machine learning and natural language processing (NLP) place you at the forefront of modern business innovation.

4. **Empowering Business Leaders of Tomorrow**: The leaders of tomorrow are not just visionaries; they are innovators who harness the power of technology to shape the future. Python is not merely a

programming language. It is a way to understand and interact with the digital world. As business students embracing Python, you are positioning yourselves as tech-savvy leaders ready to drive change, innovate, and inspire others in the complex landscape of modern business.

I.1 FEATURES OF THE BOOK

1. Parallel Exercises in Excel and Python

The most unique feature of this book is its side-by-side approach. Each concept introduced in Python is paired with a corresponding task in Excel. This comparative method not only highlights the similarities and differences between the two platforms but also reinforces your understanding by applying the same analytical concepts in two different environments.

This book comprises nine chapters, each filled with a variety of business-related exercises ranging from simple to complex, all centered around a "throughout-book" case study: the Campus Bookstore. These exercises are structured in a question-and-answer format to progressively enhance your confidence in using Python for data analysis based on the prior Excel experience. This approach is designed to facilitate a seamless transition from Excel to Python, ensuring you gain practical skills applicable to business analytics tasks.

Furthermore, the exercises in this book are carefully selected to reflect real-world business scenarios. Whether it's sales data research, financial analysis, or performance evaluation, you'll learn how to apply Python to solve practical business problems. These context-based exercises ensure that the skills you acquire are not only theoretical but immediately applicable in a professional setting.

2. Beyond Just a Readable Book: Executable Python Notebook

In the Introduction Chapter, you'll learn how to set up your Python environment using Jupyter, a popular browser-based tool for writing and sharing Python code, known for its ease of use and powerful features. The Jupyter Notebook stands out as an ideal platform for combining Python code, explanatory text, and visuals all within one document. This integration facilitates an interactive learning experience that not only demonstrates how the code works but also allows you to execute the code snippets in real time as you progress through the chapter exercises. By providing immediate feedback and results, Jupyter Notebook simplifies the process of understanding the purpose and application of Python code, experimenting with different approaches, and evaluating the effects of changes inter-actively. This hands-on approach is invaluable for learners as it bridges the gap between theoretical knowledge and practical application, making the learning process more engaging and experiential.

3. Instruct Python using the "Teachable Moment" Approach

Unlike most Python books that follow a traditional, sequential structure – starting with variable declaration, moving through programming flows, and onto data types – our approach introduces concepts as they become necessary within the context of chapter exercises. This **"teachable moment"** strategy gently guides you into the world of Python programming by intro-ducing or clarifying important concepts as they naturally arise during the problem-solving process. For instance, if a business problem is best solved by looping through an iterable data object (e.g., a list, a dictionary, or a Series, etc.), we seize the opportunity to explain what an *"iterable"* is in Python and discuss the types of iterables commonly used. Similarly, if you encounter a for-loop for the first time, we provide a **"Complementary Note"** to detail the fundamentals of looping, an essential concept for auto-mating repetitive tasks. Moreover, for an overview of specific features like Python's comment style, a **"Side Note"** is included for quick reference. Learning Python through teachable moments not only makes the material more relevant and clearer to the learner but also enhances the intuitiveness and memorability of the learning experience.

4. Transitioning from Excel to Python with Pandas

One of the primary features of this book is to introduce Pandas, a powerful library in Python for data analysis. You'll learn how to import an Excel file into a Jupyter Notebook using Pandas, an essential skill for transitioning from Excel-based data analysis to Python.

The subsequent chapters will systematically explore a range of Pandas functions, paralleling familiar tasks from Excel. We'll begin by diving into data exploration and cleaning with Pandas in Chapter 1. Moving for-ward, Chapter 2 will teach you how to add computational columns, while Chapter 3 will delve into data aggregation using Pandas' groupby and pivot tables. Chapter 4 will introduce you to creating visualizations with Pandas' plotting capabilities and the matplotlib library. Special emphasis is placed on np.where in Chapter 5, a function that facilitates column-wise conditional computations akin to Excel's conditional logic. As we progress to more advanced topics, Chapter 6 covers Boolean indexing and data classification. Chapters 7 and 8 will guide you through text and date processing, and finally, Chapter 9 will showcase how to merge and join databases. These topics are designed to deepen your understanding of Pandas' robust capabilities for sophisticated data analysis, demonstrating its advantages over Excel.

5. Embracing Python's Versatility

As of 2025, there are over 655,000 Python libraries and packages available on PyPI (Python Package Index). Pandas is just one of them. This impressive number represents a vast and diverse set of tools covering nearly every programming need imaginable, from data science and machine learning to application development and automation.

As you progress through the book, you'll come to appreciate Python's versatility. Unlike Excel, which has limitations in handling large datasets and complex calculations, Python, with its robust libraries like Pandas, Matplotlib, NumPy, and many others, offers scalability and advanced analytical capabilities. You'll learn how to harness these tools to perform more advanced operations and pave the way for data manipulation and analysis.

6. A Journey into Data Science

This book is your companion on a journey to enhancing your data analytics skills. With clear explanations, real-world examples, and practical exercises, it's designed to make your transition from Excel to Python as seamless and enjoyable as possible. Whether you're a business professional looking to upgrade your analytical skills or a student preparing for a career in a data-centric world, "Python for Excel Users: A Beginner's Guide" is the perfect starting point. It is also a stepping stone into the broader world of data science. As you become comfortable with Python, a realm of possibilities opens up. You'll be well-positioned to explore more advanced topics in Python, delve into machine learning, or even transition into a career in data science.

Now, join us in exploring the exciting intersection of business analytics and Python programming, and take your first steps into the future of data analysis.

1.2 THE "THROUGHOUT-BOOK" CASE: CAMPUS BOOKSTORE

Our goal is to help the Campus Bookstore to understand its business operations and make several business decisions. The bookstore utilizes an Excel worksheet named "Invoice" within the "Bookstore-Ch0x.xlsx" workbook series (where x denotes the chapter number) to organize its raw transaction data. This dataset captures sales transactions across the bookstore's four locations from January 1, 2023, to March 31, 2023. It details 1,000 transactions, each uniquely identified by an Invoice Number, and includes a variety of products identified by Item Numbers and names, such as Jackets, Pens, and Backpacks. The dataset provides comprehensive transactional details, including quantities sold, list prices, costs, and discounts applied, which shed light on the bookstore's pricing strategies and inventory management practices. Additionally, sales data are linked to specific employees and store locations, enabling analyses of employee performance and regional sales trends. This framework sets the stage for a detailed examination of the bookstore's transactional dynamics and operational specifics ahead of more advanced data analytics efforts.

1.3 THE FILE FOLDERS

Learning Python and Excel effectively requires hands-on practice. To supplement the text, this book includes five folders of files. The "Integrated Texts" folder houses the main content for both Excel and Python, featuring demonstrations and explanations for all chapters. The "Excel Files" folder contains the Excel files for each chapter. Excel solutions can be found in the "Excel Solutions" folder. For Python learners, the "ipynb" folder provides Jupyter Notebook files (ipynb stands for Interactive PYthon NoteBook) for all chapter exercises, complete with detailed explanations, including those for the introduction chapter. The "HTML" folder includes HTML versions of all ipynb files, making it convenient for you to view Python content directly in web browsers. Finally, the "Exercises" folder includes chapter-end exercises for both Python and Excel, featuring new datasets in each subfolder. These exercises are designed for users seeking additional practice and for instructors assessing   student performance.

I.4 EXCEL DEMONSTRATION

The primary goal of the Excel demonstration is to help readers leverage their existing Excel experience to familiarize data analytics tasks required in each exercise, thereby facilitating a smoother transition to the Python demonstrations. Detailed instructions and screenshots will guide you through using specific Excel functions to complete exercises in each chapter. The Excel functions discussed are commonly available across various versions, including Windows Excel, Mac Excel, and Office 365, unless a particular version is specified. It's important to note that the Excel interface may look slightly different from the provided screenshots, particularly for Office 365 users. While alternative screenshots for different versions of Excel are not provided, you can generally find the required functionalities close to the areas shown in the screenshots. This approach ensures all readers, regardless of their Excel version, can navigate the tools necessary for the exercises effectively.

Alongside the exercise files in the "Bookstore-Ch0x.xlsx" series, we also provide solution files titled "Bookstore-Ch0x-Completed.xlsx" for your reference. It is highly recommended that you attempt to complete the exercises using the steps outlined in each chapter before consulting the solution files.

I.5 PYTHON DEMONSTRATION

Transitioning from Excel to Python is a transformative journey, and this book is designed to guide you through it with comprehensive explanations and step-by-step tutorials using Jupyter Notebook. Unlike Excel, Jupyter Notebook is entirely free and open-source, released under the BSD License which is notably permissive. This license permits individuals, educational institutions, and commercial entities to freely use, modify, and distribute Jupyter without any licensing fees.

A Jupyter Notebook consists of cells that can contain executable code, text (formatted using Markdown), equations, visualizations, and multimedia elements. The code you write in Jupyter Notebook is highly portable, allowing you to run it across various platforms such as Windows, macOS, and Linux. For installation instructions and how to start using Jupyter Notebook, please consult the "Preparatory.html" file in the "HTML" folder, which details downloading and launching Jupyter Notebook via the Anaconda Navigator.

For the chapter exercises, all Python demonstrations are provided in both Jupyter's ipynb format and HTML format. You can engage with the Python code by opening the "Bookstore-Ch0x.ipynb" files in the "ipynb" folder or view the rendered outputs directly by accessing the "Bookstore-Ch0x.

html" files. This setup ensures that you can easily follow along with the exercises and see the results of your code.

1.6 PYTHON PREPARATION

1.6.1 What Is Python?

Python is a general-purpose programming language, and it has applicability anywhere that data plays the key role, e.g., data science, mathematical computation, or machine learning. Created by Guido van Rossum, and released in 1991, Python now is one of the most popular programming languages.

1.6.2 What Can Python Do?

Python is commonly used for, but not limited to:

- large-scale data analytics,
- complex machine learning, mathematics and statistics,
- task automation,
- enterprise software development,
- web development (server-side).

1.6.3 Why Python Is So Popular?

In a recent worldwide survey (www.tiobe.com/tiobe-index/), Python has been recognized as the most popular language. In another survey (https://pypl.github.io/PYPL.html), Python earns the highest popularity (28.98% share) among all computer languages, followed by Java and JavaScript. It is well known that for anyone from `casual coders` (or `citizen developers`, meaning those who create applications to be consumed by themselves or other users from a small-scale group, e.g., financial analysts and accountants) to professional software engineers, Python is a viable, accessible programming language that can be used for small tasks, like powering a simple welcome bot for new customers, or executing extremely complex code, such as analyzing massive amounts of financial data for a hedge fund. There are a couple of reasons as to why it is so popular:

- Python has a simple English-like syntax.
- Python's unique syntax allows developers to write programs with fewer lines than some other programming languages (a.k.a. the "Pythonic" style).

- Python runs on an interpreter system, meaning that code can be executed as soon as it is written. This means, for casual coders, you may promptly find the result and take action.
- Python works on different platforms (Windows, Mac, Linux, Raspberry Pi, etc.).
- Python's flexibility in writing code allows programmers to organize their projects in a procedural way, an object-oriented way or a functional way.

1.6.4 Advantages of Learning and Using Python

Here are a few advantages of learning and using Python:

- Popularity and access: Python has a huge community that supports a huge amount of libraries, which helps maintain its accessibility to any skill level. Most importantly, those open-source libraries are all free.
- Simple syntax: The Python coding language has an easy-to-learn syntax and uses plain English words.
- Readability: Lines of code written in Python are very easy to read. For instance, Python relies on clearer indentation to define and separate different scopes (e.g., the scope of loops, if-else, functions, and classes) while other programming languages often use curly-brackets, semicolons, or parentheses for this purpose.
- Scalability: You can start a program in Python without having to worry about the back-breaking work of rewriting code for other platforms when you are in need of scaling up.

Now, please follow the instructions below to install and launch Jupyter Notebook. Alternatively, you can open the "Preparatory.html" file located in the "HTML" folder, which provides the same step-by-step guidance for installing Jupyter Notebook.

1.6.5 How to Start?

Many PCs and Macs have python already installed. That means the fastest way to start using Python is to open your Windows Command Line (cmd. exe) or Mac Terminal application and simply type "python" or "ipython" to enter the Command-Line version of Python interpreter.

- iPython stands for interactive Python. It is an advanced interactive Python shell.
- Its interactive interpreter runs like Python, but with some easier and more pleasant features, such as color-highlighted texts, statement autocompletion, and better edit history management.
- The two main integrated development environment (IDE) tools used in this book – Jupyter and Spyder – support iPython syntactic features.

The screenshot below shows an example of using iPython in the Mac Terminal. The example simply uses Python as a calculator. The details of all arithmetic operators will be soon discussed later.

```
● ● ●     test-network — IPython: fabric-samples/test-network — ipython — 85×27
(base) Chichunde-MacBook-Air:test-network chou4291$ ipython
Python 3.9.12 (main, Apr  5 2022, 01:53:17)
Type 'copyright', 'credits' or 'license' for more information
IPython 8.2.0 -- An enhanced Interactive Python. Type '?' for help.

In [1]: 8+9
Out[1]: 17

In [2]: 8-9
[Out[2]: -1                                                              ]

In [3]: 8*9
[Out[3]: 72                                                              ]

In [4]: 8/9
[Out[4]: 0.8888888888888888                                             ]

In [5]: 8%9
[Out[5]: 8                                                              ]

In [6]: 8**9
[Out[6]: 134217728                                                       ]

In [7]: 8//9
[Out[7]: 0                                                              ]

In [8]: █
```

If you do not have Python installed on your computer, you can download it from the link: www.python.org/

Of course, if you prefer using a graphic user interface to make coding a better experience and have better interaction with Python, you are highly recommended to use Jupyter Notebook that is embedded in Anaconda Navigator.

I.6.6 Introduction to Anaconda Navigator

Anaconda Navigator is an open-source software package that includes Jupyter Notebook, Spyder, and other development tools to implement projects of data analytics and scientific computing (e.g., machine learning, large-scale data processing, etc.). For business users of Python, Anaconda Navigator is the best choice to learn, manage, and share your data analytics projects. In this book, all of the example code requiring interactive input/output is illustrated and explained using Jupyter Notebook. Be aware that all code is executable on both Jupyter and other integrated development environment (IDE) since Python is basically a highly portable, cross-platform language.

I.6.7 How to Install Anaconda Navigator?

Anaconda Navigator supports Windows, MacOS, and Linux (Ubuntu). Here's the link to download Anaconda: www.anaconda.com/download. Your email address for a quick registration is optional. The download page automatically detects your operating system (OS) and shows the installer that fits to your OS. The screenshot below is an example of the Windows installer of Anaconda Navigator that always supports the latest version of Python.

The installation is quite similar to any other application installer. You may follow the instructions to complete the installation. Most of the time, all we need to do is to accept the default settings. The screenshot below shows the beginning of the installation.

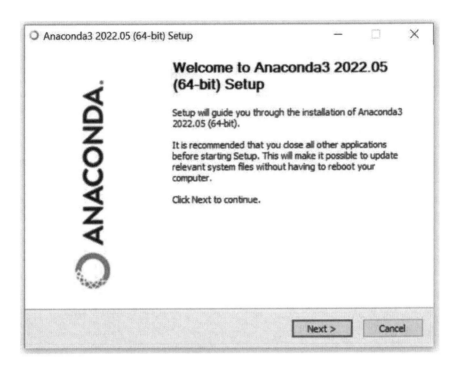

You may also choose the folder you want to install:

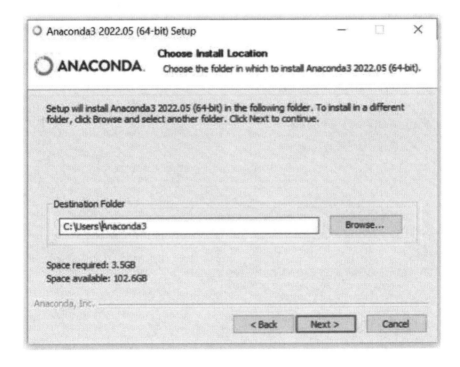

It might take a while to complete the installation after you click the `Install` button.

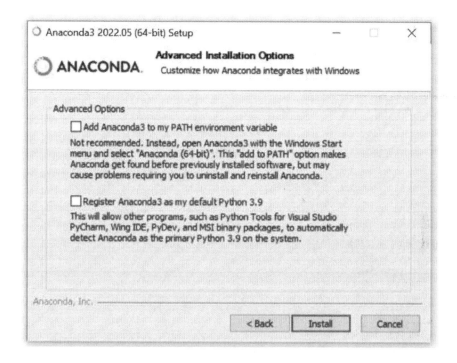

Once the installation is completed, you should be able to find the Anaconda Navigator in your Start Menu. Now you can launch it just like how you would any new application:

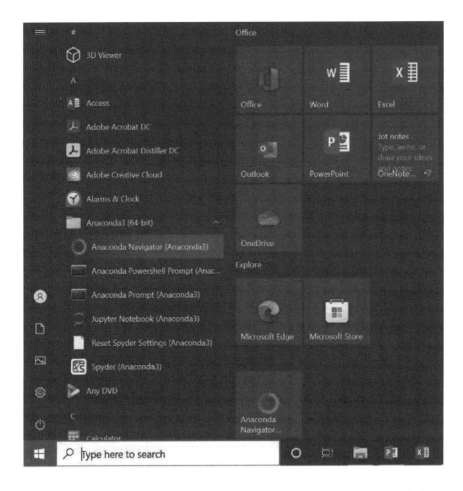

The home page of Anaconda Navigator looks like the screenshot below:

On Windows 10 or later, you can directly launch Jupyter Notebook from the Start Menu without needing to activate the entire Anaconda platform. However, if you are using a Mac, you will still need to activate Anaconda and launch Jupyter within the platform.

Note for Mac Users: Please be aware that you'll need to know your chip type to download the correct version of the Anaconda platform. This ensures compatibility and smooth installation.

- If your Mac uses an Intel chip, download the Intel version.
- If your Mac has an Apple Silicon chip (e.g., M1, M2), download the Apple Silicon version, as illustrated below:

I.6.8 Jupyter Notebook

As mentioned earlier, in this book, we mainly use Jupyter Notebook for Python code demonstration. Jupyter Notebook is a browser-based interactive development platform that supports both Python computing and documenting. When you first launch the Notebook, your default browser (Google Chrome) will open a new tab to show the root directory of the active Windows user as below:

It might just look like a file explorer but it is much more than that. The Jupyter Notebook actually contains a Python running environment and a Markdown-based documentation service.

- Markdown is a lightweight markup language (compared to Hyper Text Markup Language, HTML) for creating formatted text using a plain-text editor. Jupyter adopts Markdown as its documentation tool.
- The complete Markdown syntax is available at: www.markdownguide.org/basic-syntax/#escaping-backticks

Let's click the "New" drop-down menu on the top-right of the Jupyter Home to create your first Python Notebook project:

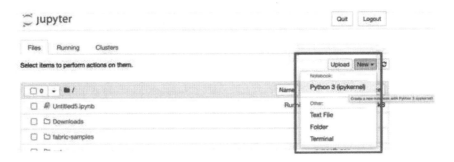

A typical notebook file is made of many "cells". The screenshot below depicts five selected components in a standard notebook file. Selected items are all framed in red and numbered. The first four items are on the top menu. Item #5 illustrates a cell to be filled with Python code or code description. You may use item #1 to insert new cells. To execute Python statements contained in one cell, we use item #2. Item #3 is a drop-down menu for you to toggle a cell as a chunk of Python code or code description in the Markdown format. Item #4 provides the complete list of Jupyter Notebook commands available for use. You may try to experience these items

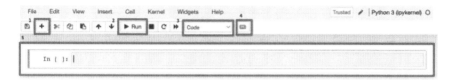

In the first project, we simply use Python as a calculator to practice some basic arithmetic operations. Below are Python's arithmetic operators:

Operator	Name	Example
+	Addition	X+Y
-	Subtraction	X-Y
*	Multiplication	X*Y
/	Division	X/Y
%	Modulus	X%Y
**	Exponentiation	X**Y
//	Floor division	X//Y

Please note that in the main book content, we use **In[#]** to refer to input cells and **Out[#]** to refer to output cells in Jupyter, following its standard convention (e.g., **In[12]:**, **Out[12]:**).

In[#]:

```
# Comments starts with a #, and Python will ignore them.

# when you input an arithmetic expression, iPython will return the
result in no time
# all you need to do is to input the expression as below and
click "Run"

8+9
```

Out[#]:

```
17
```

In[#]:

```
# Click "Run"
8-9
```

Out[#]:

```
-1
```

```
In[#]:
# You may change the input numbers below to have different outputs
8*9

Out[#]:
72

In[#]:
8/9 # divison returns the quotient as a floating number

Out[#]:
0.8888888888888888

In[#]:
8%9 # modulo returns the remainder of a floor division

Out[#]:
8

In[#]:
8**9 # exponent returns the nth power to a given number

Out[#]:
134217728

In[#]:
8//9 # floor division returns the integer quotient

Out[#]:
0
```

The calculations above look very straightforward. However, they work just like calculators. Once a calculation is completed and the result is printed out, the values in the expression will be disposed of. Sometimes, you might want to store these values in named variables for later use:

```
In[#]:
a=8; b=9 # assign 8 and 9 to two variables: a, b
# the semicolon separator is used when you want to write multiple
statements in one line
```

Unlike other formal programming languages, such as Java and C++, in Python, you don't have to declare a variable. A variable is created the moment you first assign an initial value to it.

```
In[#]:

c1=a+b # assign the result of a+b to c1 variable
print(c1) # ask Python to print c1

Out[#]:

17
```

The last line uses the most popular output function in Python: print(). We will heavily rely on this function and introduce more on it in the following sections.

I.6.9 Jupyter's Markdown

Within Jupyter, Markdown cells can be used to write rich text alongside the code, which is incredibly useful for creating detailed documentation of the code, explaining the logic, or presenting results and analysis in a readable format. You only need to use Item #3's drop-down menu to toggle from "Code" to "Markdown", then you can type explanatory text in the Markdown cell.

Markdown in Jupyter is extremely useful for creating notebooks that are not only executable but also readable and well-documented. It allows Jupyter notebooks to serve as computational essays, reports, or tutorials that combine live code, narrative text, and visualizations. The ability to combine explanatory text with code and to format this text richly ensures that Jupyter notebooks are versatile tools for data analysis, academic research, teaching, and even book writing. In fact, the Python part of our book is completely written in Jupyter and heavily relies on both "Code" and "Markdown".

Now everything looks great. You may find the "Save as" menu item in the "File" tab and save your first project "calculator" to your working folder. NOTE: You might have noticed the filename extension of a Jupyter Notebook project is .ipynb. The particular extension suggests you can only open the project using Jupyter Notebook since the project might contain lots of descriptions other than executable Python code.

- Every programming language has an extension; Python has an extension called (.py). Different from an .ipynb file, all Python files stored in the .py extension are executable in the Python interpreter. In Jupyter, you can use "Download As" in the "File" tab and save your project as "calculator.py" to make your project executable in other Python IDEs.
- If you need to share your project with someone who doesn't have Jupyter Notebook installed, you can use the Download As option under the "File" tab and save your project as an "HTML" file. This approach ensures that your project can be viewed in any web browser.

## CHAPTER 1

Data Exploration and Cleaning

O UR GOAL IS TO help the Campus Bookstore to understand its business operations and make several business decisions. Please refer to the Introduction Chapter to review the case background and the objectives of the analyses. However, before any analysis can be performed, the first step is always data exploration and data cleaning. That is, we have to take this opportunity to familiarize ourselves with the data we received, to ensure the data is aligned with what we need (e.g., does it match the business processes we are focusing on, does it include the fields we requested, etc.), to validate the data and to clean the data so it's ready for analysis, and to perform some initial analyses to explore patterns in the dataset.

1.1 BASIC CONCEPTS OF DATA EXPLORATION AND CLEANING

Data exploration and cleaning are critical steps in data analytics projects. It serves as the assurance for accurate, reliable, and insightful analysis. These steps not only improve the quality of the data but also enhance the overall effectiveness of the analysis, leading to more insightful and valuable results.

DOI: 10.1201/9781003567103-2

1. Data Exploration
- **Understanding the Data:**
  Data exploration allows analysts to gain an initial understanding of the data. This involves summarizing the main characteristics, often using visual methods. It helps in understanding the context and relevance of the data, ensuring that the data aligns with the goals of the analysis.

- **Identifying Patterns and Relationships:**
  By exploring data, analysts can identify trends, patterns, and correlations. This is crucial for developing hypotheses and guiding further analysis. It also helps in detecting anomalies, outliers, or unexpected results, which could be significant in understanding the underlying phenomena or could indicate data quality issues.

- **Data Visualization:**
  It is often useful to use visualization techniques such as histograms, scatter plots, and box plots provide a graphical representation of data, making it easier to spot patterns and outliers. Effective visualizations are also essential for communicating findings to stakeholders in a clear and understandable manner. We will delve into data visualization in Chapter 4.

2. Data Cleaning
- **Improving Data Quality:**
  Data cleaning involves correcting errors and unexpected mistakes in the data, such as fixing typos or correcting erroneous entries. It ensures that data is consistent across datasets, which might include resolving discrepancies or standardizing data formats.

- **Handling Missing Data:**
  Missing data is another common issue that data cleaning addresses. Proper handling of missing data is crucial as it can significantly impact the results and conclusions drawn from the analysis. Through methods like imputation, deletion, or flagging incomplete records, data cleaning ensures that the analysis is not biased or mistakenly skewed.

- **Removing Irrelevant Data:**
  This step involves removing data that is not relevant to the analysis, which helps in reducing noise and focusing on pertinent information. It improves the efficiency of the analysis process by reducing the volume of data that needs to be processed.

- **Enhancing Data Integrity:**
  Data cleaning also includes validating data against known standards or rules, such as database normalization. The process examines data integrity and ensures that data is reliable and suitable for analysis. It usually involves different datasets that can be integrated seamlessly, maintaining consistency and integrity across datasets. We will introduce data normalization and table join in Chapter 6.

1.2 UNDERSTANDING THE "INVOICE_RAW" WORKSHEET

To illustrate the data exploration and cleaning tasks, we have prepared a worksheet titled "**Invoice_raw,**" which contains raw transaction data prior to cleaning. This worksheet is located in the "Bookstore-Ch01.xlsx" workbook. Although it has not been cleaned yet, it provides detailed information on the Campus Bookstore's sales transactions. Below is a summary of the key components and insights you may find from the dataset:

1. **Dataset Structure – columns and rows:**
   - There are 16 columns (**A:P**) and 2026 data rows (**2:2027**) in this workbook. The first row is the header row that shows meaningful labels for each column.

2. **Transactions and Products:**
   - There are sales transactions identified by unique **Invoice Number**s ranging from one to 1,000. Each row represents a specific sale line item. Rows with the same **Invoice Number** represent multiple items sold in one sale.
   - Products sold are identified both by **Item Number** and **Item** name, including Jackets, Pens, Stuffed Mascots, Baseball Caps, Keychains, Mugs, Greeting Cards, and Backpacks.

3. **Date and Discount:**
   - All transactions occurred between **1/1/2023** and **3/31/2023**, representing the transactions made by Campus Bookstore during the first season.
   - Discounts vary by item, ranging from 0% to 20%, complying with Bookstore's discount policy.

4. **Cost, Price, and Quantity:**
   - Each item has a **List Price** and listed **Cost**. The selling price is the **List Price** subtract the discount amount (= **List Price** * **Discounts**).

- The **Quantity** of items sold varies, with multiple entries for some items suggesting one transaction might include multiple sale items, and different discount rates applied to different items.

5. **Inventory**:
   - The **Quantity in Stock** indicates the available inventory for each item on **3/31/2023**. Be aware that the **Quantity in Stock** represents the snapshots of the inventory available on a specific date and can only be updated on new transactions in a live system. In this worksheet, this dynamic feature is not provided.

6. **Employees**:
   - Sales are associated with specific employees (**Emp ID** and **Name**), suggesting that employee performance could be tracked.
   - **Start Date** and **Weekly Payment** indicate employee's tenure and salary respectively.

7. **Store Information**:
   - Transactions are linked to specific **Store ID**s and **Store Name**s (North, West, East), with addresses provided. This could indicate regional sales performance.

8. **Duplicates and Aggregation Opportunities**:
   - Some transactions share the same **Invoice Number**, indicating multiple items per purchase.
   - Aggregation could provide insights into total sales per invoice, employee sales performance, and inventory turnover.

1.3 EXPLORATION AND CLEANING TASKS

In real-world data analytics projects, various tasks arise at different stages. In this book, we use a **question-answering** approach to demonstrate how to perform these tasks using versatile Excel functions and Python's Pandas library.

Below are some examples where we will use the Bookstore dataset to demonstrate how data exploration and cleaning tasks can be completed with Excel and Python:

Q1: **How many unique stores are there in this dataset?**
Q2: **How many unique employees are there in this dataset?**

Q3: **What is the total number of sales transactions? Any missing values or zeros?**

Q4: **Any duplicated records?**

1.4 EXCEL

You may follow the step-by-step guide below to learn how to perform the selected four data exploration and cleaning tasks:

Q1: How many unique stores are there in this dataset?

Excel provides several ways to get distinct (unique) values from a column. Here are some of the most common methods:

- **UNIQUE** Function

  The **UNIQUE** function in Excel works for both numerical and categorical (text) values, as well as dates. It's a versatile function that can return a list of unique values from a range or array, regardless of the data type. Whether your data consists of numbers, text strings, or dates, **UNIQUE** will effectively identify and return the unique entries.

  Go to the "Invoice" worksheet. Use the fast key combination "Ctrl-End" to quickly go to the bottom row of this worksheet. Then move your pointer to cell O2029. Follow the following steps to complete **UNIQUE** function:

  - Type "=" to add a formula.
  - Type "unique" slowly until a dropdown list that contains some recommended functions for you to choose. Select "UNIQUE" from the list.
  - Type "O2:O2027" along with an ending parenthesis to complete the function.
  - Press "Enter" to execute the formula.
  - In the formula bar, you may find your completed formula as below:

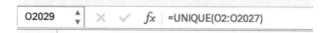

- In range (O2029:O2032), you can see the returned four distinct Store names listed as below:

North
West
East
South

- **COUNTA** Function

  To quickly find out how many different values you have, use **COUNTA** with **UNIQUE**. **COUNTA** helps count all cells that aren't empty in a **categorical** column (for numerical columns, you should use **COUNT**). When you use it with **UNIQUE**, it tells you how many unique items are there. Here's a simple way to do it:

  - Copy "**UNIQUE(O2:O2027)**".

  - Paste it into cell O2028, but add an "=" in front of it.

  - Then, wrap it with **COUNTA** as below, making sure to close the parentheses properly.

| O2028 | ↕ | ✕ ✓ | *fx* | =COUNTA(UNIQUE(O2:O2027)) |

In cell O2028, you should have four as the number of stores.

Q2: How many unique employees are there in this dataset?

Follow the steps outlined in **Q1** to count the number of employees and to create a list of all employees using column K. If done correctly, you will get the results as below:

	8
Daniel Marquez	
Kristin Lee	
Valerie Gibson	
Adriana Cisneros	
Elizabeth Rodriguez	
Nathaniel Marquez	
Bradley Marshall	
Carol Parker	

Q3: What is the total number of sales transactions? Any missing values or zeros?

As previously noted, line items with identical Invoice Numbers indicate they were sold in a single transaction. Therefore, to calculate the total number of transactions, we can effectively use **COUNT** combined with **UNIQUE**. It's important to highlight that we opt for **COUNT** rather than **COUNTA** in this context because **COUNT** is designed to count the numbers of all non-empty cells in a **numerical** column.

To test for missing values or zeros in an Excel worksheet, you can employ Excel's filter functionality. This method is particularly efficient for smaller datasets or when doing a quick check:

- Filtering for Zeros:
  - Click on the column header to select the column you want to check. For example, the **Discount** column.
  - Go to the Data tab and click Filter. This adds dropdown arrows to the column headers.

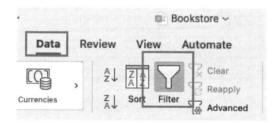

- Click the dropdown arrow for the column you are interested in (e.g., **Discount**). Then use the checkboxes to select only "0". You may first deselect all, then select "0" as shown in the screenshot below.

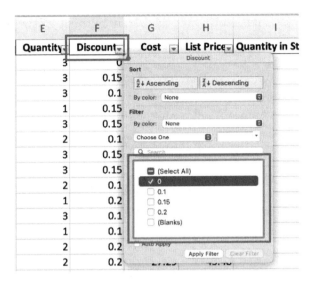

- Click "Apply Filter" button. This will filter the rows where the cell value is zero. The test results indicate the **Discount** column contains some zero(s). It is common in practice to sell items without discounts.

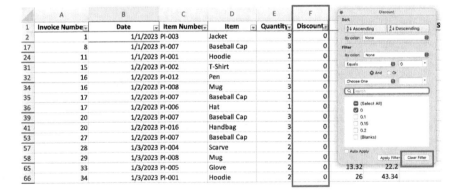

	A	B	C	D	E	F	
1	Invoice Numbe	Date	Item Number	Item	Quantity	Discount	
2	1	1/1/2023	PI-003	Jacket	3	0	
17	8	1/1/2023	PI-007	Baseball Cap	3	0	
24	11	1/1/2023	PI-001	Hoodie	1	0	
31	15	1/2/2023	PI-002	T-Shirt	1	0	
32	16	1/2/2023	PI-012	Pen	1	0	
34	16	1/2/2023	PI-008	Mug	3	0	
35	17	1/2/2023	PI-007	Baseball Cap	1	0	
36	17	1/2/2023	PI-006	Hat	1	0	
39	20	1/2/2023	PI-007	Baseball Cap	3	0	
41	20	1/2/2023	PI-016	Handbag	3	0	
53	27	1/2/2023	PI-007	Baseball Cap	2	0	
57	28	1/3/2023	PI-004	Scarve	2	0	
58	29	1/3/2023	PI-008	Mug	2	0	
65	33	1/3/2023	PI-005	Glove	2	0	13.32	22.2
66	34	1/3/2023	PI-001	Hoodie	2	0	26	43.34

- After examining the results, you may click "Clear Filter" button to restore your dataset to the original view.

- Filtering for Blanks:

- Similar to filtering for zeros, use the filter dropdown to select "(Blanks)" to see all rows where the cell value is missing. Since we don't have any missing values in the **Discount** column, it won't return any rows in this case.

- Advanced Filter for Multiple Conditions:
  One limitation of using filter dropdown to test for missing values or zeros is you can only perform it one column at a time. If you would like to test multiple columns, you can use the "Advanced Filter". The Advanced Filter feature can extract rows according to complex conditions you assign to it. For example, if you want to test for zero values in either Discount or Quantity columns, you can follow the steps below to perform the filtering:

  - Copy all column labels to Row 2041.

  - Type "0" in both AF2 and AG3 to assign "Quantity = 0 OR Discount = 0" condition for Quantity and Discount columns. Make sure the two "0"s are in different rows. If you type "0"s in the same row (Row 2), the Advanced Filter will interpret it as "Quantity = 0 AND Discount = 0", which represent a more stringent condition.

- Go to the **Data** tab.
- Click **Advanced** in the Sort & Filter group.
- Choose "Copy to another location".
- In the "List Range" field, select the whole dataset, including the column labels. The selected range should be: $A$1:$P$2027.
- In the "Criteria Range" field, select the condition area, including the labels. The selected range should be: $AB$1:$AQ$3.

- In the "Copy to" field, specify where you want to place the unique values. For example, $AB$5 and click **OK**.

- You will see the test results as below. Since **Quantity** column has no zero values, the filtering returns the same rows as when testing **Discount** column's zeros.

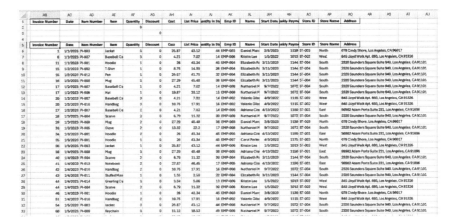

You may expand the testing scope to include other columns. Keep in mind, conditions shown in different rows are combined with "OR". On the other hand, conditions shown in one same row are combined with "AND".

Q4: Any duplicated records?
- **List Duplicates with COUNTIFS():**
  You can list duplicate rows in Excel using a combination of methods depending on your exact needs and preferences. If you want to create a list or flag duplicates without altering the original data, you can create formulas using Excel's **COUNTIFS()** to identify duplicates based on multiple columns.

  - Our data is in columns A to P and has headers in the first row.
  - In column U (or another column away from P), type "Duplicates" in U1 cell. Then starting from U2, enter the following formula:

    =COUNTIFS(A:A,A2,B:B,B2,C:C,C2,D:D,D2,E:E,E2,F:F,F2,G:G, G2,H:H,H2,I:I,I2,J:J,J2,K:K,K2,L:L,L2,M:M,M2,O:O,O2,P:P,P2)

U2		*fx* =COUNTIFS(A:A,A2,B:B,B2,C:C,C2,D:D,D2,E:E,E2,F:F,F2,G:G,G2,H:H,H2,I:I,I2,J:J,J2,K:K,K2,L:L,L2,M:M,M2,O:O,O2,P:P,P2)							
	S	T	U	V	W	X	Y	Z	AA
1			Duplicates						
2			1						

NOTE: COUNTIFS(A:A,A2) tests if any cells in column A contains the same value as A2. Since Bookstore has columns from A to P, the formula above expands the scope to include all columns. That is why it is a bit lengthy and cumbersome. You may copy and paste it to U2 instead of typing it by hand.

  - Drag the formula down through the range in column U from row 2 to 2027. This formula counts the occurrence of each row based on all A:P columns if any duplicate rows are detected.
  - Put the pointer on column U's header "Duplicate". Go to the Data tab and click Filter. This adds dropdown arrows to column U's header.

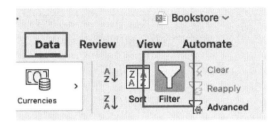

- Click the dropdown arrow for column U. Then use the checkboxes to select the counts greater than "1" ("2" in this case), as shown in the screenshot below:

- Click "Apply Filter" button. This will filter the rows whose occurrence is greater than one. The results indicate there are 10 duplicate rows (half of 20 output records) found in this dataset. This method highlights duplicate rows with their original values in the data, making them easy to spot.

C1	⌄	× ✓ *fx*	Item Number					

	A	B	U	V	W	X	Y
1	**Invoice Number**	**Date**	**Duplicate** ▼	●		Duplicate	
205	103	1/9/2023	2	**Sort**			
206	103	1/9/2023	2	↑ Ascending		↓ Descending	
360	186	1/17/2023	2	By color: None			⊟
361	186	1/17/2023	2	**Filter**			
425	221	1/19/2023	2	By color: None			⊟
426	221	1/19/2023	2	Equals	⊟	2	▾
685	350	2/1/2023	2	● And ○ Or			
687	350	2/1/2023	2	Choose One	⊟		▾
793	406	2/6/2023	2	🔍 Search			
794	406	2/6/2023	2				
908	463	2/10/2023	2	⊟ (Select All)			
909	463	2/10/2023	2	☐ 1			
969	491	2/12/2023	2	☑ 2			
971	491	2/12/2023	2				
1342	675	3/1/2023	2				
1343	675	3/1/2023	2				
1806	893	3/20/2023	2	☐ Auto Apply			
1807	893	3/20/2023	2		Apply Filter	Clear Filter	
1820	899	3/20/2023	2				
1822	899	3/20/2023	2				
2028							
2029							

◀ ▶	Item	Employee	Store	Invoice Items	Invoice Head	Invoice	+

Ready   20 of 2026 records found   Accessibility: Good to go

- **"Remove Duplicates" Feature**

  Once you spot the duplicate rows, you may decide the further actions. For a quick, manual removal without formulas, you can use the "Remove Duplicates" feature:

  - Select the data range A1:P2037, including the header.
  - Go to the **Data** tab on the Ribbon.
  - Click **Remove Duplicates**.
  - Make sure the "My data has headers" option is checked.
  - Make sure all column(s) are selected when removing duplicates and click **OK**.

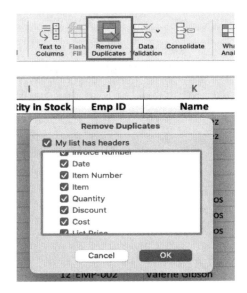

- Double check the Alert information of removing ten duplicate rows and click **OK**.

This method modifies the original data by removing duplicate entries, leaving only unique values in the dataset.

- **Remove Duplicates with Advanced Filter**
  The Advanced Filter feature can also extract unique values to a different location:
  - Go to the **Data** tab.
  - Click **Advanced** in the Sort & Filter group.
  - Select List Range as $A$1:$P$2027.
  - Choose "Copy to another location".

- In the "Copy to" field, specify where you want to place the unique values. For example, $AB$2041.
- Check the "Unique records only" box and click **OK**.

This method generates a new data range that is free from duplicates. It does not alter the original data and allows you to specify a different location for the unique values.

1.5 PYTHON

For how to use Python's Pandas library to perform data exploration and cleaning tasks using the Bookstore dataset, please refer to the Jupyter notebook file "Bookstore-Ch01.ipynb" to access the code, or view the "Bookstore-Ch01.html" file to see the outputs of all code. You should find Pandas' versatile data exploration and cleaning functions are more efficient and straightforward than Excel's indirect approaches. That is because Pandas can automatically handle missing or incomplete data, making it easier for business users to clean and preprocess their datasets.

1.5.1 Introduction to Pandas

Pandas is an open-source library written in Python Language. Pandas provides high performance, fast, easy-to-use data structures, and data analysis tools for manipulating numeric data and time series. Pandas is built on the NumPy library and written in languages like Python, Cython, and C. In Pandas, we can import data from various file formats like Microsoft Excel, JSON, SQL, etc.

As discussed earlier, Pandas is the most powerful tool to do data analytics in a business context. It allows us to clean data, transform data, manipulate data, make visualizations, and more. Specifically, Pandas offers the following advantages for business users:

1. Data Structures: Pandas provides data structures like Series and DataFrame, which are more intuitive for working with tabular data, such as spreadsheets and databases, commonly used in businesses.

2. Handling Missing Data: Pandas can automatically handle missing or incomplete data, making it easier for business users to clean and pre-process their datasets.

3. Advanced Indexing and Data Alignment: Pandas offers advanced indexing options, such as multi-level indexing and label-based indexing, which are more user-friendly for business users working with large and complex datasets.

4. Data Manipulation and Analysis Tools: Pandas has built-in functions for data aggregation, filtering, sorting, grouping, merging, and pivoting, which are essential for business users to analyze and derive insights from their data.

5. Time Series Analysis: Pandas has extensive support for working with time series data, which is commonly used in finance, sales, and other business domains.

6. Compatibility with Other Libraries: Pandas is compatible with many other data analysis and visualization libraries, such as Matplotlib, Seaborn, and Plotly, which makes it easier for business users to create visualizations and gain insights from their data. Since Pandas is built on top of NumPy, you can always use NumPy functions directly on Pandas data structures when needed.

1.5.2 Install and Import Pandas

Since Pandas is not a built-in package, when we first use it, it must be installed using the `pip install` command, as shown below. Keep in mind, once you have installed Pandas in your Jupyter, you won't need to install it next time since your Jupyter environment can recognize any installed libraries. Depending on your operating systems, sometimes you may need to restart the Jupyter kernel to activate it using the "restart the kernel" button. Below we use **In[#]** to refer to input cells and **Out[#]** to refer to output cells in Jupyter, following its standard convention (e.g., **In[12]:**).

```
In[#]:

pip install pandas
```

Out[#]:

```
Requirement already satisfied: pandas in /Users/chou4291/anaconda3/
lib/python3.11/site-packages (2.0.3)
Requirement already satisfied: python-dateutil>=2.8.2 in /Users/
chou4291/anaconda3/lib/python3.11/site-packages (from pandas) (2.8.2)
Requirement already satisfied: pytz>=2020.1 in /Users/chou4291/
anaconda3/lib/python3.11/site-packages (from pandas) (2023.3.post1)
Requirement already satisfied: tzdata>=2022.1 in /Users/chou4291/
anaconda3/lib/python3.11/site-packages (from pandas) (2023.3)
Requirement already satisfied: numpy>=1.21.0 in /Users/chou4291/
anaconda3/lib/python3.11/site-packages (from pandas) (1.24.3)
Requirement already satisfied: six>=1.5 in /Users/chou4291/anaconda3/
lib/python3.11/site-packages (from python-dateutil>=2.8.2->pandas)
(1.16.0)
Note: you may need to restart the kernel to use updated packages.
```

Then we import Pandas under the alias of pd. The pd alias is commonly used among Pandas users.

```
In[#]:

import pandas as pd
```

Now your Pandas library is readily available to provide services.

PANDAS DATAFRAME

DataFrame is a two-dimensional labeled data structure with columns of potentially different types. If you are familiar with Microsoft Excel, you may consider DataFrame as a supercharged Excel table. Most of the tasks you can do in Excel can be done in Pandas DataFrame too and vice versa. In fact, you will learn there are many areas where Pandas DataFrame outperforms Excel.

1.5.3 Data Import

Our first task is to read Bookstore.xlsx as a Pandas' data frame. For Excel files, Pandas provides the interface to read them through the pd.read_excel() method.

```
In[#]:

filepath = "/Users/chi2019/Desktop/Book/Excel Files/Bookstore-Ch01.
xlsx" # Change the path according to your file location


# For Windows users, prefix r is added:
# filepath = r"\Users\chi2019\Desktop\Book\Excel Files\Bookstore-
Ch01.xlsx"
```

In the code snippet above, we start by specifying the filepath, which directs to the file's location on your system. A comment, indicated by the "#" symbol, follows the filepath. This comment is intended for human readers; the machine will ignore it. Adding comments like this is a standard practice for annotating code lines with your notes.

Note: In Python, strings must be enclosed in either single (") or double (""") quotes. Both types of quotes are acceptable, but you should maintain consistency by not mixing them within the same string.

THE PREFIX r FOR WINDOWS USERS

In the above example: "/Users/chi2019/Desktop/Book/Excel Files/ Bookstore-Ch01.xlsx" represents the standard path format in MacOS, using forward slash as the path separator. However, if you are a Windows user, you might have "C:\Users\chi2019\Desktop\Book\Excel Files\ Bookstore-Ch01.xlsx". Backslash is the common way to present a path in Windows. However, in Python, backslash is reserved to signify special characters. For example, "hello\nworld" – the \n means a new line. You may try printing it out with print("hello\nworld").

So there is a conflict since the raw path names in Windows usually have backslashes in them. But we want them to mean actual backslashes, not special characters as Python realizes. To resolve this issue, you will need to add one letter r as the prefix of the file path to make it like:

filepath = r"C:\Users\chi2019\Desktop\Book\Excel Files\Bookstore-Ch01.xlsx".

The r stands for "raw" and will cause backslashes in a string to be interpreted as actual backslashes rather than special characters. For example, r"hello\nworld" means the characters "hello\nworld". Again, try printing it with print(r"hello\nworld").

In MacOS, the "r" is not necessary since Mac uses forward slash, instead of a backslash, in a file path. Of course, if you are specifying a relative path, not a raw Windows path, the better approach is to take advantage of Python's cross-platform path separator: "/Users/chi2019/Desktop/Book/ Excel Files/Bookstore-Ch01.xlsx".

```
In[#]:

invoice = pd.read_excel(filepath, sheet_name = "Invoice_raw", header = 0, usecols = "A:P", nrows = 2026)
```

- *read_excel()*

The read_excel() function is part of the Pandas library in Python, which is widely used for data manipulation and analysis. This function is particularly useful for reading data from Excel files (both .xls and .xlsx formats) into a Pandas DataFrame, making it easy to manipulate, analyze, and visualize data using Python. It can read data from both older .xls files and the newer .xlsx format used by more recent versions of Microsoft Excel. Pandas' read_excel() can read from a specific sheet of an Excel file by name or index, or it can load all sheets into a dictionary of DataFrames.

In addition to the first parameter to specify the file path, it offers other various parameters to customize how data is read, including:

- sheet_name: Specifies which sheet to read. The default reads the first sheet.
- header: Identifies the row (Python is zero-indexed) to use for column labels. The default is 0.
- nrows: Specifies the number of data rows to read (header is excluded).
- usecols: Limits the data read to a selection of columns either by name or index.
- index_col: Uses one of the columns as the DataFrame's index.
- skiprows: Skips a specified number of rows from the start of the sheet, useful for bypassing headers or formatting in Excel files.
- dtype: Defines column data types.

In the example above, we use read_excel() method to read data from Bookstore.xlsx and store the data to a data frame `invoice`. The first parameter is the `filepath` we just defined. The second parameter is `sheet_name` that specifies the worksheet you want to read. In this case, we assign the exact sheetname "Invoice" (case-sensitive) in Bookstore-Ch01.xlsx to this argument.

By default, the pd.read_excel() function in pandas will interpret the first row of the Excel file as the column labels (headers) for the DataFrame. This is controlled by the `header` parameter, which defaults to 0, indicating that the first row (index 0) should be used as the header. If you set (header= None), the DataFrame will not have labeled columns, and the first row of the Excel file will be treated as data. You can also specify a different row as the header by setting the header parameter to the index of that row. For example, if you want to use the fourth row (index 3) as the header, you would call header=3.

The `usecols` parameter allows you to specify which columns to read from the Excel file. You can provide a list of integers representing the indices of the columns you want to include: (usecols=[2, 3]). If the Excel file has a header row, you can specify the columns by name: (usecols= ["Column3", "Column4"]). You can also use a string that describes a range of Excel column labels to be included: (usecols = "A:D").

With header, usecols and nrows, you actually can read a specific cell from any Excel worksheet. You may try it yourself.

Now you may dump the partial content of `invoice` by calling the head() function to quickly print out the first 5 rows.

In[#]:

```
print(invoice.head()) # Dump the first 5 rows
```

Out[#]:

```
   Invoice
    Number       Date Item Number            Item  Quantity  Discount  \
0         1 2023-01-01       PI-003          Jacket         3      0.00
1         1 2023-01-01       PI-012             Pen         3      0.15
2         2 2023-01-01       PI-012             Pen         3      0.10
3         3 2023-01-01       PI-011  Stuffed Mascot         1      0.15
4         3 2023-01-01       PI-007     Baseball Cap        3      0.15
    Cost  List Price   Quantity  Emp ID          Name Start Date  \
                       in Stock
0  25.87       43.12         44  EMP-003  Daniel Marquez 2023-02-08
1  25.07       41.79         32  EMP-003  Daniel Marquez 2023-02-08
2  25.07       41.79         32  EMP-006     Kristin Lee 2022-01-05
3   1.55        2.59         22  EMP-002   Valerie Gibson 2022-04-09
4   4.21        7.02         14  EMP-002   Valerie Gibson 2022-04-09
```

```
    Weekly Payment Store ID Store Name  \
0              1139   ST-003     North
1              1139   ST-003     North
2              1013   ST-002      West
3              1115   ST-002      West
4              1115   ST-002      West


                                                  Address
0                    078 Cindy Shore, Los Angeles, CA 96017
1                    078 Cindy Shore, Los Angeles, CA 96017
2       845 Lloyd Walk Apt. 693, Los Angeles, CA 91326
3       845 Lloyd Walk Apt. 693, Los Angeles, CA 91326
4       845 Lloyd Walk Apt. 693, Los Angeles, CA 91326
```

You may also check if we have read the entire dataset by calling `tail()`:

```
print(invoice.tail(3)) # Print the last 3 rows using tail(3)
      Invoice Number       Date      Item   Item Quantity  Discount  \
                                    Number
2023             999 2023-03-31   PI-008       Mug          1       0.0
2024            1000 2023-03-31   PI-005     Glove          1       0.1
2025            1000 2023-03-31   PI-016   Handbag          2       0.0


        Cost  List Price      Quantity  Emp ID              Name  \
                             in Stock
2023   27.29       45.48            38  EMP-007      Carol Parker
2024   13.32       22.20            17  EMP-001  Bradley Marshall
2025   10.75       17.91            16  EMP-001  Bradley Marshall


      Start Date  Weekly Payment Store ID Store Name  \
2023  2022-04-03            1175   ST-003     North
2024  2022-09-27            1084   ST-001      East
2025  2022-09-27            1084   ST-001      East


                                                  Address
2023                 078 Cindy Shore, Los Angeles, CA 96017
2024  98982 Adam Ports Suite 231, Los Angeles, CA 91696
2025  98982 Adam Ports Suite 231, Los Angeles, CA 91696
```

Now we can use invoice DataFrame to perform the four data exploration and cleaning tasks.

1.5.4 Data Exploration and Cleaning

Q1: How many unique stores are there in this dataset?

To find unique values in a column of a Pandas DataFrame, you can use the unique() method applied to the column. This method returns an array of unique values in the order they appear in the column. Then you may use Python's len() function to get the number of unique values in the column.

```
In[#]:
len(invoice["Store ID"].unique())
Out[#]:
4
```

The above code is used to determine the number of unique store identifiers found within the "Store ID" column. We use Pandas' standard accessor invoice["Store ID"] as index to access the "Store ID" column in `invoice`. The result of invoice["Store ID"] is a Pandas Series, which is like one specific column in Excel worksheet. Then we combine unique() and len() to get four as the number of unique stores.

Using the same method, you may quickly get the unique numbers for other columns, such as the number of employees and the number of transactions:

Q2: How many unique employees are there in this dataset?¶

```
In[#]:
len(invoice["Emp ID"].unique())
Out[#]:
8
```

We have eight as the number of unique employees.

Q3: What is the total number of sales transactions? Any missing values or zeros?

```
In[#]:
len(invoice["Invoice Number"].unique())
Out[#]:
1000
```

We have 1,000 sales transactions in this dataframe.

To test for missing values (e.g., NaN or None) in a specific column or all columns of a Pandas DataFrame, you can use the combination of isna() method and any() method to check if there are any NaN or zeros at all. If there are any `True` values in a column, it indicates the presence of at least one row containing NaN. If `False`, it means none of the rows in a column containing NaN.

```
In[#]:
invoice.isna().any() # Check all columns to test if any missing
values exist

Out[#]:
Invoice Number        False
Date                  False
Item Number           False
Item                  False
Quantity              False
Discount              False
Cost                  False
List Price            False
Quantity in Stock     False
Emp ID                False
Name                  False
Start Date            False
Weekly Payment        False
Store ID              False
Store Name            False
Address               False
dtype: bool
```

The test results of missing values indicate no columns contain any missing values because all columns return `False`.

To test for zeros in a specific column or all columns of a Pandas DataFrame, you can use a simple comparison as index to look for zeros. Then use the any() method on the result to check if there are any zeros at all. If there are any `True` values in a column, it indicates the presence of at least one row containing zeros. If `False`, it means none of the rows in a column containing zeros.

```
In[#]:
(invoice == 0).any()

Out[#]:
Invoice Number        False
Date                  False
Item Number           False
Item                  False
Quantity              False
Discount               True
Cost                  False
List Price            False
```

```
Quantity in Stock    False
Emp ID               False
Name                 False
Start Date           False
Weekly Payment       False
Store ID             False
Store Name           False
Address              False
dtype: bool
```

The (invoice == 0) is a logical test (a.k.a. `boolean indexing`) that performs element-wise across the entire invoice DataFrame. Elements in `invoice` return True if their value is zero, and False otherwise. On the resulting element-wise boolean values, we further call any() to check along each column for any True values. Columns return True if there is at least one True value in that column, indicating at least one zero in that column of the invoice DataFrame. If any() finds no True values in a column, the corresponding output is False.

The (invoice == 0).any() operation is a concise and efficient way to quickly identify columns that contain zero values within a DataFrame, making it a useful tool for preliminary data exploration, cleaning, and handling of missing or placeholder values in data analytics.

The test results of zeros indicate only column "Discount" contains some zero(s). That is common in practice, actually. But if you would like to list the records that contain zeros. You may further use `boolean indexing`. This technique allows you to filter the DataFrame based on the condition(s) you specify. Here's how you can list records with missing values or zeros in a particular column:

In[#]:

```
# List records with zeros in column "Discount"
zero_records = invoice[invoice["Discount"] == 0] # Boolean indexing
technique

print("Records with zeros in column "Discount":")
print(zero_records) # the result shows 521 rows are with zeros in
"Discount"
```

Out[#]:

```
Records with zeros in column "Discount":
        Invoice        Date Item Number          Item Quantity Discount \
         Number
0             1  2023-01-01      PI-003        Jacket        3       0.0
15            8  2023-01-01      PI-007  Baseball Cap        3       0.0
22           11  2023-01-01      PI-001        Hoodie        1       0.0
29           15  2023-01-02      PI-002       T-Shirt        1       0.0
30           16  2023-01-02      PI-012           Pen        1       0.0
...          ...         ...         ...           ...      ...       ...
```

```
2015        996 2023-03-31    PI-006         Hat     1     0.0
2020        998 2023-03-31    PI-006         Hat     3     0.0
2021        998 2023-03-31    PI-007  Baseball Cap   1     0.0
2023        999 2023-03-31    PI-008         Mug     1     0.0
2025       1000 2023-03-31    PI-016      Handbag    2     0.0

        Cost  List Price    Quantity in  Emp ID                 Name \
                               Stock
0      25.87      43.12            44  EMP-003       Daniel Marquez
15      4.21       7.02            14  EMP-006          Kristin Lee
22     26.00      43.34            45  EMP-004  Elizabeth Rodriguez
29      8.75      14.59            26  EMP-004  Elizabeth Rodriguez
30     25.07      41.79            32  EMP-004  Elizabeth Rodriguez
...      ...        ...           ...      ...                  ...
2015   19.87      33.12            15  EMP-008    Nathaniel Marquez
2020   19.87      33.12            15  EMP-008    Nathaniel Marquez
2021    4.21       7.02            14  EMP-008    Nathaniel Marquez
2023   27.29      45.48            38  EMP-007         Carol Parker
2025   10.75      17.91            16  EMP-001     Bradley Marshall

      Start Date  Weekly Payment Store ID Store Name \
0     2023-02-08            1139   ST-003      North
15    2022-01-05            1013   ST-002      West
22    2023-03-11            1144   ST-004      South
29    2023-03-11            1144   ST-004      South
30    2023-03-11            1144   ST-004      South
...          ...             ...      ...        ...
2015  2022-09-07            1072   ST-004      South
2020  2022-09-07            1072   ST-004      South
2021  2022-09-07            1072   ST-004      South
2023  2022-04-03            1175   ST-003      North
2025  2022-09-27            1084   ST-001      East

                                              Address
0                  078 Cindy Shore, Los Angeles, CA 96017
15            845 Lloyd Walk Apt. 693, Los Angeles, CA 91326
22      2320 Saunders Square Suite 940, Los Angeles, C...
29      2320 Saunders Square Suite 940, Los Angeles, C...
30      2320 Saunders Square Suite 940, Los Angeles, C...
...                                               ...
2015    2320 Saunders Square Suite 940, Los Angeles, C...
2020    2320 Saunders Square Suite 940, Los Angeles, C...
2021    2320 Saunders Square Suite 940, Los Angeles, C...
2023               078 Cindy Shore, Los Angeles, CA 96017
2025    98982 Adam Ports Suite 231, Los Angeles, CA 91696

[521 rows x 16 columns]
```

Q4: Any duplicated transactions?

Duplicate rows are rows that have been registered more than one time. Sometimes your dataset contains duplicate rows. It usually means redundant records were mistakenly stored. To list the duplicate rows in a Pandas DataFrame, you can use the duplicated() method in conjunction with Pandas' boolean indexing. The duplicated() method has a parameter keep which you can adjust to specify which duplicates to mark:

```
keep="first" (default): Marks all duplicates as True except for the
first occurrence.
keep="last": Marks all duplicates as True except for the last
occurrence.
keep=False: Marks all duplicates as True.
```

Here we want to list the duplicates except the first occurrence:

In[#]:

```
duplicates = invoice[invoice.duplicated()] # keep="first" (default)
print(duplicates)
```

Out[#]:

```
      Invoice Number        Date Item Number           Item  Quantity \
204              103  2023-01-09       PI-006            Hat         3
359              186  2023-01-17       PI-003         Jacket         1
424              221  2023-01-19       PI-013       Notebook         2
685              350  2023-02-01       PI-009       Keychain         1
792              406  2023-02-06       PI-011  Stuffed Mascot        1
907              463  2023-02-10       PI-011  Stuffed Mascot        1
969              491  2023-02-12       PI-006            Hat         1
1341             675  2023-03-01       PI-007   Baseball Cap         3
1805             893  2023-03-20       PI-012            Pen         3
1820             899  2023-03-20       PI-009       Keychain         1

      Discount   Cost  List Price  Quantity in Stock    Emp ID \
204       0.10  19.87       33.12                 15   EMP-003
359       0.00  25.87       43.12                 44   EMP-007
424       0.20  27.87       46.45                 17   EMP-008
685       0.15  11.12       18.53                 49   EMP-001
792       0.15   1.55        2.59                 22   EMP-001
907       0.10   1.55        2.59                 22   EMP-004
969       0.15  19.87       33.12                 15   EMP-003
1341      0.20   4.21        7.02                 14   EMP-002
1805      0.10  25.07       41.79                 32   EMP-002
1820      0.15  11.12       18.53                 49   EMP-002

                    Name Start Date  Weekly  Store ID Store Name \
                                     Payment
204       Daniel Marquez 2023-02-08    1139    ST-003      North
359         Carol Parker 2022-04-03    1175    ST-003      North
424    Nathaniel Marquez 2022-09-07    1072    ST-004      South
685     Bradley Marshall 2022-09-27    1084    ST-001       East
792     Bradley Marshall 2022-09-27    1084    ST-001       East
907   Elizabeth Rodriguez 2023-03-11   1144    ST-004      South
969       Daniel Marquez 2023-02-08    1139    ST-003      North
1341       Valerie Gibson 2022-04-09   1115    ST-002       West
1805       Valerie Gibson 2022-04-09   1115    ST-002       West
1820       Valerie Gibson 2022-04-09   1115    ST-002       West

                                                   Address
204              078 Cindy Shore, Los Angeles, CA 96017
359              078 Cindy Shore, Los Angeles, CA 96017
424    2320 Saunders Square Suite 940, Los Angeles, C...
```

```
685    98982 Adam Ports Suite 231, Los Angeles, CA 91696
792    98982 Adam Ports Suite 231, Los Angeles, CA 91696
907    2320 Saunders Square Suite 940, Los Angeles, C...
969              078 Cindy Shore, Los Angeles, CA 96017
1341      845 Lloyd Walk Apt. 693, Los Angeles, CA 91326
1805      845 Lloyd Walk Apt. 693, Los Angeles, CA 91326
1820      845 Lloyd Walk Apt. 693, Los Angeles, CA 91326
```

In[#]:

```
len(duplicates) # you may quickly check the number of duplicates
```

Out[#]:

```
10
```

Before you make any changes or generate useful information from the dataset, it is recommended to remove all duplicates. To delete duplicate rows in a pandas DataFrame and keep only the unique rows, you can use the drop_duplicates() method. By default, this method keeps the first occurrence of each duplicate row and removes the subsequent duplicates.

In[#]:

```
# Remove duplicates, keeping the first occurrence
invoice = invoice.drop_duplicates()
len(invoice) # check the number of records after deletion of duplicates
```

Out[#]:

```
2016
```

1.6 DISCUSSIONS

In this chapter, you've learned to import Python's Pandas library and use the read_excel() function to load Excel worksheets into Pandas DataFrames. The exercises have introduced you to Pandas' robust functions for identifying unique values, duplicates, and missing data. You may have noticed that Pandas provides a more efficient and straightforward approach to data exploration and cleaning than Excel's comparatively circuitous methods. This efficiency arises from Pandas' automated handling of missing or incomplete data, which greatly simplifies the process for business users to clean and preprocess their datasets.

1.7 EXERCISES

The Campus Bookstore also operates a coffee shop, which maintains its transaction records in a separate dataset. The file "Exercise-Ch01.xlsx" contains purchase records from the coffee shop. Using the concepts covered in this chapter, complete the following exercises with "Exercise-Ch01.xlsx" as your dataset:

E1:   **How many unique product items are there in this dataset?**

E2:   **How many unique suppliers are there in this dataset?**

E3:   **What is the total number of purchase transactions? Any missing values or zeros?**

E4:   **Any duplicated records?**

## CHAPTER 2

Basic Computation

D ATA ANALYTICS IS FAR more than just computation; it includes the crucial steps of framing the right questions, exploring data, and effectively telling stories based on analytical findings. Nevertheless, without sound computational practices, analytics can yield limited or even misleading insights. For instance, consider a business owner keen to understand the impact of late customer payments. To assess the severity of a payment delay, it is essential to calculate the number of days elapsed since the agreed-upon due date. Once the "age" of the delayed payments is accurately calculated, the business owner can leverage this information to make informed decisions, such as initiating follow-up actions on overdue payments or adjusting the credit terms for customers who frequently delay their payments.

2.1 BASIC CONCEPTS OF COMPUTATION

An effective computation in different business scenarios hinges on several key attributes:

1. **Correctness:**

   Correctness is fundamental to any analytical computation, ensuring that results are accurate and reliable. This ensures that computation results are both mathematically accurate and aligned with

DOI: 10.1201/9781003567103-3

domain-specific requirements. Mathematical correctness verifies that all formulas, from simple expressions to complex iterations and conditionals, are error-free. Domain-specific correctness, on the other hand, ensures these formulas are meaningful within the given context, such as adhering to specific accounting methods for calculating depreciation. This dual-layered approach to correctness is crucial, as it prevents the generation of misleading or erroneous conclusions that could impact decision-making processes adversely.

2. **Efficiency:**
Efficiency in computation addresses the optimization of resources while maintaining correctness. Efficient computation identifies solutions that minimize the use of computational resources and time. This aspect is particularly important in large-scale data analytics where the volume of data can be vast. Efficient computation not only speeds up processing times but also can significantly reduce operational costs. The challenge lies in balancing correctness and efficiency, particularly when dealing with complex data sets or algorithms, to ensure that the most resource-effective methods do not compromise the accuracy of the results.

3. **Extensibility:**
This refers to the ability of a computation to adapt and expand, facilitating further analysis that can provide deeper insights. In the context of customer payment delays, extensibility might allow an analyst to further categorize payments by their age, enhancing more advanced analytics to understand customers' payment behavior, credibility, and risk segmentation.

Together, these computational attributes ensure that analytics are not only accurate and resource-efficient but also adaptable to evolving business needs and capable of driving deeper insights into data. These features also remind us of the multifaceted nature of data analytics. They transcend computation from mere mechanical tasks to incorporate a broader, process-oriented perspective.

2.2 COMPUTATION – FROM BASIC TO COMPLEX

The complexity of computation varies greatly depending on the scenario. For straightforward tasks such as calculating the total cost by multiplying item price by order quantity in daily transactions, a simple and clear formula suffices. However, for more involved tasks like aggregating the total amounts from thousands of transactions, each with multiple items, the computational design becomes more complex, as this is a classic example of an aggregation problem. Despite the complexity of analytics ranging widely from basic formulas to sophisticated deep neural network (DNN)-based algorithms, the underlying principles of computation remain rooted in mathematics. The key difference lies in the computational architecture required to address your problems. Fortunately, most business analytics scenarios do not demand the computational sophistication of DNN models. What you will learn from this book will equip you to handle the majority of business analytics scenarios effectively. In this chapter, we will concentrate on simple computational scenarios that require only a minimal number of formulas. Later chapters will explore the more complex computational designs needed to tackle advanced analytics problems.

2.3 BASIC COMPUTATIONS WITH BOOKSTORE DATASET

In this chapter, we will be using the "Bookstore-Ch02.xlsx" file for our demonstration. Before we dive into basic computations, make sure you are familiar with the "**Invoice**" worksheet – a cleansed version that has had duplicate transactions removed (as detailed in the previous chapter) from the "**Invoice_raw**" worksheet. It is highly recommended to review **Chapter 1** for the data structure of the "**Invoice**" worksheet. We will use this refined dataset to showcase how to manage basic computations using Excel and Python, focusing on the following examples:

Q1: **What are the extensions (the product of price and quantity) before and after discount?**

Q2: **Calculate the margins earned for each sales item (defined as Margin = (Sale Price – Cost) * Quantity).**

Q3: **Calculate the new margins if we apply a 5% markup to the list prices due to a CPI adjustment.**

2.4 EXCEL

Excel is renowned for its "what you see is what you get" functionality, which is especially useful for handling simple calculations like the three questions mentioned above.

Q1: What are the extensions (the product of price and quantity) before and after discount?

- **Extension before discount**
  To calculate the extension before discount, you can follow these steps to insert a new column and create the necessary formula:

  1. **Insert a New Column**:
     - Right-click on the column header of the **List Price** to bring up the context menu.
     - Select "Insert" from the menu to add a blank column to the right of the List Price column.

E	F	G	H	I	J
Quantity	Discount	Cost	List Price	Quantity in Stock	Emp ID
3	0	25.87	43.12	44	EMP-003
3	0.15	25.07	41.79		
3	0.1	25.07	41.79		
1	0.15	1.55	2.59		
3	0.15	4.21	7.02		
2	0.1	11.12	18.53		
3	0.15	11.12	18.53		
3	0.15	27.29	45.48		
2	0.1	25.07	41.79		
1	0.2	3.04	5.06		
3	0.1	25.43	42.38		
1	0.1	13.32	22.2		
2	0.2	25.87	43.12		
2	0.2	27.29	45.48		

  2. **Label the New Column**:
     - In the new column, enter the label "**Extension - No Discount**" at the top in cell I1.

E	F	G	H	I
Quantity	Discount	Cost	List Price	Extension - No Discount
3	0	25.87	43.12	
3	0.15	25.07	41.79	
3	0.1	25.07	41.79	

  3. **Create the Formula**:
     - Click in cell I2 to start entering your formula.

- Type "=" to begin the formula.
- Click on cell H2 to reference the List Price in your formula.
- Type "*" to add the multiplication operator.
- Click on cell E2 to reference the **Quantity**.
- Your completed formula in cell I2 should look like: "=H2*E2"

E	F	G	H	I
Quantity	Discount	Cost	List Price	Extension - No Discount
3	0	25.87	43.12	=H2*E2

- Press "Enter" and this formula will calculate the product of **List Price** and **Quantity**.

E	F	G	H	I
Quantity	Discount	Cost	List Price	Extension - No Discount
3	0	25.87	43.12	129.36
3	0.15	25.07	41.79	

4. **Fill the Formula Down**:
Now we'd like to fill the formula of the first row to all other rows. When dealing with thousands of rows in Excel, filling a formula efficiently down an entire column is crucial for saving time and minimizing potential errors. Among all different methods, we highly recommend you to "double-click the fill handle":

- Position your cell pointer on the lower-right corner (looks like a green tiny dot) of cell I2 (the first formula) until your pointer turns into a small black cross (this is the fill handle).

E	F	G	H	I
Quantity	Discount	Cost	List Price	Extension - No Discount
3	0	25.87	43.12	129.36
3	0.15	25.07	41.79	

- Double-click the fill handle. Excel will automatically copy the formula down the column to the last adjacent row with data. This method assumes there's data in the column directly beside it, which defines where to stop.

Extension - No Discount
129.36
125.37
125.37
2.59
21.06
37.06
55.59
136.44
83.58
5.06
127.14
22.2
86.24
90.96

- **Extension after discount**

To calculate the extension after a discount, you can use a similar process to add a new column J with the label "**Extension - Discounted**" and modify the formula slightly. Your completed formula in cell J2 should be: "=H2*E2*(1-F2)" to take into account the discount offered:

E	F	G	H	I	J
Quantity	Discount	Cost	List Price	Extension - No Discount	Extension - Discounted
3	0	25.87	43.12	129.36	=H2*E2*(1-F2)

The modified formula allows you to compute the discounted extension for each item. You can then visually compare the first few rows of both columns side-by-side to see the effect of the discount:

Extension - No Discount	Extension - Discounted
129.36	129.36
125.37	106.5645
125.37	112.833
2.59	2.2015
21.06	17.901
37.06	33.354
55.59	47.2515
136.44	115.974
83.58	75.222
5.06	4.048
127.14	114.426

Q2: Calculate the margins earned for each sales item.

To calculate margin earned (defined as Margin = (Sale Price – Cost) * Quantity), we will add an extra column: "**Cost**" since margin is determined by the difference between the sale price (defined as the discounted price) and the cost. With that in mind, you can follow a similar process to add a new column K with the label "**Margin**" and create the formula based on the definition of margin. We leave this to you as an exercise. Your completed formula in cell K2 should be: "=(H2*(1-F2)-G2)*E2" to take into account the discounted price or sale price, as shown below:

K
Margin
=(H2*(1-F2)-G2)*E2

NOTE: To accurately formulate the margin calculation, please ensure that you manage the parentheses correctly to reflect the appropriate order of operations. Please verify the first few rows of your calculation results against the screenshot provided below:

K
Margin
51.75
31.3545
37.623
0.6515
5.271
11.114
13.8915
34.104
25.082
1.008

Q3: Calculate the new margins if we apply a 5% markup to the list prices due to a CPI adjustment.

We aim to determine how the margins would be affected if we increased the list prices of all items by 5%. To address this, it is not efficient to create a new column filled with the 5% value for each row, as it is unnecessary to repeat a constant value thousands of times. Each row is supposed to store data values that might vary across a dataset. If we have a constant to reference, repeating the constant value for a thousand times is absolutely not a good idea. Instead, we need a better solution to add the constant into our formula.

The most straightforward approach is to directly increase the List Price by 5% like H2*(1+5%). That is, adding the numerical value to the formula. However, this approach has limitations in terms of extensibility, a key attribute we discussed earlier. The issue with "hard-coding" the 5% directly into the formula is that it becomes cumbersome to update if, in the future, you decide to test different increase rates like 8%, 10%, or other percentages.

- **Absolute Reference**
  A better strategy involves using an "absolute reference" to a cell that contains the constant value. This method allows for easy adjustments without modifying the formula extensively each time the percentage changes. Before we implement "absolute reference" in Q3, let's discuss Excel's different reference methods.

COMPLEMENTARY NOTE – EXCEL'S REFERENCE METHODS

Excel offers two main types of cell references when creating formulas: **relative references** and **absolute references**. Understanding the distinction between these is crucial for effective formula construction and managing data dynamically across your spreadsheets.

Relative Reference

A relative reference in Excel is the default behavior when you use cell addresses in formulas. It means that when a formula is copied and pasted into another cell, the reference changes relative to the position of the formula. For example, if you have a formula in cell A1 as =B1+C1 and you copy this formula to A2, it will automatically adjust to =B2+C2. This adjustment happens because Excel shifts the reference according to the formula's new location, making it very useful for applying the same operation across multiple rows or columns.

Absolute Reference

An absolute reference in Excel is created by placing a dollar sign ($) before the column label and/or the row number in the cell reference. This tells Excel to keep the reference constant, no matter where the formula is moved or copied. For example, if you put =$B$1+C1 in cell A1 and copy it to A2, the formula will change to =$B$1+C2. Here, B1 is an absolute reference and will not change as the formula is copied down the column, while C1 is a relative reference and adjusts to C2.

Mixed Reference

Besides purely relative or absolute, Excel also allows mixed references, where either the row or the column remains fixed. For example, =B$1+ C1 ensures that while the column B might change when the formula is moved horizontally, the row 1 remains fixed. Conversely, =$B1+C1 will keep column B constant but allows the row number to change when the formula is copied vertically.

Tip: The F4 key

Technically, you might find toggling reference methods with the F4 key is very handy. The F4 key is a powerful shortcut that allows you to toggle through different cell reference methods quickly while editing a formula. This helps you easily switch between relative, absolute, and mixed references without manually typing dollar signs.

Usage Scenarios

- **Relative references** are useful for operations that need to apply a consistent process across multiple data points. For example, calculating the total cost for different items listed in each row.
- **Absolute references** are vital when you need to refer to a specific, unchanging cell, such as a tax rate or a unit conversion factor that needs to be used across various calculations in a worksheet.
- **Mixed references** come into play when you need a hybrid behavior, maintaining some parts of the formula constant while allowing others to adjust. This can be useful in budget sheets or tax tables where certain parameters change based on one dimension (either row or column) but remain constant across the other.

Understanding and applying these types of references correctly can significantly enhance your efficiency in Excel, allowing you to create more dynamic and robust spreadsheets.

Now, based on the Complementary Note above, you can add the absolute reference to the formula following the steps below:

- Insert a new column L with the label "**Margin – What-IF Analysis**."
- Move your cell pointer to column U and enter "Markup" as the label for the CPI adjustment rate
- Type either 5% or 0.05 in cell U2, as shown below:

- Develop the formula based on the mathematical relationships between List Price, Discount, Markup, and Quantity. When referring to the markup rate from cell U2, use the F4 key to toggle the reference to an absolute format: $U$2. The finalized formula should be: "= (H2*(1-F2)*(1+$U$2)-G2)*E2", as illustrated below:

L
Margin - What-If analysis
=(H2*(1-F2)*(1+$U$2)-G2)*E2

- Double-click the fill handle to fill column L with the formula.
- Verify the first few rows of your what-if analysis against the screenshot provided below:

L
Margin - What-If analysis
58.218
36.682725
43.26465
0.761575
6.16605
12.7817
16.254075

SIDE NOTE – COLUMN WIDTH ADJUSTMENT:

Occasionally, a cell may contain a value that exceeds the current column width, leading to visual confusions like overlapping between columns or hashtag symbols (#) that obscure the cell content. In these cases, it's standard practice to adjust the column width to accommodate the longer data. You may move your cell pointer to the boundary on the column header between the two columns you want to adjust. The cursor will change to a column resizing icon, which looks like a vertical bar with a left and right arrow. Then click and drag the boundary to the right to increase the width of the left column, or to the left to decrease it. Alternatively, you can double-click the column boundary (the resizing icon), and Excel will automatically adjust the width to fit the longest entry in that column.

• **Excel's Named Range – the "Define Name" Feature**

In Excel, using an absolute reference ensures that the cell reference stays constant (or locked), no matter where in the worksheet the formula is moved or copied. However, its redundant prefix $ can lead to both readability and maintenance issues, especially as formulas or datasets grow larger and more complex. In addition, the concept of absolute references is specific to spreadsheet software like Excel and doesn't universally apply to other applications and programming languages.

Excel's "Define Name" Allows users to create a human-readable name that refers to a cell, range of cells, formula, or constant value. These names can then be used in formulas. It enhances formula readability and manageability. For example, using =SUM(QuantitySold) is clearer than = SUM($E$2:$E$2017). Here QuantitySold is a defined range from E2 to E2017, hypothetically.

To use the "Define Name" feature, first position the cell pointer on cell U2, which contains the 5% markup rate. Next, click on the "Formulas" tab at the top of the screen. From the Formulas ribbon, locate the dropdown menu for "Define Names" and select "Define Names" as shown below:

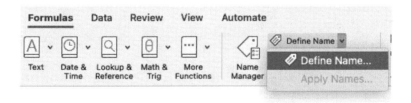

In the pop-up window that appears, start by entering the variable name "markup" in the "Name" box. Next, expand the "Scope" dropdown menu and select "Invoice" if you wish to limit the usage of "markup" to the current worksheet only. This step is optional; if you want "markup" to be a global variable accessible across different worksheets, leave the scope unchanged. In the "Comment" box, you can add any notes about the variable for future reference. Finally, ensure that the "Refers to" box correctly points to cell U2. Once everything is verified and correct, click "OK" to finalize the creation of the new "markup" variable:

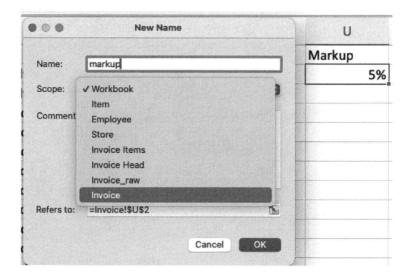

Now, add a new column M and label it as "**Margin - What-If with Defined Variable**". Next, place the cursor in cell M2 to construct a new formula for margin. This time, reference the newly defined variable "markup" instead of using an absolute reference. Begin typing "m" for "markup" in the formula bar. Excel's intelligent autofill function will then display a list of variables and functions. Select "markup" from this list to incorporate it into your formula without needing to type it manually, as illustrated below:

After filling the entire column with the first formula, you will quickly notice that the results are identical to those obtained using an absolute reference.

Using the "Named Range" feature in Excel offers numerous benefits that can enhance both the functionality and manageability of your spreadsheets. Specifically, this functionality can: 1) improve readability and understandability of your formulas, 2) simplify formula creation, 3) enhance formula accuracy, 4) make maintenance and updates easier, 5) track and navigate formulas more efficiently, and 6) support advanced excel features such as Macros and VBA. More importantly, those defined names in Excel are similar to variables in programming. They provide a more flexible way to label data or a calculation with a meaningful name, reducing errors and improving code readability.

SIDE NOTE – NAME MANAGER

As you work with increasingly complex Excel projects, managing multiple defined names becomes crucial. Excel's Name Manager is an essential tool designed to help you efficiently oversee all the variables you have defined within your workbook.

The Name Manager is a feature in Excel that allows you to view, edit, delete, and create new names used in your workbook. These names can refer to single cells, ranges of cells, formulas, or constants, and are used to make formula creation easier and more readable.

You can access the Name Manager from the Formulas tab in Excel. Click on "Formulas" tab, then click on "Name Manager" in the ribbon. A dialog box will open showing all the names currently defined in the workbook. For example, the "markup" variable we just defined can be found in the Name Manager:

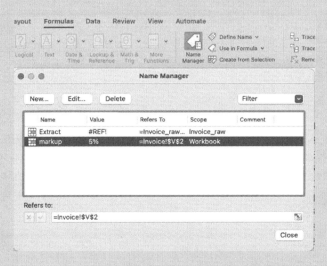

> **Note:** You may observe that the reference for "markup" shifted from cell U2 to cell V2. This occurred because we inserted a new column M after defining "markup". Excel intelligently recognizes such positional changes and automatically adjusts the reference accordingly. This automatic adjustment for position shifts also applies to both relative and absolute references when you add or move a referenced column or row after formulas have already been established.
>
> Using the Name Manager helps maintain an organized approach to managing names, especially in large or complex spreadsheets. It ensures that names are used consistently and can be updated or corrected centrally, reducing errors and improving clarity in your Excel projects.

2.5 PYTHON

Please refer to the Jupyter notebook file "Bookstore-Ch02.ipynb" to access the code, or view the "Bookstore-Ch02.html" file to see the outputs of all code.

2.5.1 Basic Concepts of Programming

As its title suggests, programming is about how to "program" your tasks and ask computer to execute the program. That said, the first thing is to figure out what you want to accomplish. These tasks might be as simple as an arithmetic calculation or might be as complicated as developing a machine learning model for the prediction of future stock prices. Regardless of its complexity, each task has the same basic elements: `input`, `process`, and `output`.

For example, if you plan to develop Python programs to automatically generate financial statements (such as income statement and balance sheet) based on journal entry data stored in a structured Excel workbook. In this scenario, clearly the `input` data is the Excel workbook that contains the transaction journal data in a structured form. The `output` is the standard make-ups of an income statement and a balance sheet (as a business major student, you should have learned the process in your introductory accounting courses). The most critical part is the `process` to aggregate entries for the financial reporting purpose. The challenge lies in how to convert the process (accounting rules) into Python code (Python rules) `without errors`.

In order to reach the goal, you need to learn what is the Python way of doing the analytics tasks. If this is your first class of programming, please keep in mind the `Python way`, just like other programming languages, is built on `coding conventions`. That said, Python requires you to use English-like statements to communicate with it. It is not like those non-code dropdown menus in Excel, which you might be more familiar with in the past.

2.5.2 Why Learn Python When We Already Have Excel?

You might view transitioning to Python as entering a challenging new realm, so why bother learning Python if you're already familiar with Excel?

Firstly, Python can perform tasks well beyond Excel's capabilities. While Excel's user-friendly interface is highly effective for numerous tasks, it has its limitations. For instance, Excel struggles with processing unstructured data like social media posts, reviews, and other web content. It also cannot handle complex machine learning algorithms. Python is a Turing Complete language capable of executing any computation you might need. In fact, most of the state-of-the-art Large Language Models (such as GPT models) and other Generative AI models are built on Python.

Secondly, Python is better suited than Excel for handling very large datasets. Excel has a row limit (1,048,576 rows per sheet) and can become sluggish with large files. Python, with libraries like Pandas and NumPy, can efficiently handle millions of rows of data for complex data analysis and machine learning without the performance limitation. On the other hand, Excel's WYSIWYG (what you see is what you get) approach, with which any change you make to the dataset is immediately visible, can be useful for small datasets. However, it becomes overwhelming with larger ones.

Thirdly, Python's widespread use and famous community support make Python an invaluable skill in many fields. Python is open-source, which means it is free to use, even for commercial applications. This can be a significant advantage over licensed software in cost-sensitive environments. Being open-source also means that Python is continuously improved by a global community of developers, ensuring that the language and its libraries are on the cutting edge of technology and security practices. In fact, the breadth of Python's libraries significantly extends what you can accomplish without starting from scratch. As of mid-2025, Python's standard library includes over 220 modules that offer a wide range of functions and data types. Beyond these, there's a vast array of over 614,000 third-party libraries available through the Python Package Index (PyPi) (Source: Wikipedia). These libraries, such as the open-source Pandas which we will use heavily in this book, provide powerful data structures and tools for fast, efficient data analysis. Installing these libraries is straightforward using Python's package manager, pip, enhancing Python's utility and efficiency for various tasks.

Lastly, Python boasts a simple, English-like syntax that is particularly approachable for beginners. Compared to other popular programming languages like C and Java, Python is far more accessible, especially for students with a business background. This ease of use is why many seasoned programmers recommend Python to newcomers.

In conclusion, while Excel is a potent tool for many small-size business applications, Python opens up a broader range of possibilities, making it a critical skill for those looking to expand their analytical and technical expertise. Python's popularity continues to surge, making it a top choice if you're looking to master a single programming language.

2.5.3 Using Variables in Python

Python's approach of defining variables is quite flexible. There is no need to declare a variable with a specific data type beforehand, and variables can switch types dynamically after their initial assignment. This flexibility in changing a variable's data type is somewhat akin to how Excel handles values in named cells, adapting to whatever content is placed. To get a better understanding, let's begin with a few basic examples before diving into the Bookstore questions:

```
In[#]:

x = 5 # x is an integer (int)
print("x =", x)
x = "Carlos Santana" # now x is a string (str)
print("x Now is:",x)

Out[#]:

x = 5
x Now is: Carlos Santana
```

• Python Comments

As you've observed in the previous examples, comments in Python are used to clarify code. They begin with a hash symbol, #, and continue until the end of the line. Comments can be placed at the beginning of a line or following executable code. Here's how you can use them:

```
In[#]:
# This is a comment
print("Hello, World!")  # This is also a comment
Out[#]:
Hello, World!
```

• Python's print()

Python's print() function can handle various data types seamlessly within a single statement, eliminating the need for type conversions. Additionally, it supports multiple string formatting techniques and the use of placeholders, which will be discussed in more detail in upcoming chapters. Here's a basic example demonstrating how to concatenate variables of different types:

```
In[#]:
name = "John"
weight = 70.8
print("My name is " + name + " and my weight is " + str(weight)) # no
formatting print
Out[#]:
My name is John and my weight is 70.8
```

You can assign values to multiple variables simultaneously in a single line by separating each variable with commas:

```
In[#]:
x, y, z = "Aerosmith", "Boston", "Chicago"
print(x, y, z) # To print all three variables at once
Out[#]:
Aerosmith Boston Chicago
```

You have the option to assign the same value to several variables at once using chained assignment. This approach streamlines variable initialization and can make your code cleaner and more concise:

```
In[#]:

Greatest_Band = Best_In_England = Love_Forever = "Beatles"
print(Greatest_Band, Best_In_England, Love_Forever)

Out[#]:

Beatles Beatles Beatles
```

• Python's Naming Convention

The naming convention for Python variables is very simple: 1) they can only contain alpha-numeric characters and underscores (A-z, 0-9, and _), 2) they cannot start with a number, and 3) they are case-sensitive (great, Great, and GREAT represent three different variables).

2.5.4 Basic Data Types

Variables can store data of different types. With different data types, you can do different things. Like other programming languages, Python supports many built-in data types. For business users, you should at least learn some of the frequently used types. We define Python's basic (or `atomic`) data types as simple values stored in one variable. For example, you may store an integer like 5, or a decimal number like 3.14, or a string like "Python", or even a logical value like `True` or `False` to one variable:

- Numeric Types: `int` (integer), `float` (decimal number)
- Boolean Type: `bool` (Boolean logical values: True/False)
- String Type: `str` (string)

In this chapter, we will concentrate on the numeric data type, with plans to explore other types in upcoming chapters.

• Numeric Type

Python supports a variety of arithmetic operations for handling numeric data. Let's refresh our understanding of these basic Python arithmetic operators:

Operator	Name	Example
+	Addition	X+Y
-	Subtraction	X-Y
*	Multiplication	X*Y
/	Division	X/Y
%	Modulus	X%Y
**	Exponentiation	X**Y
//	Floor division	X//Y

In the Introduction Chapter, we used Python as a calculator to explore some fundamental arithmetic operations. Now, let's advance our understanding by integrating these arithmetic operations with variable usage:

```
In[#]:

x1 = 5
x2 = 6
y = x1 - x2 # assign (x1-x2) to y
print(x1, "-", x2, "=", y) # print() can concatenate x1, x2, and y
with strings

Out[#]:

5 - 6 = -1
```

You can also specify the data type of a variable by using casting functions like int(), float(), and str(). These functions convert values into integer, floating-point number, and string data types respectively:

```
In[#]:

x1 = float(1)      # x will be 1.0
x2 = float(2.1)    # y will be 2.1
x3 = float("3")    # z will be 3.0
x4 = int(4.2) # w will be 4
x5 = str(3)
print(x1,x2,x3,x4,x5)

Out[#]:

1.0 2.1 3.0 4 3
```

2.5.5 Compound Assignment Operators

Python, like many programming languages, incorporates compound assignment operators to streamline code by combining an arithmetic operation with an assignment. Instead of writing a = a + b, you can use the compound assignment syntax a += b, which simplifies and shortens the code. This concept, originally introduced in the C programming language, is now widely adopted in various popular languages, including C, Java, C#, and Python. Understanding these operators is essential because they are commonly used and can significantly enhance the efficiency of your code. The following table provides a summary of all compound assignment operators available in Python.

Compound Assignment Operator	Description
+=	a+=b means a=a+b(assign a+b to a)
-=	a-=b means a=a-b(assign a-b to a)
*=	a*=b means a=a*b(assign a*b to a)
/=	a/=b means a=a/b(assign a/b to a)
%=	a%=b means a=a%b(assign a%b to a)
**=	a**=b means a=a**b(assign a**b to a)
//=	a//=b means a=a//b(assign a//b to a)

In[#]:

```
a=0
b=10
a+=b
print(a)
```

Out[#]:

```
10
```

In the example above, the compound assignment a += b is used as a shorthand for the expression a = a + b. This is why, after the operation, the value of a becomes 10. This simplification not only makes the code cleaner but also slightly faster to execute in many programming languages, including Python.

2.5.6 Data Import

As we discussed in Chapter 1, Pandas facilitates the import of Excel worksheets using the pd.read_excel() method, which requires the file path as input. After loading the data, we store it in a DataFrame named "invoice". To confirm the successful import of all rows, we display the last five rows of the DataFrame. This step is a practical way to quickly verify that the data has been correctly loaded into Pandas.

In[#]:

```
import pandas as pd

filepath = "/Users/chi2019/Desktop/Book/Excel Files/Bookstore-Ch02.
xlsx" # Change the path according to your file location

# For Windows users, prefix r is added:
# filepath = r"C:\Users\chou4291\Desktop\Book\Bookstore-Ch02.xlsx"
```

In[#]:

```
invoice = pd.read_excel(filepath, sheet_name = "Invoice", header = 0,
usecols = "A:P", nrows = 2016)
print(invoice.tail(5)) # Display the last five rows of the invoice
DataFrame
```

Out[#]:

	Invoice Number	Date	Item Number	Item	Quantity	Discount \
2011	998	2023-03-31	PI-007	Baseball Cap	1	0.0
2012	999	2023-03-31	PI-004	Scarf	3	0.2
2013	999	2023-03-31	PI-008	Mug	1	0.0
2014	1000	2023-03-31	PI-005	Gloves	1	0.1
2015	1000	2023-03-31	PI-016	Handbag	2	0.0

	Cost	List Price	Quantity in Stock	Emp ID	Name \
2011	4.21	7.02	14	EMP-008	Nathaniel Marquez
2012	6.79	11.32	39	EMP-007	Carol Parker
2013	27.29	45.48	38	EMP-007	Carol Parker
2014	13.32	22.20	17	EMP-001	Bradley Marshall
2015	10.75	17.91	16	EMP-001	Bradley Marshall

	Start Date	Weekly Payment	Store ID	Store Name \
2011	2022-09-07	1072	ST-004	South
2012	2022-04-03	1175	ST-003	North
2013	2022-04-03	1175	ST-003	North
2014	2022-09-27	1084	ST-001	East
2015	2022-09-27	1084	ST-001	East

	Address
2011	2320 Saunders Square Suite 940, Los Angeles, C...
2012	078 Cindy Shore, Los Angeles, CA 96017
2013	078 Cindy Shore, Los Angeles, CA 96017
2014	98982 Adam Ports Suite 231, Los Angeles, CA 91696
2015	98982 Adam Ports Suite 231, Los Angeles, CA 91696

For detailed explanations and uses of the parameters sheet_name, header, usecols, and nrows in the read_excel() method, please refer to Chapter 1.

2.5.7 Basic Computation Exercises

Q1: What are the extensions (the product of price and quantity) before and after discount?
From Chapter 1, we learned that in Pandas, you can access column data using square brackets with the column label, like invoice["Quantity"]. To introduce a new column (e.g., "Extension - No Discount") calculated from existing columns, you can use the following approach:

```
invoice["Extension - No Discount"] = invoice["Quantity"] *
invoice["List Price"]
```

In this formula, the left-hand side invoice["Extension - No Discount"] specifies a new column, as it doesn't previously exist in the DataFrame. On the right-hand side, the formula utilizes Pandas' capability for element-wise operations to multiply the contents of two existing columns and assigns the result to the newly created column. It's important to note that only existing columns can be referenced on the right-hand side of the equation. Now, let's put this into practice:

In[#]:
```
invoice["Extension - No Discount"] = invoice["Quantity"] *
invoice["List Price"]
print(invoice.head(5)) # Display the first five rows for verification
```

Out[#]:

```
   Invoice         Date Item Number           Item  Quantity  Discount \
    Number
0        1   2023-01-01       PI-003         Jacket         3      0.00
1        1   2023-01-01       PI-012            Pen         3      0.15
2        2   2023-01-01       PI-012            Pen         3      0.10
3        3   2023-01-01       PI-011 Stuffed Mascot         1      0.15
4        3   2023-01-01       PI-007   Baseball Cap         3      0.15

    Cost  List Price  Quantity in  Emp ID             Name       Start
                            Stock                                Date \
0  25.87       43.12           44 EMP-003  Daniel Marquez  2023-02-08
1  25.07       41.79           32 EMP-003  Daniel Marquez  2023-02-08
2  25.07       41.79           32 EMP-006     Kristin Lee  2022-01-05
3   1.55        2.59           22 EMP-002  Valerie Gibson  2022-04-09
4   4.21        7.02           14 EMP-002  Valerie Gibson  2022-04-09

   Weekly Payment Store ID Store Name \
0            1139    ST-003      North
1            1139    ST-003      North
2            1013    ST-002       West
3            1115    ST-002       West
4            1115    ST-002       West

                                Address  Extension - No Discount
0         078 Cindy Shore, Los Angeles, CA 96017          129.36
1         078 Cindy Shore, Los Angeles, CA 96017          125.37
2 845 Lloyd Walk Apt. 693, Los Angeles, CA 91326          125.37
3 845 Lloyd Walk Apt. 693, Los Angeles, CA 91326            2.59
4 845 Lloyd Walk Apt. 693, Los Angeles, CA 91326           21.06
```

From the output, it's evident that the new "Extension - No Discount" column has been successfully added as the last column in the DataFrame.

• The Order of Columns

By default, new columns in Pandas are appended to the end. However, if the order of columns matters to your data presentation or analysis, you can reposition the newly added column to a desired place using advanced techniques below:

In[#]:

```
cols = invoice.columns.tolist()
type(cols)
```

Out[#]:

```
list
```

In[#]:

```
c = cols.pop()
cols
```

Out[#]:

```
["Invoice Number",
"Date",
"Item Number",
"Item",
"Quantity",
"Discount",
"Cost",
"List Price",
"Quantity in Stock",
"Emp ID",
"Name",
"Start Date",
"Weekly Payment",
"Store ID",
"Store Name",
"Address"]
```

In[#]:

```
cols.insert(8, c)
cols
```

Out[#]:

```
["Invoice Number",
"Date",
"Item Number",
"Item",
"Quantity",
"Discount",
"Cost",
"List Price",
"Extension - No Discount",
"Quantity in Stock",
"Emp ID",
```

```
"Name",
"Start Date",
"Weekly Payment",
"Store ID",
"Store Name",
"Address"]
```

In[#]:

```
# The code snippet below involves advanced techniques and is
therefore optional.

columns = invoice.columns.tolist()  # Get a list of all column names

# Move the last column to the desired position. In this case, the
intended position is at index 8
middle_index = 8
columns.insert(middle_index, columns.pop())  # pop() removes and
returns the last item

# Assign the re-ordered columns back to a copy of invoice to keep the
original DataFrame clean
invoice_copy = invoice[columns] # The invoice_copy has the
desired order
print(invoice_copy.head(5))
```

Out [#]:

```
        Invoice         Date Item Number         Item Quantity Discount  \
        Number
0             1   2023-01-01       PI-003       Jacket        3     0.00
1             1   2023-01-01       PI-012          Pen        3     0.15
2             2   2023-01-01       PI-012          Pen        3     0.10
3             3   2023-01-01       PI-011 Stuffed Mascot      1     0.15
4             3   2023-01-01       PI-007  Baseball Cap       3     0.15

     Cost  List Price  Extension - No Discount    Quantity  Emp ID  \
                                                  in Stock
0   25.87       43.12                   129.36          44 EMP-003
1   25.07       41.79                   125.37          32 EMP-003
2   25.07       41.79                   125.37          32 EMP-006
3    1.55        2.59                     2.59          22 EMP-002
4    4.21        7.02                    21.06          14 EMP-002
              Name Start Date  Weekly Payment Store ID Store Name  \
0   Daniel Marquez 2023-02-08            1139    ST-003      North
1   Daniel Marquez 2023-02-08            1139    ST-003      North
2      Kristin Lee 2022-01-05            1013    ST-002       West
3   Valerie Gibson 2022-04-09            1115    ST-002       West
4   Valerie Gibson 2022-04-09            1115    ST-002       West

                                      Address
0           078 Cindy Shore, Los Angeles, CA 96017
1           078 Cindy Shore, Los Angeles, CA 96017
2   845 Lloyd Walk Apt. 693, Los Angeles, CA 91326
3   845 Lloyd Walk Apt. 693, Los Angeles, CA 91326
4   845 Lloyd Walk Apt. 693, Los Angeles, CA 91326
```

As you may have noticed, Pandas' column aggregation capability is highly effective. It allows for the aggregation of entire columns (conceptually similar to vectors in mathematics) without the need for explicit repetitive loops or additional filling operations.

Using this efficient pattern, we can quickly derive the formula for the "Extension - Discounted" column:

In[#]:

```
invoice["Extension - Discounted"] = invoice["Quantity"] *
invoice["List Price"] * (1 - invoice["Discount"])
print(invoice.head(5))
```

Out[#]:

	Invoice Number	Date	Item Number	Item	Quantity	Discount \
0	1	2023-01-01	PI-003	Jacket	3	0.00
1	1	2023-01-01	PI-012	Pen	3	0.15
2	2	2023-01-01	PI-012	Pen	3	0.10
3	3	2023-01-01	PI-011	Stuffed Mascot	1	0.15
4	3	2023-01-01	PI-007	Baseball Cap	3	0.15

	Cost	List Price	Quantity in Stock	Emp ID	Name	Start Date \
0	25.87	43.12	44	EMP-003	Daniel Marquez	2023-02-08
1	25.07	41.79	32	EMP-003	Daniel Marquez	2023-02-08
2	25.07	41.79	32	EMP-006	Kristin Lee	2022-01-05
3	1.55	2.59	22	EMP-002	Valerie Gibson	2022-04-09
4	4.21	7.02	14	EMP-002	Valerie Gibson	2022-04-09

	Weekly Payment	Store ID	Store Name \
0	1139	ST-003	North
1	1139	ST-003	North
2	1013	ST-002	West
3	1115	ST-002	West
4	1115	ST-002	West

	Address	Extension - No Discount \
0	078 Cindy Shore, Los Angeles, CA 96017	129.36
1	078 Cindy Shore, Los Angeles, CA 96017	125.37
2	845 Lloyd Walk Apt. 693, Los Angeles, CA 91326	125.37
3	845 Lloyd Walk Apt. 693, Los Angeles, CA 91326	2.59
4	845 Lloyd Walk Apt. 693, Los Angeles, CA 91326	21.06

	Extension - Discounted
0	129.3600
1	106.5645
2	112.8330
3	2.2015
4	17.9010

Q2: Calculate the margins earned for each sales item.

Building on what we've covered in Q1, adding a new calculated column in Pandas is quite straightforward. Therefore, we can quickly establish the formula for the margins earned (defined as Margin = (Sale Price – Cost) * Quantity) as follows:

In[#]:

```
invoice["Margin"] = invoice["Quantity"] * (invoice["List Price"] * (1 -
invoice["Discount"]) - invoice["Cost"])
print(invoice.head(5))
```

Out[#]:

	Invoice Number	Date	Item Number	Item	Quantity	Discount \
0	1	2023-01-01	PI-003	Jacket	3	0.00
1	1	2023-01-01	PI-012	Pen	3	0.15
2	2	2023-01-01	PI-012	Pen	3	0.10
3	3	2023-01-01	PI-011	Stuffed Mascot	1	0.15
4	3	2023-01-01	PI-007	Baseball Cap	3	0.15

	Cost	List Price	Quantity in Stock	Emp ID	Name	Start Date \
0	25.87	43.12	44	EMP-003	Daniel Marquez	2023-02-08
1	25.07	41.79	32	EMP-003	Daniel Marquez	2023-02-08
2	25.07	41.79	32	EMP-006	Kristin Lee	2022-01-05
3	1.55	2.59	22	EMP-002	Valerie Gibson	2022-04-09
4	4.21	7.02	14	EMP-002	Valerie Gibson	2022-04-09

	Weekly Payment	Store ID	Store Name \
0	1139	ST-003	North
1	1139	ST-003	North
2	1013	ST-002	West
3	1115	ST-002	West
4	1115	ST-002	West

	Address	Extension - No Discount \
0	078 Cindy Shore, Los Angeles, CA 96017	129.36
1	078 Cindy Shore, Los Angeles, CA 96017	125.37
2	845 Lloyd Walk Apt. 693, Los Angeles, CA 91326	125.37
3	845 Lloyd Walk Apt. 693, Los Angeles, CA 91326	2.59
4	845 Lloyd Walk Apt. 693, Los Angeles, CA 91326	21.06

	Extension - Discounted	Margin
0	129.3600	51.7500
1	106.5645	31.3545
2	112.8330	37.6230
3	2.2015	0.6515
4	17.9010	5.2710

Q3: Calculate the new margins if we apply a 5% markup to the list prices due to a CPI adjustment.

As previously mentioned, Python's flexibility with variables is highly advantageous. For a "what-if" analysis like Q3, you simply need to define a variable for the markup rate and then incorporate it into the formula for calculating the "what-if" margin:

In[#]:

```
markup = 0.05 # Note that Python does not support numbers in the
percentage format. That's why we use decimal.
invoice["Margin - What-If analysis"] = invoice["Quantity"] *
(invoice["List Price"] * (1 + markup) * (1 - invoice["Discount"]) -
invoice["Cost"])
print(invoice.head(5))
```

Out[#]:

	Invoice Number	Date	Item Number	Item	Quantity	Discount	\
0	1	2023-01-01	PI-003	Jacket	3	0.00	
1	1	2023-01-01	PI-012	Pen	3	0.15	
2	2	2023-01-01	PI-012	Pen	3	0.10	
3	3	2023-01-01	PI-011	Stuffed Mascot	1	0.15	
4	3	2023-01-01	PI-007	Baseball Cap	3	0.15	

	Cost	List Price	Quantity in Stock	Emp ID	Name	Start Date	\
0	25.87	43.12	44	EMP-003	Daniel Marquez	2023-02-08	
1	25.07	41.79	32	EMP-003	Daniel Marquez	2023-02-08	
2	25.07	41.79	32	EMP-006	Kristin Lee	2022-01-05	
3	1.55	2.59	22	EMP-002	Valerie Gibson	2022-04-09	
4	4.21	7.02	14	EMP-002	Valerie Gibson	2022-04-09	

	Weekly Payment	Store ID	Store Name	\
0	1139	ST-003	North	
1	1139	ST-003	North	
2	1013	ST-002	West	
3	1115	ST-002	West	
4	1115	ST-002	West	

	Address	Extension - No Discount	\
0	078 Cindy Shore, Los Angeles, CA 96017	129.36	
1	078 Cindy Shore, Los Angeles, CA 96017	125.37	
2	845 Lloyd Walk Apt. 693, Los Angeles, CA 91326	125.37	
3	845 Lloyd Walk Apt. 693, Los Angeles, CA 91326	2.59	
4	845 Lloyd Walk Apt. 693, Los Angeles, CA 91326	21.06	

	Extension - Discounted	Margin	Margin - What-If analysis
0	129.3600	51.7500	58.218000
1	106.5645	31.3545	36.682725
2	112.8330	37.6230	43.264650
3	2.2015	0.6515	0.761575
4	17.9010	5.2710	6.166050

2.6 DISCUSSIONS

• **The Advantages of Variable Declaration in Programming Languages**
In this chapter, you have learned how to use Excel's absolute references, "define name" feature, and Python's variable declaration to consistently refer to data within computations. You probably have noticed using variables to facilitate computations is more advantageous.

In programming, variables are used to store data values. A variable in a program can be declared to represent a particular value or data structure and can be referred to multiple times throughout the program. Variables in programming are more dynamic compared to Excel's absolute references and named ranges. They can hold different data types and structures, change values throughout the execution of the program, and are integral to controlling program flow and logic.

Additionally, variables can be reassigned and manipulated extensively. They are crucial for handling complex logic and data processing tasks in programming. Named ranges in Excel share some similarities with variables as they both serve as aliases for data references, but variables in programming are generally more powerful due to their integral role in data manipulation and control flow.

• **Pandas' Column Aggregation**
Pandas' column aggregation capability offers several significant advantages that make data manipulation and analysis more efficient and user-friendly. Below are some key benefits:

1. Simplified Code
   Column aggregation allows complex operations to be expressed in a single line of code, reducing the need for lengthy and intricate loops. This leads to cleaner, more readable code.

2. Efficiency and Performance
   Pandas leverages vectorized operations, meaning computations are performed on entire columns at once rather than iterating through each element. This results in faster execution times, especially when working with large datasets.

3. Ease of Use
   Pandas provides high-level functions for common aggregation tasks (e.g., sum(), mean(), max(), min(), see upcoming chapters), making it

straightforward to apply these operations without needing deep programming expertise.

In summary, Pandas' column aggregation capability is a powerful feature that offers significant benefits in terms of efficiency, simplicity, and flexibility, making it an essential tool for data analysis in Python.

2.7 EXERCISES

Using the concepts covered in this chapter, complete the following exercises with "Exercise-Ch02.xlsx" as your dataset. Please note that "Exercise-Ch02.xlsx" is a cleaned version of "Exercise-Ch01.xlsx", with duplicate transactions removed as covered in the previous chapter.

E1: **What are the extensions (the product of unit cost and quantity ordered) before and after discount?**

E2: **Calculate the new costs if we apply a 5% delivery expense to each order based on the extensions (after discount) calculated in E1.**

## CHAPTER 3

Aggregating Data Using Group-By and Pivot Tables

A FUNDAMENTAL ASPECT OF DATA analytics, especially within tabular datasets, is the mastery of summarizing data, which is critical for generating actionable insights. Humans are typically not adept at processing large amounts of detailed, unclassified data. By grouping and aggregating data, we reduce cognitive load, transforming complex datasets into more manageable and comprehensible segments. Consequently, in a dataset containing both categorical and numerical data columns, it is very common to run aggregations on some numerical columns based on the result of value grouping in a categorical column. For instance, analyzing sales figures by region or customer demographics, or computing other statistical measures enables businesses to extract multidimensional insights from the data. Structuring data in this manner facilitates the identification of relationships, patterns, and anomalies that might be overlooked in more detailed representations.

 DOI: 10.1201/9781003567103-4

3.1 GENERAL GUIDELINES FOR GROUP-BY AGGREGATIONS

Group-by aggregations are a powerful tool in data analysis, allowing you to summarize and analyze subsets of data based on shared characteristics. Here are some general guidelines to effectively use group-by aggregations:

1. **Set Clear Objectives**

   Understand the purpose of your analysis. Are you trying to make comparisons, identify trends, or find inefficiencies? Your goal will guide how you group and what aggregations you use.

2. **Identify Key Variables**

   Determine which categorical variables you will use to group the data. These could be attributes like time periods (refer to Chapter 9), geographic locations, product categories, or customer segments.

3. **Select Appropriate Aggregations**

   Decide on the aggregation functions that will best generate the desired output from the data you're analyzing. Common functions include:

   - **Sum**: Totaling up numerical data within each group.

   - **Average (Mean)**: Calculating the average value within each group.

   - **Count**: Counting the number of entries in each group.

   - **Max/Min**: Identifying the highest or lowest values within each group.

   - **Standard Deviation**: Measuring the variation or dispersion of data within each group.

4. **Clean and Prepare Data**

   Ensure your data is clean and appropriately preprocessed before grouping. This might involve data exploration and cleaning tasks introduced in Chapter 1:

   - Removing or imputing missing values.

   - Eliminating duplicates or addressing extreme outliers (e.g., unusually high or low values).

   - Standardizing categorical data (e.g., ensuring consistency in labels or categories).

   - Converting data types as needed (e.g., converting days into age categories, refer to Chapter 9).

5. **Use Software Tools Efficiently**

   Utilize the capabilities of your data analysis tools. In Excel, functions like PivotTables can facilitate quick grouping and aggregation. In Python, libraries such as Pandas offer extensive functions for complex group-by operations.

6. **Visualize Results**

   Present your aggregated data visually to enhance comprehension. Use charts, graphs, and tables to illustrate the trends and summaries discovered through your group-by operations (refer to Chapter 4).

7. **Check for Accuracy and Consistency**

   Validate the results. Ensure your aggregations logically reflect the grouped data and check for any anomalies or unexpected results that could indicate issues with the data or the group-by logic.

8. **Iterate and Refine**

   Refine your groupings and aggregations based on initial findings. Analysis might reveal new patterns or questions that require different groupings or additional aggregation functions.

By following these guidelines, you can harness the full potential of group-by aggregations to derive meaningful insights from your data, facilitating better decision-making and strategic planning.

3.2 AGGREGATIONS WITH BOOKSTORE DATASET

We will be using the "Bookstore-Ch03.xlsx" file to demonstrate group-by aggregation. This file contains the "Invoice" worksheet, which concludes the extension and margin calculations from Chapter 2. Please ensure you understand its layout before attempting the exercises below:

Q1: Calculate the total and average amounts, and determine the maximum and minimum values for both extension and margin.

Q2: Compute the total and average amounts of extension and margin, grouped by store and employee, respectively.

Q3: Generate a report comparing the margin contributed by each store for each item.

3.3 EXCEL

3.3.1 Excel Tables

Excel Tables are a structured feature in Microsoft Excel that make working with data easier than in traditional range-based worksheets. By converting a range of data into a table, you gain enhanced functionality that can improve both productivity and accuracy. Below are some key features of Excel Tables:

- **Structured References:** Excel Tables allow you to use column names instead of cell references, which makes formulas easier to understand and maintain.
- **Auto-Expansion:** As you add data to a table, it automatically expands to include the new data, along with any formulas that are part of the table.
- **Built-In Filtering, Sorting, and Searching:** Tables come with built-in controls that make it easier to manage large sets of data.
- **Integrated Total Row:** Quickly add a bottom row for totals or other summary functions without manually entering formulas.

Comparison with Traditional Range-Based Worksheets:

- **Data Modeling:** Excel Tables allow users to create data models that can analyze groups of related datasets (refer to Chapter 6). This powerful database-like functionality is not supported in traditional worksheets.
- **Formula Management:** Excel Tables use structured referencing, which is generally more intuitive and less error-prone than the traditional A1-style referencing in range-based sheets. In addition, common tasks that require manual setups in traditional ranges, such as formula filling and updates, are automated in Tables.
- **Scalability:** Tables perform better in terms of greater scale. As your data grows, features like automatic formula expansion and filtering make it easier to handle large datasets in tables than in regular ranges.
- **Additional Functionality:** While traditional ranges are flexible and suitable for various tasks, tables offer additional functionalities, like slicers for filtering that are not available in regular ranges.

Overall, Excel Tables offer a more efficient and error-resistant way to handle data compared to traditional range-based approaches, especially as the complexity and volume of data increase. Therefore, in this chapter, we will leverage Tables for demonstrating group-by aggregations.

COMPLEMENTARY NOTE – EXCEL TABLES' REFERENCE

Excel Tables use a structured reference system that is quite different from the traditional cell address notation used in regular worksheets. The notations used in Excel Tables' reference system include:

1. **Table Names:** Each table can be named, and this name is used as the base for referencing any data within it. For example, for a table named Sales, you can refer to the table by using Sales in your formula.
2. **Column References:** Instead of referring to columns by label letters, you refer to them by their header names enclosed in square brackets. For example, if you have a column named "Revenue" in the Sales table, you can refer to this column as Sales[Revenue].
3. **Other References:**
   - **Header Row:** To refer to the header of a column, you might use Sales[#Headers], [Revenue].
   - **The Current Row:** When writing formulas within a row, you can refer to the current row by adding @ in front of the column name. For example, [@Revenue] refers to the cell in the current row of Revenue.
   - **Total Row:** To reference the total row, you would use something like Sales[#Totals], [Revenue].

In general, structured references make formulas in Excel Tables easier to read and write, as they use meaningful column names rather than generic cell addresses. This is particularly useful in maintaining large datasets where huge amount of various traditional cell references (e.g., relative, absolute, mixed) can become confusing and error prone.

However, the new reference system can sometimes be confusing for beginners to memorize its reference notations. Fortunately, when working with Table's structured references, you often don't need to manually type out the entire reference. Excel provides a very user-friendly way to build these references using the "point-and-click" method. For example, for column references, you can simply click on the column headers while in the formula bar, and Excel will automatically insert the correct structured reference for that column.

3.3.2 Converting Bookstore Dataset to Excel Table

As previously discussed, to convert the "Invoice" worksheet into an Excel Table, follow these steps:

1. Navigate to the "Insert" tab and select the "Table" button.

2. In the dialog box that appears, confirm the auto-selected range for your table. Make sure to tick the "My table has headers" box if your dataset includes headers in the first row. For the "Invoice" worksheet, the range should be $A$1 to $R$2017, as shown below:

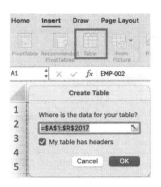

3. Upon converting your "Invoice" worksheet into an Excel Table, you'll notice several immediate changes:

- A new "Table" tab appears, specifically designed for configuring Excel Tables. Its visibility is contingent on whether your pointer is positioned within the table's range.

- You can rename the table using the "Table Name" box.

- Pivot tables and slicers are readily available for Tables.

- The table can be converted back to a traditional range if necessary.

- Removing duplicates is straightforward – simply click "Remove Duplicates".

- Visibility checkboxes allow you to toggle the display of header rows, total rows, filter buttons, etc. You can also choose to enable or disable banded rows/columns, which use alternating colors for better readability, often referred to as "zebra striping".

- Select your preferred built-in style from the options available on the right side.

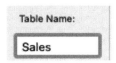

4. Before we proceed, first rename the new table to "Sales" for clearer identification. It is strongly advised to give your newly created tables meaningful names before you create any formulas.

Table Name:

Sales

Now, we are prepared to explore the three examples.

Q1: Calculate the total and average amounts, and determine the maximum and minimum values for both extension and margin.

- **Use "Total Row"**
  In Excel Tables, the fastest way to quickly get the total and the average for a column is to utilize the "Total Row" checkbox:

  1. Once you activate the "Total Row" checkbox, Excel will automatically scroll to the bottom of the table, and you will see the "Total" row as below:

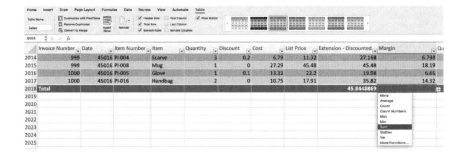

  2. Next, move your cursor to the cell in the "Total" row under the "Extension - Discounted" column. From the dropdown menu that appears, select "Average" to quickly get the average extension

per item of 45.845, as shown above. Repeat this process for the "Margin" column, but this time choose "Sum" to obtain the total margin across all sale items, which is 30062.032.

3. Feel free to explore different aggregation functions available in the dropdown menu to further utilize the convenient "Total Row" feature.

- **Use Aggregation Functions**

  One limitation of the "Total Row" feature is that you can only select one aggregation function per column at a time. If you wish to display various aggregations like SUM, COUNT, AVERAGE, MAX, and MIN for the same column, you'll need to manually develop additional formulas to handle these calculations. To avoid altering the settings of the "Sales" table, we will use a separate sheet named "Aggregation Functions" to demonstrate the advantages of using Excel Tables for formula development:

  1. In cell B2 of the "Aggregation Functions" sheet, navigate to the Home tab, open the "AutoSum" dropdown menu, and select Sum from the list:

This is what you will have in cell B2:

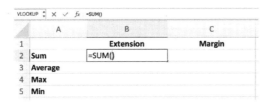

2. With the cursor within the parentheses of the SUM() function, navigate to the Sales table (located in the Invoice sheet) and position

the cell pointer over the label of the "Extension - Discounted" column. Wait for the cursor to change to a down-arrow shape, then click on the column label. The formula should now appear as: "= SUM(Table1[Extension - Discounted])":

	List Price	Extension - Discounted	Margin
1946	42.38	33.904	
1947	11.32	9.056	
1948	41.79	83.58	
1949	41.79	66.864	
1950	33.12	29.808	
1951	46.45	92.9	

VLOOKUP | × ✓ fx =SUM(Sales[Extension - Discounted]+Invoice!)
SUM(number1, [number2], ...)

3. Press Enter to accept the formula. Excel will automatically return you to the "Aggregation Functions" sheet. You can then verify if the result is 92423.292:

	A	B	C
1		Extension	Margin
2	Sum	92423.292	
3	Average		
4	Max		
5	Min		

4. Now, repeat Steps 1 to 3 to develop Average, Max, and Min formulas for the Extension column. Alternatively, you can copy the SUM() formula by dragging the fill handle down through the entire "Extension" column and then changing the function names to Average, Max, and Min as needed. Once you've set up all the aggregation functions for the "Extension" column, you can select all four formulas as a range and copy the entire range to the "Margin" column. This shortcut method is feasible because the Margin column is right next to the "Extension - Discounted" column. After completing these steps, verify your results against the figures provided below:

	A	B	C
1		**Extension**	**Margin**
2	**Sum**	92423.292	30062.032
3	**Average**	45.8448869	14.91172222
4	**Max**	139.35	55.74
5	**Min**	2.072	0.522

Q2: Compute the total and average amounts of extension and margin, grouped by store and employee.

Q1 illustrates examples of unclassified aggregations. Next, we will explore how to perform classified aggregations using Excel's conditional aggregation functions like SUMIF(), AVERAGEIF(), COUNTIF(), as well as the powerful Pivot Tables.

- **Conditional Aggregation Functions**
  Excel's conditional aggregation functions (or group-by aggregation) allow us to apply conditions to the data being aggregated. These functions are particularly useful when you want to analyze certain subsets of data without creating separate tables. There are three commonly used conditional aggregation functions:

- **SUMIF()**: This function adds up the values in a range that meet a specified criterion. For example, SUMIF(range, criteria, sum_range) can be used to sum cell values in the sum_range where the cells in the range meet the criteria.

- **AVERAGEIF()**: Similar to SUMIF, this function calculates the average of values in a range that meet specified criteria using the general formula: AVERAGEIF(range, criteria, average_range).

- **COUNTIF()**: This function counts the number of cells within a range that meet the given condition using the general formula: COUNTIF(range, criteria).

  Now, let's follow these steps to address Q2:

1. Begin by navigating to the "Aggregations by Store" worksheet, which currently only contains header rows:

	A	B	C	D	E	F	G
1			Extension			Margin	
2		Sum	Average	Count	Sum	Average	Count
3							
4							
5							

2. The group-by aggregation requires all unique instances that appear in one column. In Chapter 1, we have introduced Excel's UNIQUE() function that can meet the requirement without manually searching for all unique cell values. Position your cursor in cell A3 and enter "=UNIQUE()". Within the parentheses, direct your cursor to the Sales table, click on the "Store Name" column label, and then accept the completed formula:

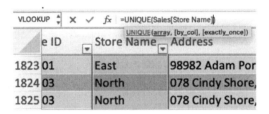

3. This will create a list of unique instances of the "Store Name" column in cell A3:

	A	B	C	D	E	F	G
1			Extension			Margin	
2		Sum	Average	Count	Sum	Average	Count
3	North						
4	West						
5	East						
6	South						

4. Next, place your pointer on cell B3 and enter "=SUMIF(". With the parentheses open, click on the "*fx*" icon to launch the "Formula Builder" on the right-hand side:

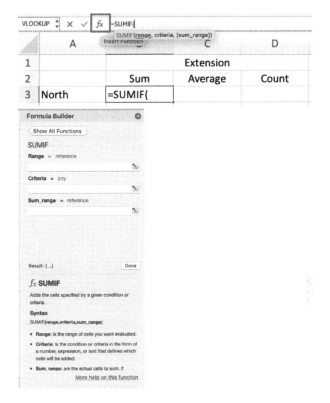

5. Excel's "Formula Builder" is a powerful assistant for configuring parameters within an Excel function. It is particularly useful when developing complex functions, such as conditional aggregations. It also provides brief descriptions for each parameter defined in the function. For SUMIF(), as discussed earlier, there are three mandated parameters: (range, criteria, sum_range). You may refer back to previous steps to fill in the "Range" with "Sales[Store Name])", "Criteria" with the cell value in A3 ("North" in this row), and "Sum_range" with "Sales[Extension – Discounted]". Once all parameters are correctly assigned, you can view the outcome in the "Result" preview section:

6. Now, place your pointer on cell C3 and complete "AVERAGEIF()" with the same parameter values as those used in "SUMIF()". After completing the entry, verify your results:

	A	B	C	D
			Extension	
1				
2		Sum	Average	Count
3	North	21546.2335	44.1521178	
4	West			
5	East			
6	South			

fx =AVERAGEIF(Sales[Store Name],A3,Sales[Extension - Discounted])

7. For the "COUNTIF()" function, which requires only two parameters, reuse the values for "Range" and "Criteria" from the previous functions and omit the "Sum_range", as shown below:

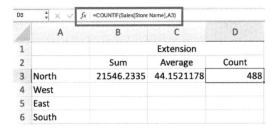

fx =COUNTIF(Sales[Store Name],A3)

	A	B	C	D
			Extension	
1				
2		Sum	Average	Count
3	North	21546.2335	44.1521178	488
4	West			
5	East			
6	South			

8. Now, you can copy the three completed formulas across all other stores:

	A	B	C	D
1			Extension	
2		Sum	Average	Count
3	North	21546.2335	44.1521178	488
4	West	22974.9715	45.3155256	507
5	East	23126.8215	45.4357986	509
6	South	24775.2655	48.3891904	512

9. For the Margin section, follow Steps 2 to 8 as described above, but adjust the "Sum_range" parameter to reference "Sales[Margin]" instead to complete the formulas:

E3   fx =SUMIF(Sales[Store Name],A3,Sales[Margin])

	A	B	C	D	E	F	G
1			Extension			Margin	
2		Sum	Average	Count	Sum	Average	Count
3	North	21546.2335	44.1521178	488	6943.7035	14.2289006	488
4	West	22974.9715	45.3155256	507	7475.4115	14.7444014	507
5	East	23126.8215	45.4357986	509	7599.3715	14.9300029	509
6	South	24775.2655	48.3891904	512	8043.5455	15.7100498	512

10. Repeat Steps 2 to 9 above for the conditional aggregations grouped by the "Name" column, which includes employees' names. Verify your results using the "Aggregations by Name" sheet:

B3   fx =SUMIF(Sales[Name],A3,Sales[Extension - Discounted])

	A	B	C	D	E	F	G
1			Extension			Margin	
2		Sum	Average	Count	Sum	Average	Count
3	Daniel Marquez	9534.6885	41.8188092	228	3128.3185	13.7206952	228
4	Kristin Lee	12333.5345	44.5253953	277	4002.8645	14.4507744	277
5	Valerie Gibson	10641.437	46.2671174	230	3472.547	15.0980304	230
6	Adriana Cisneros	12138.6625	46.6871635	260	3988.6525	15.3409712	260
7	Elizabeth Rodriguez	11908.3985	45.2790817	263	3819.8885	14.5242909	263
8	Nathaniel Marquez	12866.867	51.6741647	249	4223.657	16.9624779	249
9	Bradley Marshall	10988.159	44.1291526	249	3610.719	14.5008795	249
10	Carol Parker	12011.545	46.19825	260	3815.385	14.6745577	260

- **Pivot Tables**
  Excel's Pivot Table is a powerful tool to summarize and present large datasets in a concise and dynamic manner. It allows users to extract

the group-by results from a dataset by easily reorganizing and summarizing selected columns and rows. Pivot tables are particularly useful for a quick group-by analysis without extensive use of formulas, making them invaluable for business applications.

Now, follow the steps below to use Pivot Table in Q2:

1. Make sure your cursor is positioned within the Sales table. Then, in the Table ribbon, click the "Summarize with PivotTable" button:

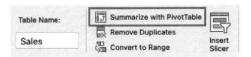

Note: An alternative method to create a pivot table is by selecting the "PivotTable" button from the Insert ribbon while your cursor is on the Sales table, as shown below:

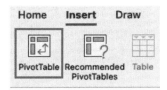

2. In the dialog box that pops up, confirm the Sales table is selected and choose to create your new pivot table in a new worksheet, as illustrated below:

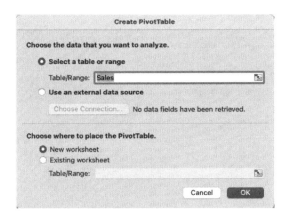

3. A new "PivotTable Analyze" tab will appear, enabling you to configure the new pivot table. For instance, you can rename the newly created pivot table to "ByStore". Additionally, you may also rename the sheet to "Pivot – by Store". On the "PivotTable Analyze" ribbon, the toggleable "Field List" button controls the visibility of the main configuration panel on the right-hand side, labeled "PivotTable Fields", as illustrated below:

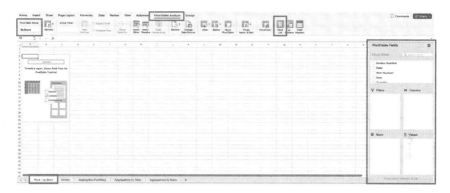

4. The "PivotTable Fields" panel offers drag-and-drop functionality for configuring pivot tables. For instance, to develop a group-by-store aggregation, you can first drag the "Store Name" from the field list to the "Rows" section. Then, further drag the "Extension - Discounted" to the Values section, as illustrated below:

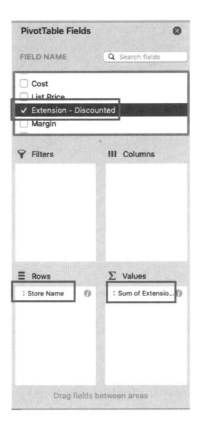

Now, you can view the outcomes of the first two drag-and-drop actions presented in the canvas area on the left-hand side:

	A	B
1		
2		
3	**Row Labels** ▾	**Sum of Extension - Discounted**
4	East	23126.8215
5	North	21546.2335
6	South	24775.2655
7	West	22974.9715
8	**Grand Total**	**92423.292**

5. You may have observed that the order of store names in Column A differs from what is shown in the "Aggregations by Store" worksheet. To rearrange a Row Label, right-click it, select

"Move", and then choose the appropriate movement options, as demonstrated below:

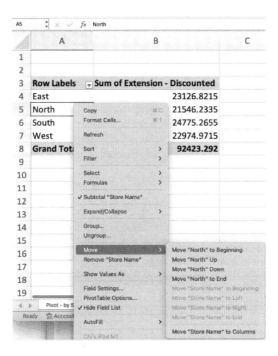

After a few movements, you will have the same order as occurs in the "Aggregations by Store" worksheet:

	A	B
1		
2		
3	**Row Labels** ▾	**Sum of Extension - Discounted**
4	North	21546.2335
5	West	22974.9715
6	East	23126.8215
7	South	24775.2655
8	**Grand Total**	**92423.292**

6. To include the average amount in the pivot table, simply drag the "Extension - Discounted" field to the Values section once more. Then change its aggregation function by clicking the ⏀ icon icon located at the end of the item in the Values section:

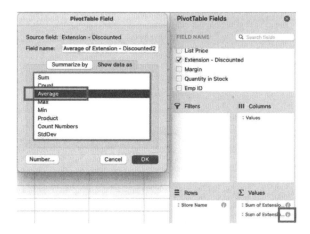

Repeat the same process to include a record count in the pivot table. Now, your Values section should look like as follows:

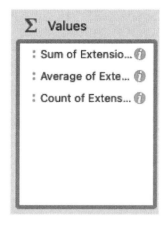

7. Next, let's change the labels in the pivot table to maintain consistency with the "Aggregations by Store" worksheet. Double-click on "Row Labels" and directly rename the label for Column A to "Stores". For the other columns, double-click their labels and use the dialog box that appears to rename them to "Sum-Ex", "Average-Ex", and "Count-Ex", respectively, as shown below:

8. Merge the cells above the labels "Sum-Ex", "Average-Ex", and "Count-Ex", and label them as "Extension" by using the Merge & Center on the Home ribbon. This will give you a neatly formatted table as follows:

	A	B	C	D
1				
2			**Extension**	
3	**Store** ⏷	**Sum-Ex**	**Average-Ex**	**Count-Ex**
4	North	21546.2335	44.15211783	488
5	West	22974.9715	45.31552564	507
6	East	23126.8215	45.43579862	509
7	South	24775.2655	48.38919043	512
8	**Grand Total**	**92423.292**	**45.8448869**	**2016**

9. For Margin aggregations, drag the "Margin" field to the Values section three times. To switch the aggregation functions, an alternative method is double-clicking the labels in cells F3 and G3 and use the dialog box that appears to change to "Average" and "Count", respectively, as illustrated below:

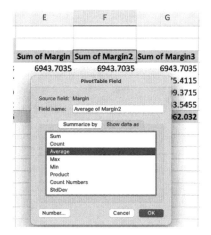

10. After refining the format, the finalized pivot table will be as shown below:

	A	B	C	D	E	F	G
1							
2			Extension			Margin	
3	Store ▾	Sum-Ex	Average-Ex	Count-Ex	Sum-Margin	Average-Margin	Count-Margin
4	North	21546.2335	44.15211783	488	6943.7035	14.22890061	488
5	West	22974.9715	45.31552564	507	7475.4115	14.74440138	507
6	East	23126.8215	45.43579862	509	7599.3715	14.93000295	509
7	South	24775.2655	48.38919043	512	8043.5455	15.7100498	512
8	Grand Total	92423.292	45.8448869	2016	30062.032	14.91172222	2016

11. To create the by-Employee pivot table, there's no need to start from scratch. The quickest method is to make a copy of the "Pivot – by Store" worksheet. Simply right-click on the tab named "Pivot – by Store" and select "Move or Copy" from the menu. In the dialog box that appears, tick "Create a copy" and click OK. Rename the duplicated sheet to "Pivot – by Employee":

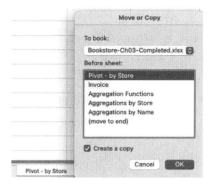

12. Next, drag the "Name" field to the Rows section and remove "Store Name" from the Rows section:

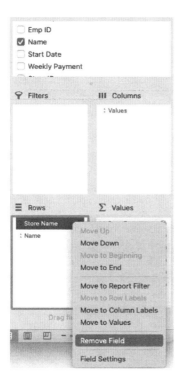

This action will prompt Excel to automatically update the contents of the new pivot table to reflect by-Employee aggregations:

	A	B	C	D	E	F	G
1							
2			Extension			Margin	
3	Store	Sum-Ex	Average-Ex	Count-Ex	Sum-Margin	Average-Margin	Count-Margin
4	Adriana Cisneros	12138.6625	46.68716346	260	3988.6525	15.34097115	260
5	Bradley Marshall	10988.159	44.12915261	249	3610.719	14.50087952	249
6	Carol Parker	12011.545	46.19825	260	3815.385	14.67455769	260
7	Daniel Marquez	9534.6885	41.81880921	228	3128.3185	13.72069518	228
8	Elizabeth Rodriguez	11908.3985	45.27908175	263	3819.8885	14.52429087	263
9	Kristin Lee	12333.5345	44.52539531	277	4002.8645	14.45077437	277
10	Nathaniel Marquez	12866.867	51.67416466	249	4223.657	16.96247791	249
11	Valerie Gibson	10641.437	46.26711739	230	3472.547	15.09803043	230
12	Grand Total	92423.292	45.8448869	2016	30062.032	14.91172222	2016

The in-place replacement of the group-by dimension highlights the dynamic updating capability of Excel's Pivot Tables. When you add or rename columns within the table, any formulas associated with those columns will automatically adjust to reflect the changes.

Q3: Generate a report comparing the margin contributed by each store for each item.

Q2 addresses the by-store and by-employee aggregations independently, while Q3 integrates the by-store and by-item dimensions. One strategy is to retain both "Store Name" and "Item" in the Rows section, creating a two-tier, waterfall-like hierarchical table:

However, when dealing with more complex combinations across two dimensions, the visual clarity of a waterfall-like table may be less effective:

	A	B
1		
2		
3	Row Labels ▼	Sum of Margin
4	⊙ **East**	**7599.3715**
5	Backpack	902.556
6	Baseball Cap	126.823
7	Gloves	450.66
8	Greeting Card	106.225
9	Handbag	362.4015
10	Hat	578.062
11	Hoodie	947.271
12	Jacket	677.086
13	Keychain	266.728
14	Magnet	227.178
15	Mug	795.776
16	Notebook	843.0675
17	Pen	819.364
18	Scarf	300.16
19	Stuffed Mascot	51.4285
20	T-Shirt	144.585
21	⊙ **North**	**6943.7035**
22	Backpack	680.089
23	Baseball Cap	80.457
24	Gloves	367.41
25	Greeting Card	97.402
26	Handbag	204.006
27	Hat	495.248
28	Hoodie	600.451
29	Jacket	674.944

The preferred method is to shift one dimension to the Columns section, which typically enhances the visual presentation:

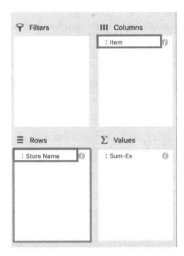

This "pivot" effect is the primary reason such two-dimensional analyses are termed "pivot analysis". With the pivot table layout, you can quickly pinpoint specific data points through "coordinate" navigation. For instance, you can easily see that the West store contributes a margin of $641 for hats.

Sum of Margin	Column Labels																Grand Total
Store	Backpack	Baseball Cap	Glove	Greeting Card	Handbag	Hat	Hoodie	Jacket	Keychain	Magnet	Mug	Notebook	Pen	Scarve	Stuffed Mascot	T-Shirt	Grand Total
North	680.085	80.457	367.41	97.402	204.006	495.248	600.451	674.944	396.396	274.57	773.044	1003.32	624.9805	245.242	64.7035	361.4425	6943.7035
West	779.66	167.246	418.47	116.325	239.5575	641	784.702	741.78	267.6545	259.789	720.75	824.4875	984.4505	197.098	57.28	281.1615	7475.4115
East	902.556	126.823	450.66	106.225	362.4015	578.062	947.271	677.086	266.728	227.178	795.776	843.0675	819.364	300.16	51.4285	144.585	7599.3715
South	745.76	152.823	466.2	90.334	352.547	682.406	721.851	970.358	306.5655	299.253	1011.784	989.385	856.983	125.158	53.092	219.046	8043.5455
Grand Total	3108.065	527.349	1702.74	410.286	1152.512	2396.716	3054.275	3064.168	1237.344	1060.79	3301.354	3660.26	3285.778	867.858	226.502	1006.235	30062.032

When analyzing multidimensional data, the "waterfall-like" method, while useful for sequential data relationships, can become visually cumbersome. In contrast, the pivot method, by distributing dimensions across both rows and columns, can improve readability and quick access to specific data intersections, making it a superior choice for more intricate analyses. This distinction is crucial for you to consider when designing pivot tables to best meet the analytical needs.

3.4 PYTHON

Please refer to the Jupyter notebook file "Bookstore-Ch03.ipynb" to access the code, or view the "Bookstore-Ch03.html" file to see the outputs of all code.

3.4.1 Data Aggregations in Pandas

Data aggregation in Pandas is a crucial technique used to combine data from multiple rows of data into single summary statistics or values, which can be more informative for decision-making. Aggregating data helps in summarizing complex or large datasets into more manageable forms. This makes it easier to understand the data at a glance and draw conclusions from key statistics like sum, mean, median, or count. In Pandas, aggregation methods such as `sum()`, `mean()`, `max()`, `min()`, and others offer a way to quickly summarize and understand large datasets by applying these functions either across rows or columns.

Similar to Excel spreadsheets, Pandas DataFrames often comprise columns with heterogeneous data types. As previously explored, in datasets containing both categorical and numerical data, it is common to perform aggregations on specific numerical columns based on categorical groupings. Pandas allows you to group data based on certain criteria (e.g., categories or time intervals) and then apply aggregation functions to these groups respectively. This group-by analysis lets you compare metrics across different segments or categories within the data. For example, consider a sales dataset for a company that operates across various regions. This dataset includes columns for the region, product sold, sale date, and sale amount. You might want to group the data by region or product to calculate total and average sales for each, enabling a comparison of sales performance across different regions or product items.

To facilitate the classification and grouping of data for in-depth analysis, Pandas offers two user-friendly methods: `groupby()` and `pivot_table()`. These methods are robust tools for group-by aggregation in Python, helping you organize and summarize data effectively.

3.4.2 Pandas' Aggregation Methods

Pandas' aggregation methods allow for flexible data aggregation across different axes (rows or columns) of a DataFrame or Series. These methods are part of Pandas' capabilities and are designed to operate directly on DataFrame and Series objects, providing a powerful set of tools for statistical analysis and data exploration:

1. sum(): Calculates the arithmetic total.

2. mean(): Calculates the arithmetic mean.

3. max(): Finds the maximum value.

4. min(): Finds the minimum value.

5. std(): Calculates the standard deviation, which measures the dispersion of a dataset relative to the mean.

6. count(): Counts the number of non-null values.

7. median(): Finds the median of the dataset.

3.4.3 Create a Test DataFrame

To illustrate the use of Pandas' aggregation methods on both rows and columns, we'll begin by constructing a test DataFrame from scratch. Creating a DataFrame manually is a standard practice for testing purposes. The following code generates a DataFrame consisting solely of numerical data, enabling us to perform aggregations across both rows and columns. This DataFrame specifically represents sales data for three regions over four quarters:

```
In[#]:

import pandas as pd

# Define data as a dictionary
dic = {
        "Quarter 1": [15000, 12000, 13000],
        "Quarter 2": [16000, 14000, 13500],
        "Quarter 3": [17000, 15000, 14500],
        "Quarter 4": [18000, 16000, 15500]
}

# Create DataFrame
df = pd.DataFrame(dic, index=["North", "Central", "South"])

# Display the DataFrame
df

Out[#]:
```

	Quarter 1	Quarter 2	Quarter 3	Quarter 4
North	15000	16000	17000	18000
Central	12000	14000	15000	16000
South	13000	13500	14500	15500

• Code Explanations:

1. The `dic` dictionary (see the Side Note below):

The keys represent the column labels (i.e., the four quarters), and the values are lists containing sales figures for each region. Using a dictionary to create a DataFrame is indeed a common and effective method in Pandas. This approach leverages the natural correspondence between the `key-value` pairs in a dictionary and the `column-labels-to-data-rows` structure in a DataFrame.

2. DataFrame method:

The pd.DataFrame() function creates the DataFrame. The `index` parameter specifies the row labels, which are the regions ("North", "Central", "South").

• Side Note – Dictionary

Dictionary is one of Python's collective data types (you may consider them as data containers). Other common collective data types include `list`, `tuple`, and `set`. A dictionary (`dict`) is a mapping data type that associates a value with a key, pretty similar to a real dictionary when we look up the meaning of a word by using the alphabetical order as the key. Dictionaries are captured in a pair of `curly brackets` with one or more `key:value` pairs inside. The keys can be of any data types (usually strings and numbers are preferred). The data values can also be of any data types, including collective data such as lists, tuples or dicts. That's why, in the above example, we can assign a list of regional sales [15,000, 12,000, 13,000] to "Quarter 1".

Create a Dictionary Using {}

Below is a simple example of a dictionary that contains a few "username:password" pairs:

```
In[#]:
passwords = {"Mary":"12345",
             "John":"98765"}
print(passwords)

Out[#]:
{"Mary": "12345", "John": "98765"}
```

Using dict() to Create Dictionaries

You can also use the dict() constructor to create dictionaries by directly passing a set of arguments to the dict(), where keys are the argument names and values are the argument values:

```
In[#]:

passwords = dict(Mary = "12345",
                 John = "98765")
passwords

Out[#]:

{"Mary": "12345", "John": "98765"}
```

Access Members in a Dictionary

In previous chapters, you have learned how to use the `square brackets` retriever along with the index (e.g., column label or row index number, etc.) to access items in a DataFrame. Dictionaries employ the same standard method for data retrieval. For example, passwords["Mary"] will return the value paired with the key "Mary":

```
In[#]:

print(passwords["Mary"]) # Get Mary's password: "12345"

Out[#]:

12345
```

• Side Note – List

Among Python's built-in collective data types, `list` is the most commonly used. Let's briefly go over some key usage of Python's `list`.

Create a List Using []

The simplest way to create a list is to wrap a bunch of data items in a pair of square brackets and assign the data items to a variable:

```
In[#]:

list_a = [1,2,3,4,5]
print(list_a)

Out[#]:

[1, 2, 3, 4, 5]
```

Using list() to Create a List

List can also be constructed using the `list()` method:

```
In[#]:
list_b = list([1,2,3])
print(list_b)
```

```
Out[#]:
[1, 2, 3]
```

You may also combine the `range()` method in the `list()` constructor to create a list of a series of numbers:

```
In[#]:
list_c = list(range(10)) # Note that range(10) generates numbers
from 0 to 9
print(list_c)
list_d = list(range(3, 9)) # range(3, 9) generates numbers
from 3 to 8
print(list_d)
```

```
Out[#]:
[0, 1, 2, 3, 4, 5, 6, 7, 8, 9]
[3, 4, 5, 6, 7, 8]
```

You may include data points of different data types in a list:

```
In[#]:
list_e = [89, "abc", 3.14, True, -240, "happy"] # list_e has items of
int, float, str and boolean
print(list_e)
```

```
Out[#]:
[89, "abc", 3.14, True, -240, "happy"]
```

Access Members in a List

Just like dictionaries and DataFrames, lists also employ square brackets for data retrieval. To access a list item, we always use an index number enclosed by square brackets (e.g., `[0]`) since lists are ordered iterables.

```
In[#]:
print(list_e[1]) # This returns "abc", which has the index
number of 1
```

```
Out[#]:
Abc
```

3.4.4 Aggregations in a DataFrame

• Aggregation for Columns
Now, let's begin by using sum() to quickly calculate the totals for each quarter column in the DataFrame `df`:

```
In[#]:

df.sum()

Out[#]:

Quarter 1    40000
Quarter 2    43500
Quarter 3    46500
Quarter 4    49500
dtype: int64
```

This is quite straightforward, isn't it? While we can apply the same structure to quickly execute other aggregation methods like mean(), max(), min(), and count(), this approach might seem cumbersome or non-Pythonic (we'll explain what Pythonic means later). Rather than replicating the above code structure multiple times, we can simplify the process using the `agg()` method, which accepts other methods as arguments:

```
In[#]:

df.agg(["sum", "mean", "max", "min", "count"])

Out[#]:
```

	Quarter 1	Quarter 2	Quarter 3	Quarter 4
sum	40000.000000	43500.0	46500.0	49500.0
mean	13333.333333	14500.0	15500.0	16500.0
max	15000.000000	16000.0	17000.0	18000.0
min	12000.000000	13500.0	14500.0	15500.0
count	3.000000	3.0	3.0	3.0

As illustrated above, by passing a list of aggregation method names to the `agg()` method, we can efficiently obtain all aggregation results with just one line of code. The `agg()` method is one of Python's `high-order functions`. A high-order function is a function that either accepts one or more functions as arguments or returns a function as its result. This is a powerful concept in functional programming and is supported in Python.

In Python, some common examples of higher-order functions include `agg()`, map(), apply(), filter(), and sorted().

• Aggregation for Specific Column(s)
Aggregation methods can also be applied to specific column(s) rather than the entire DataFrame. We simply need to specify which column(s) should be aggregated:

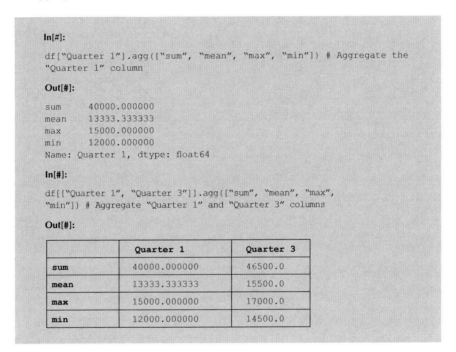

```
In[#]:

df["Quarter 1"].agg(["sum", "mean", "max", "min"]) # Aggregate the
"Quarter 1" column

Out[#]:

sum       40000.000000
mean      13333.333333
max       15000.000000
min       12000.000000
Name: Quarter 1, dtype: float64

In[#]:

df[["Quarter 1", "Quarter 3"]].agg(["sum", "mean", "max",
"min"]) # Aggregate "Quarter 1" and "Quarter 3" columns

Out[#]:
```

	Quarter 1	Quarter 3
sum	40000.000000	46500.0
mean	13333.333333	15500.0
max	15000.000000	17000.0
min	12000.000000	14500.0

• Aggregations for Rows
The DataFrame df is a homogeneous dataset as it comprises only numerical data across two dimensions: quarter and region. For such datasets, Pandas enables not only vertical but also horizontal aggregations. To perform horizontal aggregation, we must specify `axis=1` as an additional argument in the aggregation method. Let's begin this process with the sum() method:

```
In[#]:

df.sum(axis = 1)

Out[#]:

North      66000
Central    57000
South      56500
dtype: int64
```

You may also apply the `axis=1` for `agg()`:

```
In[#]:
df.agg(["sum", "mean", "max", "min", "count"], axis = 1)
Out[#]:
```

	sum	mean	max	min	count
North	66000.0	16500.0	18000.0	15000.0	4.0
Central	57000.0	14250.0	16000.0	12000.0	4.0
South	56500.0	14125.0	15500.0	13000.0	4.0

• Aggregation for Specific Row(s)

Aggregating specific rows requires the use of special accessors `loc` or `iloc`, which we will introduce in Chapter 4. For the moment, let's use the example below to demonstrate the use of the `loc` accessor:

```
In[#]:
df.loc["North"].agg(["sum", "mean", "max", "min"])
Out[#]:
sum      66000.0
mean     16500.0
max      18000.0
min      15000.0
Name: North, dtype: float64
```

• Summarizing Pandas' Axis Settings

The diagram below illustrates the two directions of aggregation determined by the axis argument. Please note that the default value for `axis` is zero. Therefore, when performing column aggregation, the `axis` argument can be omitted since it defaults to vertical aggregation.

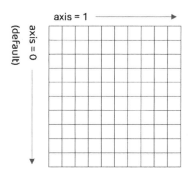

3.4.5 Aggregation Exercises with Pandas

Now, let's use the read_excel() method to import the "Invoice" sheet from the "Bookstore-Ch03.xlsx" file into a Pandas DataFrame:

```
In[#]:

import pandas as pd

filepath = "/Users/chi2019/Desktop/Book/Excel Files/Bookstore-Ch03.
xlsx" # Change the path according to your file location

# For Windows users, prefix r is added:
# filepath = r"C:\Users\chi2019\Desktop\Book\Excel Files\Bookstore-
Ch03.xlsx"

sales = pd.read_excel(filepath, sheet_name = "Invoice", header = 0,
usecols = "A:R", nrows = 2016)
print(sales.head(5))

Out[#]:
      Invoice            Date Item            Item Quantity  Discount  \
      Number                 Number
0           1 2023-01-01   PI-003            Jacket        3      0.00
1           1 2023-01-01   PI-012               Pen        3      0.15
2           2 2023-01-01   PI-012               Pen        3      0.10
3           3 2023-01-01   PI-011   Stuffed Mascot        1      0.15
4           3 2023-01-01   PI-007    Baseball Cap        3      0.15

      Cost  List Price            Extension -   Margin  Quantity in Stock  \
                                   Discounted
0    25.87       43.12              129.3600  51.7500                 44
1    25.07       41.79              106.5645  31.3545                 32
2    25.07       41.79              112.8330  37.6230                 32
3     1.55        2.59                2.2015   0.6515                 22
4     4.21        7.02               17.9010   5.2710                 14

      Emp ID             Name Start Date  Weekly  Store ID Store Name  \
                                          Payment
0    EMP-003  Daniel Marquez 2023-02-08     1139    ST-003      North
1    EMP-003  Daniel Marquez 2023-02-08     1139    ST-003      North
2    EMP-006     Kristin Lee 2022-01-05     1013    ST-002       West
3    EMP-002  Valerie Gibson 2022-04-09     1115    ST-002       West
4    EMP-002  Valerie Gibson 2022-04-09     1115    ST-002       West

                                            Address
0           078 Cindy Shore, Los Angeles, CA 96017
1           078 Cindy Shore, Los Angeles, CA 96017
2   845 Lloyd Walk Apt. 693, Los Angeles, CA 91326
3   845 Lloyd Walk Apt. 693, Los Angeles, CA 91326
4   845 Lloyd Walk Apt. 693, Los Angeles, CA 91326
```

Q1: Calculate the total and average amounts, and determine the maximum and minimum values for both extension and margin.

To address Q1, we can call the agg() function to quickly get the sum, mean, max, and min for both extension and margin:

In[#]:

```
q1 = sales[["Extension - Discounted", "Margin"]].agg(["sum", "mean",
"max", "min"])
q1
```

Out[#]:

	Extension - Discounted	Margin
sum	92423.292000	30062.032000
mean	45.844887	14.911722
max	139.350000	55.740000
min	2.072000	0.522000

Hmm, that was fast! However, for Q2, we will need the help from the groupby() method.

Groupby()

The `groupby()` function is used to split the data into groups based on some criteria, apply a function to each group independently, and combine the results into a data structure. It's particularly useful for aggregating data, performing transformations, or filtering data, depending on your needs. The following code snippet groups the data in the sales DataFrame by the values found in the "Store Name" column:

In[#]:

```
by_store = sales.groupby("Store Name") # Call sales' groupby()
function to create a GroupBy object by "Store Name"
```

Technically, the result of the groupby() function is not a new DataFrame. Instead, it creates a GroupBy object:

In[#]:

```
type(by_store) # The type() function identifies the type of the input
data object
```

Out[#]:

```
pandas.core.groupby.generic.DataFrameGroupBy
```

The GroupBy object is a collection of groups pending for further aggregations. You can think of it as a sort of blueprint that describes how the DataFrame is split into groups. Unlike DataFrames, the content of a GroupBy object cannot be printed directly:

```
In[#]:

print(by_store) # This won't work
<pandas.core.groupby.generic.DataFrameGroupBy object at
0x166c2a7b0>
```

Instead, you must use a `for` loop to explore the content of a GroupBy object. The Complementary Note below offers detailed explanations of Python's `for` loop:

• Complementary Note – Python's for Loop

The `for` loop in Python repeats a group of embedded statements for each element in a sequence of numbers, or a string, or a collective data type (such as a `list`, a `tuple`, a `dictionary`, or a `set`). It is important to understand that iteration (or loop) allows computers to perform repeated operations, which is fundamental in programming for automating tasks that would be tedious or impractical to perform manually. Iterative processes are also the foundation for more complex algorithms in fields such as machine learning.

Loop Through a List

Among Python's built-in collective data types, `list` is the most commonly used. In previous chapters, you have learned how to use the zero-based `indexes` and the `square brackets` retriever to access items in a DataFrame. Lists employ the same standard method for data retrieval. Let's start with defining a simple list and retrieve the elements in the list:

```
In[#]:

bands = ["Aerosmith", "Boston", "Chicago"] # Create a list named
"bands" that includes three iconic rock'n roll bands
print(bands[0], bands[1], bands[2]) # Use direct index retrieval to
enumerate and print out all three members in the "bands" list

Out[#]:

Aerosmith Boston Chicago
```

The issue with the enumeration method is that it becomes cumbersome and impractical with lists containing a large number of elements. Let's now demonstrate how to create a `for` loop to easily iterate through the entire "bands" list:

```
In[#]:

for band in bands: # The `for` statement to iterate over each member
in "bands"
        print(band) # The indented code to be executed for every member
in "bands"

Out[#]:

Aerosmith
Boston
Chicago
```

As shown above, the two-line `for` loop can efficiently manage lists of any length. This exemplifies the power of iteration. Let's discuss the two-line `for` loop in more details:

The For Band in Bands Approach

Unlike `for` loops in other programming languages where you must specify minimum or maximum loop bounds, Python allows you to use a more natural, English-like syntax (`for band in bands:`) to iterate over each element in an iterable and access its data. The variable "band" acts as an iterator that represents each item in the "bands" list during each iteration. In this case, it refers to "Aerosmith", "Boston", and "Chicago", respectively.

The Indentation Prompt ":"

In the `for` example above, you probably have noticed we added a colon at the end of the `for` statement. The `colon` is also required at the end of `while`, `if`, `else`, and other Python keywords that leads to a block of indented code. This required `label:` prompts Python to execute code in the scope that follows it.

The Indentation Length

Note that Python uses indentation to specify the scope of a block of code that follows a specific Python keyword (e.g., `for`, `if`, `else`, etc.). The ending label: prompts Python to execute the indented code. Despite the number of spaces can be any (a minimum of one space is required), Python suggests four spaces (or a tab) as the default indentation.

Compare with the Conventional Approach

Of course, you can also use the traditional index retrieval method to facilitate a for loop, though it is generally not recommended since its syntax is less intuitive:

```
In[#]:

for i in range(len(bands)): # Combine `len()` with `range()` to
create counters for indexing
    print(bands[i])

Out[#]:

Aerosmith
Boston
Chicago
```

As demonstrated above, the traditional method requires using a counter i that ranges from zero to the length of the "bands" list minus one (which is two in this case). This old-fashioned approach to developing a for loop combines the len() method with the range() function to determine the number of iterations. Due to its syntactic complexity, this method is less favored by most Python programmers compared to the simpler, more computational efficient for band in bands approach.

A Pythonic Choice

In addition to its superiority in simplicity, readability, computational efficiency, less and cleaner code, the for band in bands approach is more in line with Python's design philosophy, often referred to as Pythonic, which encourages readability and simplicity. This Pythonic method is widely adopted in the Python community and is generally considered best practice for looping through items in a list and other iterable data types.

Loop Through a String

In fact, looping through an iterable is very common in Python applications. For example, in Chapter 2, we briefly introduce Python's string type.

Python's strings (str) are more like an ordered list of characters. You may consider str type as a special case of list.

Since strings are lists, you may also loop through the characters in a string, with a for loop:

```
In[#]:

s = "Python"
for char in s: # a temporary iterator "char" is specified to represent
each character in s
    print(char)

Out[#]:

P
y
t
h
o
n
```

Non-Index Loop

Sometimes, you only need a loop that iterates a specific number of times without the need to use or reference the loop's index or iterator. You may use an underscore _ as a placeholder variable when the loop index is not needed. In the following example, the loop executes exactly three times, as dictated by the specified range(3). Since the print() function outputs the same string without needing the use of the iterator, we use an underscore _ as a placeholder:

```
In[#]:

for _ in range(3):
    print("I love Python!")

Out[#]:

I love Python!
I love Python!
I love Python!
```

Now, let's return to the GroupBy object by_store. As by_store is iterable, we can use a for loop to iterate through it and print out its content:

In[#]:

```
for store in by_store:
    print(store)
```

Out[#]:

```
(Full results are truncated due to length. Please refer to the HTML
output for the complete details.)
("East", Invoice       Date        Item     Item Quantity Discount \
         Number                    Number
5              4 2023-01-01    PI-009  Keychain        2      0.10
6              4 2023-01-01    PI-009  Keychain        3      0.15
7              4 2023-01-01    PI-008       Mug        3      0.15
25            12 2023-01-02    PI-003    Jacket        2      0.10
26            12 2023-01-02    PI-004     Scarf        2      0.10
...          ...         ...       ...       ...     ...       ...

[509 rows x 18 columns])
("North", Invoice      Date Item Number            Item  Quantity \
          Number
0              1 2023-01-01    PI-003        Jacket         3
1              1 2023-01-01    PI-012           Pen         3
16             9 2023-01-01    PI-008           Mug         3
17             9 2023-01-01    PI-016       Handbag         1
18             9 2023-01-01    PI-016       Handbag         3
...          ...         ...       ...          ...       ...

[488 rows x 18 columns])
("South", Invoice Date       Item     Item Quantity    Discount \
          Number           Number
11             6 2023-01-01  PI-005    Gloves        1       0.10
12             6 2023-01-01  PI-003    Jacket        2       0.20
19            10 2023-01-01  PI-004     Scarf        1       0.20
20            10 2023-01-01  PI-013  Notebook        3       0.20
21            10 2023-01-01  PI-016   Handbag        2       0.10
...          ...         ...     ...       ...     ...        ...

[512 rows x 18 columns])
("West", Invoice   Date Item Number             Item  Quantity \
         Number
2              2 2023-01-01   PI-012             Pen         3
3              3 2023-01-01   PI-011  Stuffed Mascot         1
4              3 2023-01-01   PI-007   Baseball Cap         3
8              5 2023-01-01   PI-012             Pen         2
9              5 2023-01-01   PI-014   Greeting Card         1
...          ...         ...      ...            ...       ...

[507 rows x 18 columns])
```

From the output, it's evident that the sales DataFrame has been divided into four groups: "East", "North", "South", and "West". Each group contains data rows corresponding to one of the unique values found in the "Store Name" column.

Now, let's create the by_employee GroupBy using "Name" column and dump its content:

```
In[#]:
by_employee = sales.groupby("Name") # Call groupby() to create a
GroupBy object by "Name" (employee)
for employee in by_employee:
    print(employee)

Out[#]:
(Full results are omitted due to length. Please refer to the HTML
output for the complete details.)
```

Combine Groupby() with Aggregation Methods

With the two GroupBy objects, we can now leverage Python's versatile aggregation methods to implement the groupby aggregations. Again, let's start with Pandas' sum() method for margin amounts:

```
In[#]:
sum_ex = by_store["Margin"].sum()
sum_ex

Out[#]:
Store Name
East     7599.3715
North    6943.7035
South    8043.5455
West     7475.4115
Name: Margin, dtype: float64
```

Note: It is worth noting that although the sales DataFrame has been divided into groups in the by_store GroupBy object, the original labels are retained for further actions, such as aggregations. However, if you try to print by_store["Margin"], it does not display data directly. That is because by_store["Margin"] is still a preparatory object waiting for a specific command to perform calculations. The results are shown only after an aggregation method like .sum() is applied.

```
In[#]:
print(by_store["Margin"]) # It is still a preparatory object, not a
data object
Out[#]:
<pandas.core.groupby.generic.SeriesGroupBy object at 0x166c4b170>
```

Q2: Compute the total and average amounts of extension and margin, grouped by store and employee, respectively.

- **Using groupby() and agg()**

Now that we have a clear understanding why it is essential to pair groupby() with aggregation methods, we are prepared to tackle Q2:

In[#]:

```
bystore_agg = by_store[["Extension - Discounted", "Margin"]].
agg(["sum", "mean"])
bystore_agg
```

Out[#]:

Store Name	Extension - Discounted		Margin	
	sum	mean	sum	mean
East	23126.8215	45.435799	7599.3715	14.930003
North	21546.2335	44.152118	6943.7035	14.228901
South	24775.2655	48.389190	8043.5455	15.710050
West	22974.9715	45.315526	7475.4115	14.744401

In[#]:

```
byEmployee_agg = by_employee[["Extension - Discounted", "Margin"]].
agg(["sum", "mean"])
byEmployee_agg
```

Out[#]:

Name	Extension - Discounted		Margin	
	sum	mean	sum	mean
Adriana Cisneros	12138.6625	46.687163	3988.6525	15.340971
Bradley Marshall	10988.1590	44.129153	3610.7190	14.500880
Carol Parker	12011.5450	46.198250	3815.3850	14.674558
Daniel Marquez	9534.6885	41.818809	3128.3185	13.720695
Elizabeth Rodriguez	11908.3985	45.279082	3819.8885	14.524291
Kristin Lee	12333.5345	44.525395	4002.8645	14.450774
Nathaniel Marquez	12866.8670	51.674165	4223.6570	16.962478
Valerie Gibson	10641.4370	46.267117	3472.5470	15.098030

Once you grasp how to combine groupby() and agg(), you can perform any classified aggregation in a Pandas DataFrame quickly. In fact, a more efficient approach is to bypass the explicit declaration of GroupBy objects and utilize Python's method chaining feature. This allows you to directly combine groupby() and agg() into a single line of code, and is more Pythonic:

In[#]:

```
bystore_agg_chain = sales.groupby("Store Name")[["Extension -
Discounted", "Margin"]].agg(["sum", "mean"])
bystore_agg_chain
```

Out[#]:

	Extension - Discounted		Margin	
Store Name	sum	mean	sum	mean
East	23126.8215	45.435799	7599.3715	14.930003
North	21546.2335	44.152118	6943.7035	14.228901
South	24775.2655	48.389190	8043.5455	15.710050
West	22974.9715	45.315526	7475.4115	14.744401

The aggregation examples provided above do not include max() and min(). To incorporate these, simply add ["max", "min"] to the agg() method as demonstrated previously and rerun the modified code. We'll leave this as an exercise for you to complete.

• **Using Pivot Tables**
Another way to address Q2 is by using Pandas' pivot_table. Similar to Excel's Pivot Tables, Pandas provides this powerful method to summarize and reorganize your data by creating a new table based on the original DataFrame. It allows you to perform data aggregation and transformation, making it easier to analyze and visualize the data. Its syntax is also quite straightforward:

In[#]:

```
pivot_bystore = pd.pivot_table(sales, values=["Extension -
Discounted", "Margin"],
                    index="Store Name", aggfunc=["sum", "mean"])
print(pivot_bystore)
```

Out[#]:

```
                               sum                          mean
          Extension - Discounted  Margin  Extension - Discounted    Margin
Store Name
East              23126.8215    7599.3715            45.435799   14.930003
North             21546.2335    6943.7035            44.152118   14.228901
South             24775.2655    8043.5455            48.389190   15.710050
West              22974.9715    7475.4115            45.315526   14.744401
```

In the example above, we constructed a pivot table from the `sales` DataFrame. We began by assigning the `values` parameter to the target columns: ["Extension - Discounted", "Margin"]. The `index` parameter, representing the row, was set to "Store Name" for the by_store analysis. The `aggfunc` parameter functions similarly to the `agg()` method we discussed earlier. It accepts a list of aggregation functions, and in this instance, we used "sum" and "mean". Now, we can quickly copy and paste the above cell and change its index to "Name" for the by_Employee analysis:

In[#]:

```
pivot_byEmp = pd.pivot_table(sales, values=["Extension - Discounted",
"Margin"],
                    index="Name", aggfunc=["sum", "mean"])
print(pivot_byEmp)
```

Out[#]:

```
                                 sum                          mean   \
                Extension - Discounted  Margin  Extension - Discounted
Name
Adriana Cisneros            12138.6625  3988.6525            46.687163
Bradley Marshall            10988.1590  3610.7190            44.129153
Carol Parker                12011.5450  3815.3850            46.198250
Daniel Marquez               9534.6885  3128.3185            41.818809
Elizabeth Rodriquez         11908.3985  3819.8885            45.279082
Kristin Lee                 12333.5345  4002.8645            44.525395
Nathaniel Marquez           12866.8670  4223.6570            51.674165
Valerie Gibson              10641.4370  3472.5470            46.267117

                        Margin
Name
Adriana Cisneros     15.340971
Bradley Marshall     14.500880
Carol Parker         14.674558
Daniel Marquez       13.720695
Elizabeth Rodriquez  14.524291
Kristin Lee          14.450774
Nathaniel Marquez    16.962478
Valerie Gibson       15.098030
```

Q3: Generate a report comparing the margin contributed by each store for each item.

Earlier, when using Excel's Pivot Table for Q3, we discussed the benefits of employing a pivot-like report for analyzing data with two or more dimensions. Pandas' pivot_table() supports similar pivot-like analysis. To utilize this, you simply need to specify both the index and the columns arguments:

```
In[#]:

pivot_q3 = pd.pivot_table(sales, values="Margin",
                index="Store Name", columns="Item", aggfunc="sum")
print(pivot_q3)

Out[#]:

Item       Backpack  Baseball Cap  Gloves  Greeting Card  Handbag      Hat \
Store Name
East        902.556       126.823  450.66        106.225  362.4015  578.062
North       680.089        80.457  367.41         97.402  204.0060  495.248
South       745.760       152.823  466.20         90.334  352.5470  682.406
West        779.660       167.246  418.47        116.325  233.5575  641.000


Item        Hoodie   Jacket  Keychain   Magnet       Mug  Notebook \
Store Name
East       947.271  677.086  266.7280  227.178   795.776  843.0675
North      600.451  674.944  396.3960  274.570   773.044  1003.3200
South      721.851  970.358  306.5655  299.253  1011.784   989.3850
West       784.702  741.780  267.6545  259.789   720.750   824.4875


Item            Pen    Scarf  Stuffed Mascot   T-Shirt
Store Name
East       819.3640  300.160         51.4285  144.5850
North      624.9805  245.242         64.7015  361.4425
South      856.9830  125.158         53.0920  219.0460
West       984.4505  197.098         57.2800  281.1615
```

You can verify the results with those we obtained in Excel.

• The Power of Iteration

We'd like to use the final example in this chapter to demonstrate the power of iteration. We start by creating a list of the three categorical columns in the sales DataFrame. Then, using a simple for loop, we can generate pivot tables for these three dimensions in just two lines of code. This type of iteration-based automation is extremely challenging to achieve in Excel, even with VBA support. With Python, however, you can harness such powerful capabilities with joy.

In[#]:

```
dimensions = ["Store Name", "Name", "Item"]

for dim in dimensions:
    pivot = pd.pivot_table(sales, values="Margin", index=dim, aggfunc="sum")
    print(pivot)
```

Out[#]:

```
                     Margin
Store Name
East          7599.3715
North         6943.7035
South         8043.5455
West          7475.4115
                          Margin
Name
Adriana Cisneros       3988.6525
Bradley Marshall       3610.7190
Carol Parker           3815.3850
Daniel Marquez         3128.3185
Elizabeth Rodriguez    3819.8885
Kristin Lee            4002.8645
Nathaniel Marquez      4223.6570
Valerie Gibson         3472.5470
                     Margin
Item
Backpack          3108.065
Baseball Cap       527.349
Gloves            1702.740
Greeting Card      410.286
Handbag           1152.512
Hat               2396.716
Hoodie            3054.275
Jacket            3064.168
Keychain          1237.344
Magnet            1060.790
Mug               3301.354
Notebook          3660.260
Pen               3285.778
Scarf              867.658
Stuffed Mascot     226.502
T-Shirt           1006.235
```

3.5 DISCUSSIONS

In this chapter, you have learned how to use Pandas' groupby(), agg(), and pivot_table() functions along with the powerful for loop. Pandas' aggregation functions provide several advantages over Excel's SUMIF(), AVERAGEIF(), and Pivot Tables, particularly when working with large datasets or requiring automations and reproducibility. Some of the key comparisons are summarized as follows:

1. Ease of Use:
   1) Pandas: Once familiar with Python and Pandas, these functions are highly intuitive for data manipulation. Python scripts can be more readable and easier to debug than complex Excel formulas. The ability to write code allows for more explicit and understandable steps in data processing.
   2) Excel: Excel is user-friendly for those not familiar with programming, providing drag and drop items in Pivot Tables. Formulas like SUMIF() and AVERAGEIF() are straightforward for simple tasks but can become cumbersome as conditions and datasets grow more in complexity.

2. Scalability:
   1) Pandas: Excellently suited for handling large datasets, far surpassing Excel's row and column limits. Pandas efficiently processes data that can run into millions of rows with ease and the performance is optimized.
   2) Excel: Has a limitation on the number of rows and the amount of data it can handle, which can make it less suitable for very large enterprise datasets.

3. Reusability and Automation:
   1) Pandas: Python scripts can be saved, reused, and automated. Its powerful for loop allows for the automation of repetitive tasks through scripts, which can be executed with minimal user interaction, thereby increasing efficiency.
   2) Excel: While macros can automate tasks, they generally require manual setup and are less flexible in handling changes in data structure compared to Python scripts.

4. Flexibility and Functionality:
   1) Pandas: Offers extensive functionalities for complex calculations, transformations, and more sophisticated statistical operations. groupby() and pivot_table() can handle multiple aggregation functions simultaneously, and custom functions can be applied using agg().
   2) Excel: Pivot Tables provide robust summary tools, but applying different aggregations or custom calculations can quickly become limiting and less straightforward.

Overall, while Excel remains a fantastic tool for many business professionals for ad-hoc analysis and smaller datasets, Pandas provides a more robust, scalable, and automation-friendly environment suitable for modern data analytics needs.

3.6 EXERCISES

Using the concepts covered in this chapter, complete the following exercises with "Exercise-Ch03.xlsx" as your dataset.

E1: Generate descriptive statistics for purchase cost, including total cost, average cost per order, maximum cost, and minimum cost.

E2: Compute the total and average amounts of purchase cost, and number of orders, grouped by supplier.

E3: Create a report comparing purchase quantities for each store and item.

## CHAPTER 4

Data Visualization and Ranking

D ATA VISUALIZATION PLAYS A critical role in data analytics by transforming complex data into graphical representations, making it easier to identify patterns, trends, and insights. It is a powerful tool to bridge the gap between data and decision-making by making insights more accessible and understandable to humans. "Words are not as effective as tables, while tables are not as effective as pictures; a picture is worth a thousand words." This Chinese proverb highlights the idea that visual representations are generally more powerful and clearer than textual descriptions or tabular data, aligning with the idea that data visualization is a universal language for communicating findings to audiences from diverse backgrounds. By combining the right visual techniques with thoughtful design, data visualization enables business analysts and stakeholders to extract value from data, communicate effectively, and make data-driven decisions.

On the other hand, data ranking is the process of sorting data points based on specific criteria, typically from highest to lowest (or vice versa) in terms of value, relevance, or importance. It is a key technique in data analysis, helping to identify top performers, outliers, or trends. Data ranking is often paired with data visualization because visualizations can effectively communicate the results of ranked data. Charts such as bar charts, pie

DOI: 10.1201/9781003567103-5

charts, and heatmaps are commonly used to represent rankings, making it easier for users to compare data points, identify trends, and highlight top or bottom performers. By combining ranking with visualization, complex datasets become more accessible, allowing users to quickly grasp key insights, spot outliers, or observe patterns.

4.1 GENERAL GUIDELINES FOR DATA VISUALIZATION

To effectively use data visualization, it's important to understand some key concepts and guidelines. The following guidelines can help you create clear, effective, and insightful visualizations for your audience to better understand information and make actions.

1. **Types of Charts and Graphs**
   - **Pie Chart**: Represents parts of a whole using slices of a circle. It is best used for simple, proportional comparisons.
   - **Bar Chart**: Displays categorical data with rectangular bars, where the length of the bar represents the value. It's commonly used to compare quantities across categories.
   - **Line Chart**: Shows data trends over time or continuous variables. It's useful for visualizing time-series data or trends.
   - **Heatmap**: Uses color to represent data values, often used to show the intensity of data across a matrix or grid (e.g., correlation matrices).
   - **Histogram**: Displays the distribution of a dataset by grouping data into bins. It helps visualize the frequency of data points within specific ranges.
   - **Scatter Plot**: Used to show relationships or correlations between two numerical variables. Patterns in the plot can indicate relationships, trends, or clusters.

2. **Choosing the Right Visualization**

   The type of chart should be selected based on the kind of data and the analysis goal. For example:
   - Use a **pie chart** or a **bar chart** for comparing categories.
   - Use a **line chart** for showing trends over time.
   - Use a **heatmap** for visualizing matrix data or correlations.

- Use a **scatter plot** for understanding relationships between two variables.

3. Detailed Designs
   - **Color**: Plays a critical role in helping users focus on key data points. However, colors should be used carefully to avoid clutter or confusion.
   - **Simplicity**: Keeping visualizations simple and avoiding excessive use of design elements is essential for clarity. Over-complicating the design can obscure the data rather than highlight key insights.
   - **Consistent Formatting**: Consistency in design elements (fonts, colors, chart types) across different visualizations to maintain a professional and polished look.

4. **Storytelling with Data**
   - **Narrative Flow**: Data visualizations are often used to tell a story, guiding the audience through a sequence of insights. For effective storytelling, the visuals should be arranged logically, leading to a clear conclusion.
   - **Emphasizing Key Points**: Highlighting important data points (using color, size, or annotations) helps guide the audience to focus on the key message.
   - **Context-Aware**: Consider the context in which the visualization will be used, whether for a report, presentation, or interactive dashboard.
   - **Know Your Audience**: Tailor the visualization to the knowledge level and needs of your audience. Technical experts might want detailed data, while executives may prefer high-level summaries.

4.2 GENERAL GUIDELINES FOR DATA RANKING

Ranking provides a clearer view of data distribution and makes it easier to prioritize decision-making based on metrics like sales, or other quantitative performance measures. However, care should be taken when interpreting ranked data, as the criteria for ranking can influence outcomes and insights:

1. **Choose the Ranking Dimension**
   Ranking dimension refers to the specific categories or entities by which you want to rank data. In your example, product items, customers,

and stores would be the **dimensions** or **criteria** used to rank the data based on a chosen metric, such as sales, quantity, or revenue.

2. **Select the Right Metric**

   Ensure the variable or metric you're using to rank is relevant to the analysis or decision-making context (e.g., revenue, customer satisfaction, or sales volume). Use domain-specific knowledge to ensure the rankings reflect the underlying reality and don't mislead.

3. **Use Visualization Aids**

   Visualize rankings through charts or graphs to improve understanding. Highlight top or bottom performers clearly in visualizations for ease of interpretation. Additionally, bar charts, scatter plots, and heatmaps are also effective tools for displaying ranked data.

4. **Beware of Outliers**

   Rankings can be skewed by outliers or extreme values. Review the dataset for outliers and consider whether they should be included or addressed through data exploration techniques. If necessary, apply appropriate filters to exclude extreme values that could distort the ranking.

4.3 DATA RANKING AND VISUALIZATION WITH BOOKSTORE DATASET

We will use the "Bookstore-Ch04.xlsx" file to demonstrate how to utilize data visualization tools in both Excel and Python. In Chapter 3, we covered the benefits of using **Excel Tables** for advanced analysis. The "Invoice" worksheet in "Bookstore-Ch04.xlsx" has already been formatted as an Excel Table named "sales". Before proceeding with the exercises below, please take a moment to familiarize yourself with the fundamental operations of Excel Tables.

Q1: **Identify the top ten invoices with the highest total amounts.**

Q2: **Which product is the most popular? What are the top three most popular products? Does your answer change when using different measures of "popularity", such as the number of transactions, quantity sold, or total sales?**

Q3: **Create a pie chart displaying the top ten products with the highest total amounts.**

Q4: **Create a bar chart comparing the margin and sales for each store.**

Q5: **Create a line chart comparing the sales made by each store in the past three months.**

Q6: **Develop a heat map to analyze the sales performance of each store over the past three months.**

4.4 EXCEL

Q1: Identify the top ten invoices with the highest total amounts.

Q1 is a typical example of data ranking, where the ranking dimension is the invoice identifier (i.e., invoice number), and the ranking metric is the invoice amount. To calculate the total amount for each invoice, we can use pivot tables as introduced in Chapter 3:

1. Create a pivot table from the "Sales" table by dragging "Invoice Number" to the Rows section and "Extension – Discounted" to the Values section.

This will display the sum of extensions for each invoice in the table area:

	A	B
1		
2		
3	**Row Labels** ▼	**Sum of Extension - Discounted**
4	1	235.9245
5	2	112.833
6	3	20.1025
7	4	196.5795
8	5	193.696
9	6	88.972
10	7	72.768
11	8	30.168
12	9	181.899
13	10	152.774
14	11	259.8605

2. Rename Column A to "Invoice Number" and Column B to "Invoice Amount". Then, place the pointer on any cell in Column B:

	A	B
1		
2		
3	**Invoice Number** ⌄↑	**Invoice Amount**
4	1	235.9245
5	2	112.833
6	3	20.1025
7	4	196.5795
8	5	193.696

First, we'll use Excel's traditional "Conditional Formatting" to highlight the top ten invoices. Then, we'll show how sorting and filtering with a pivot table can more effectively meet our needs.

- **Use Conditional Formatting**
  1. On the Home ribbon, open the "Conditional Formatting" menu, select "Top/Bottom Rules", and choose "Top Ten Items", as shown below:

2. In the pop-up window, click "OK" to accept the default "Top Ten" settings:

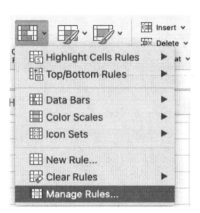

3. Open the "Conditional Formatting" menu again and select "Manage Rules":

	A	B
740	737	78.351
741	738	110.024
742	739	155.063
743	740	37.74
744	741	134.992
745	742	80.4
746	743	260.26
747	744	12.65
748	745	41.496
749	746	120.048

4. In the pop-up window, update the "Applies to:" range from "$B$4" to "$B$4:$B$1003" to exclude the bottom row (Grand Total):

5. Scroll down the table to view the highlighted "Top Ten" invoices:

	A	B
739	736	111.48
740	737	78.351
741	738	110.024
742	739	155.063
743	740	37.74
744	741	134.992
745	742	80.4
746	743	260.26
747	744	12.65
748	745	41.496
749	746	120.048

As you may have noticed, while traditional "Conditional Formatting" offers excellent visual aids for highlighting data based on specific conditions, it can become inefficient when applied to large datasets like Bookstore workbook. In contrast, sorting and filtering directly in a pivot table or using other data analysis techniques can provide faster, more scalable solutions for large datasets. These methods are more efficient in handling and summarizing large amounts of data while still allowing for clear insights.

- **Use Pivot Table's Sorting and Filtering**
    1. We begin by clearing the previous highlighting from conditional formatting. Open the "Conditional Formatting" menu and select "Manage Rules". In the pop-up window, choose the formatting rule you want to remove:

Click the graphic icon Φ icon and press OK to delete the selected rule:

    2. Then, right-click any cell in Column B, choose "Sort" from the pop-up menu, and select "Sort Largest to Smallest":

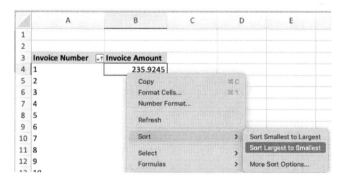

The sorted dataset will appear as shown below:

	A	B
1		
2		
3	**Invoice Number** ⬇	**Invoice Amount**
4	601	299.173
5	840	294.89
6	218	291.5145
7	489	281.1
8	180	275.208
9	643	262.031
10	743	260.26
11	11	259.8605
12	468	259.4025

3. Right-click any cell in Column A, choose "Filter" from the pop-up menu, and select "Top 10":

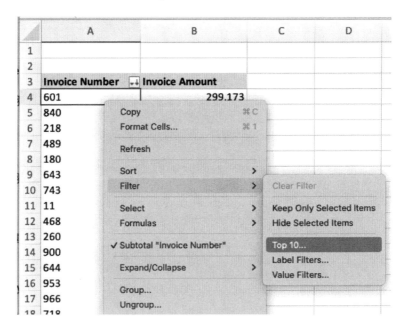

4. The "Top 10 Filter" enables you to filter data to display the top or bottom n values (default is 10) or find items that make up a specific percent or items that add up to a specific total. In this example, choose "Top 10 Items" as shown below:

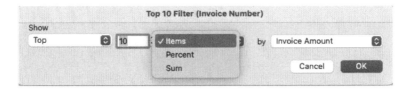

The invoices with the top 10 highest amounts will appear as shown below:

	A	B
1		
2		
3	**Invoice Number** ↓T	**Invoice Amount**
4	601	299.173
5	840	294.89
6	218	291.5145
7	489	281.1
8	180	275.208
9	643	262.031
10	743	260.26
11	11	259.8605
12	468	259.4025
13	260	257.376
14	**Grand Total**	**2740.8155**

Q2: Which product is the most popular? What are the top 3 most popular products? Does your answer change when using different measures of "popularity", such as the number of transactions, quantity sold, or sales amount?

Q1 demonstrates how to use a pivot table's sorting and filtering for data ranking by invoice. In Q2, we shift the ranking dimension to product items and expand the ranking metrics to include three measures: number of transactions, quantity sold, and sales amount. Despite the increased complexity, the ranking process follows the same steps as in Q1. We will leave this question for you to complete, but you can verify your answers using the completed pivot tables shown below:

1. Pivot table without filters (sorted by sales amount in descending order):

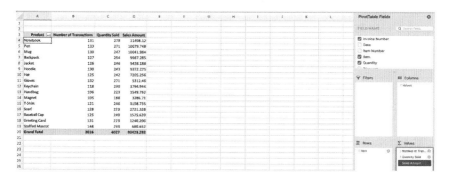

2. Top 3 by number of transactions:

	A	B	C	D
1				
2				
3	**Product** 🔽	**Number of Transactions**	**Quantity Sold**	**Sales Amount**
4	Stuffed Mascot	148	293	680.652
5	Pen	133	271	10079.748
6	Glove	132	271	5312.46
7	**Grand Total**	**413**	**835**	**16072.86**

3. Top 3 by quantity sold:

	A	B	C	D
1				
2				
3	**Product** 🔽	**Number of Transactions**	**Quantity Sold**	**Sales Amount**
4	Stuffed Mascot	148	293	680.652
5	Notebook	131	278	11408.12
6	Greeting Card	131	273	1240.206
7	Scarve	128	273	2721.328
8	**Grand Total**	**538**	**1117**	**16050.306**

There are four products listed due to a tie between Notebook and Greeting Card. If the tie isn't a significant issue, it's generally unnecessary to implement a "tie-break" strategy.

4. Top 3 by sales amount:

	A	B	C	D
1				
2				
3	**Product** 🔽	**Number of Transactions**	**Quantity Sold**	**Sales Amount**
4	Notebook	131	278	11408.12
5	Pen	133	271	10079.748
6	Mug	130	247	10041.984
7	**Grand Total**	**394**	**796**	**31529.852**

For the question "Which product is the most popular?", we'll leave it to your judgment, as it should be easy to identify the top product from the three completed tables above based on your personal or contextual criteria.

Q3: Create a pie chart displaying the top 10 products with the highest total amounts.

Q3 is an example of combining data ranking with data visualization. We start by creating a pivot table, using product items as the ranking dimension and sales amount as the ranking metric:

1. Sort the pivot table by sales amount in descending order, then use the "Top 10" filter to identify the top 10 products:

	A	B
1		
2		
3	**Product** ↓T	**Sales Amount**
4	Notebook	11408.12
5	Pen	10079.748
6	Mug	10041.984
7	Backpack	9567.285
8	Jacket	9428.188
9	Hoodie	9372.275
10	Hat	7205.256
11	Gloves	5312.46
12	Keychain	3794.944
13	Handbag	3549.762
14	**Grand Total**	**79760.022**

2. There are several ways to create charts from a pivot table. The most common approach is to go to the Insert tab and choose the chart type from the drop-down menu. You can also select from various chart layouts. In the case of a pie chart, choose "3-D Pie" from the "Pie" drop-down menu, as shown below:

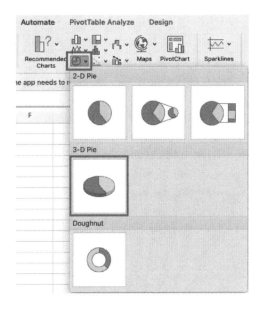

3. On the right to the pivot table, you should immediately have the pie chart as below:

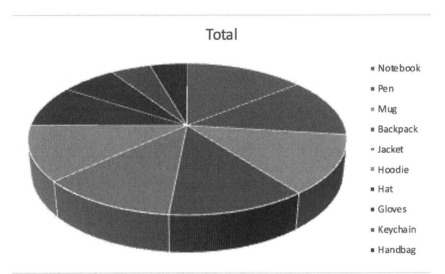

4. Excel's chart settings are highly user-friendly, allowing each element of the chart to be customized individually. Simply point and click on an element, and the "Format" panel will appear on the right-hand side. Here are a few simple examples to try out:

- Click on the chart title and rename it to "Sales by Product".
- Select the legend and change its position from "Right" to "Bottom".

The pie chart below reflects the reconfigurations made after the two changes above:

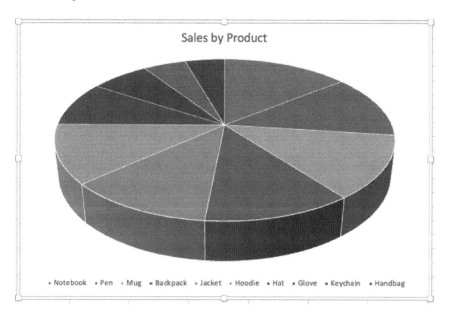

5. To add or modify more features on the pie chart, point and click the entire pie chart and follow the steps below:
   - Open the "**Add Chart Element**" menu from the Design ribbon, as shown below:

- Choose "**Data Labels** -> **Outside End**" to display data values on each slice of the pie chart:

- Point and click any of the newly added data labels:

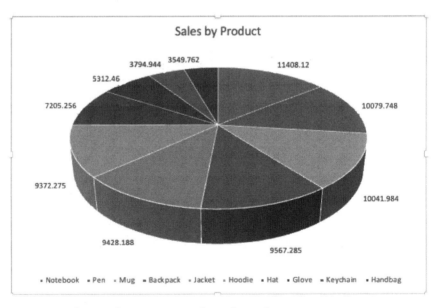

- In the configuration panel on the right:
  1) Go to the **Label Options** tab and expand the options.
  2) Uncheck **Value** and check **Percentage** to change the data labels to percentage values, as shown below:

3) Expand the **Number** options, select **Percentage** from the **Category** menu, and set the **Decimal places** to 1, as shown below:

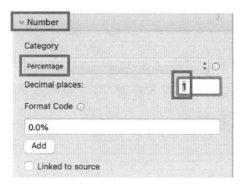

4) The modified percentage labels are particularly useful for comparing portions in a pie chart:

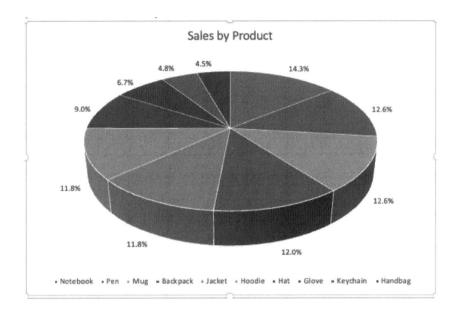

- Sometimes, you may want to emphasize a specific slice of the pie chart, such as the "Mug" product, to draw the audience's attention. To do this, simply double-click the Mug slice and drag it outward from the pie. This effect is known as a "slice explosion":

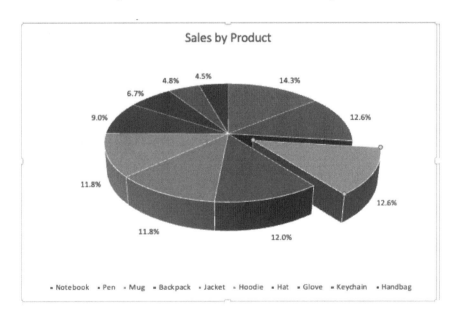

Q4: Create a bar chart comparing the margin and sales for each store.

Q4 can be completed using a simpler process than Q3, as it doesn't require specific ranking:

1. Begin by creating a pivot table, using store names in the Rows section, and both margin ("Margin") and sales amount ("Extension - Discounted") in the Values section. Adjust the column labels in the header row accordingly:

	A	B	C
1			
2			
3	Store ▼	Total Sales	Total Margin
4	East	23126.8215	7599.3715
5	North	21546.2335	6943.7035
6	South	24775.2655	8043.5455
7	West	22974.9715	7475.4115
8	Grand Total	92423.292	30062.032

2. Creating a bar chart (or column chart) from a pivot table is straight-forward. Place the cursor on any cell within the pivot table, go to the "PivotTable Analyze" ribbon, and click "Pivot Chart":

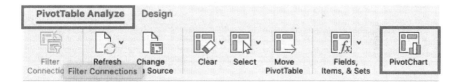

3. The bar chart is typically the default chart type for a quick comparison in a pivot table. Optionally, you can easily use the "Add Chart Elements" menu to add a title, include data labels formatted as "Currency", and remove the gridlines by selecting and deleting them, as shown in the completed bar chart below:

COMPLEMENTARY NOTE – SLICER

Slicer is a visual filtering tool that allows users to quickly and easily filter data in pivot tables, pivot charts, and Excel Tables. It provides a user-friendly interface with clickable buttons representing the values of a specific field, making it easy for users to filter data by simply clicking on the desired buttons. Using Q4 as an example, below are the steps to create a slicer of product items for the pivot chart:

1. Select the pivot chart. In the "PivotChart Analyze" ribbon, click the "Insert Slicer" button:

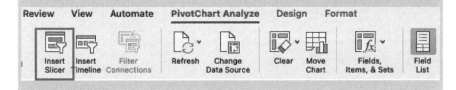

2. In the pop-up list of available fields, choose "Item":

3. Adjust the slicer that appears to display all products. Press and hold the "Ctrl" key (or "Command" on Mac), then click "Hoodie", "Jacket", and "T-Shirt" to filter and display only the apparel-related products:

4. You may have noticed that the data in both the pivot table and pivot chart have dynamically updated to reflect the filtered results:

5. Optionally, you can use the "Fill Color" menu to apply a light gray background to the entire worksheet. To do this, select the entire worksheet by clicking the top-left corner icon, then choose the desired color:

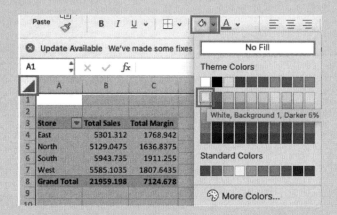

6. This will hide the gridlines on the worksheet, giving it a clean, dashboard-like slicer:

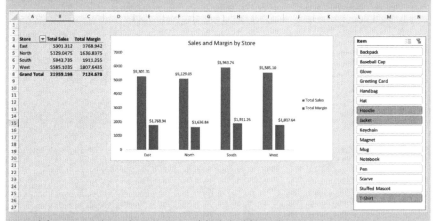

Feel free to explore this slicer-enabled dashboard on your own. In practice, you can create multiple charts on a separate worksheet and use slicers with advanced settings to control the dynamics of all connected charts.

Q5: Create a line chart to compare sales made by each store over the past three months.

Trend analysis helps identify patterns or movements in data over a period of time. An effective trend analysis shows whether your data is increasing, decreasing, or remaining stable, and can detect cyclical patterns, seasonality, or long-term trends. It is widely used in finance, economics, marketing, and business analytics to guide time-series decisions and make predictions. Among different trend analysis tools, the **line chart** serves as a fundamental visualization tool that simplifies the identification of these trends.

The Invoice worksheet contains transactions made from the first quarter of 2023. To create the line chart comparing the monthly sales of each store, we still can use pivot table to group sales by the "Date" column.

1. To create a pivot table from the "Sales" table, drag "Date" to the Rows section, "Store name" to the Columns section, and "Extension - Discounted" to the Values section. Excel will automatically add two date attributes: Months and Days to the Rows section for selection:

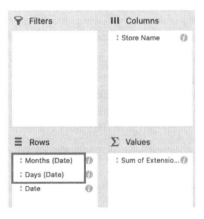

2. Since the goal is to create monthly sales figures for each store, remove "Days" and "Date" from the Rows section by right-clicking on them and selecting "Remove Field":

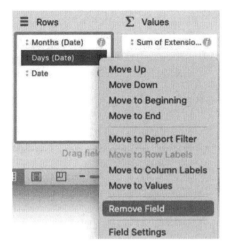

After renaming the labels, the pivot table will look as follows:

	A	B	C	D	E	F
1						
2						
3	**Sales**	**Store**	▼			
4	**Month**	▼ **East**	**North**	**South**	**West**	**Grand Total**
5	Jan	7558.5825	7108.679	8971.066	7043.711	30682.0385
6	Feb	7033.2535	6441.9285	7490.5355	8162.8765	29128.594
7	Mar	8534.9855	7995.626	8313.664	7768.384	32612.6595
8	**Grand Total**	**23126.8215**	**21546.2335**	**24775.2655**	**22974.9715**	**92423.292**

3. Position your cursor within the pivot table, navigate to the "PivotTable Analyze" ribbon, and select "Pivot Chart". As illustrated earlier, this action will generate a default bar chart as shown below:

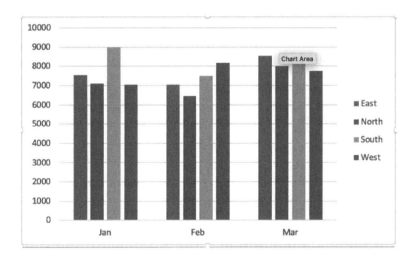

4. Select the bar chart and navigate to the Design ribbon. Open the "Change Chart Type" menu to switch the current bar chart to the desired line chart:

5. In the "Change Chart Type" menu, choose "Line" to view different line chart layouts and choose "Line with Markers":

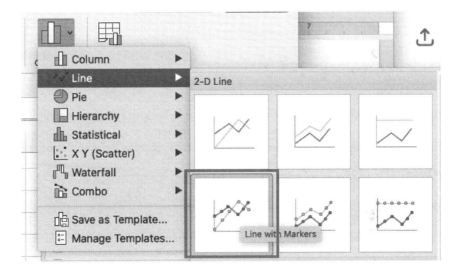

The updated line chart will look like as follows:

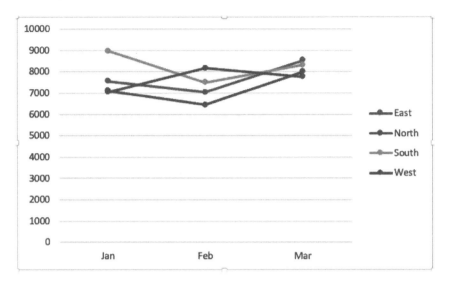

6. Optionally, you can adjust the scale of the vertical axis for a better presentation of sales trends:

- Click on the vertical axis to launch the Format Axis panel on the right-hand side. Expand "Axis Options", and increase the Minimum value in the Bounds section to 5,000, as illustrated below:

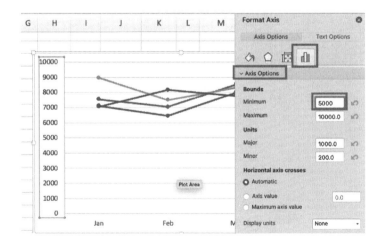

- After rescaling the value axis and adding the chart title, your completed line chart should appear as:

One of the insights gained from the line chart above is the West store generated its highest sales in February, whereas other stores experienced their lowest sales during that month. You are encouraged to explore and discover additional valuable insights from all the charts introduced in this chapter.

Q6: Develop a heat map to analyze the sales performance of each store over the past three months.

Heatmaps can be particularly useful when you want to engage your audience with a spectrum of colors representing varying data values. We will use the same pivot table from Q5, which summarizes the store sales by month, to demonstrate how to use "Conditional Formatting" to create heatmaps in Excel.

1. Select the range of all 12 data points in the store-by-month pivot table. Make sure that you do not include any totals. Navigate to the Home ribbon, open the Conditional Formatting menu, and select "Color Scales" to browse all the available color scales:

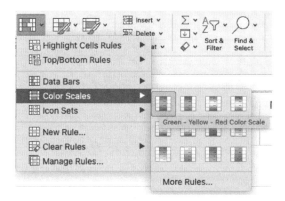

2. In the case of "Green-Yellow-Red" color scale, green often represents higher values, suggesting positive outcomes or high performance. Yellow signals medium range values, indicating moderate perform-ance. Red indicates lower values, which might represent poor per-formance or areas of concern that need addressing. The screenshot below displays the pivot table as a heatmap, using the "Green-Yellow-Red" color scale:

Sales	Store ▾				
Month ▾	East	North	South	West	Grand Total
Jan	7558.5825	7108.679	8971.066	7043.711	30682.0385
Feb	7033.2535	6441.9285	7490.5355	8162.8765	29128.594
Mar	8534.9855	7995.626	8313.664	7768.384	32612.6595
Grand Total	23126.8215	21546.2335	24775.2655	22974.9715	92423.292

As depicted above, the South store's January sales are the highest among all 12 data points, and thus appear in the deepest green. On the other hand, the North store's February sales are the lowest, and therefore appear in the red color.

4.5 PYTHON

Please refer to the Jupyter notebook file "Bookstore-Ch04.ipynb" to access the code, or view the "Bookstore-Ch04.html" file to see the outputs of all code.

Python offers a variety of powerful visualization libraries. For business users, Pandas' built-in plotting functions combined with Matplotlib are the most commonly used.

4.5.1 Pandas Plotting

Pandas provides convenient, high-level plotting functions through its DataFrame.plot() method, which integrates with Matplotlib. This allows users to generate basic visualizations directly from data stored in DataFrames with minimal code. Specifically, Pandas plotting allows you to create various types of plots directly from DataFrames and Series.

1. Basic plots:
   • Bar plot: df.plot(kind="bar") or df.plot.bar()

- Pie chart: s.plot(kind="pie") or s.plot.pie()
- Line plot: df.plot(kind="line") or df.plot.line()
- Scatter plot: df.plot(kind="scatter", x="column1", y="column2") or df.plot.scatter(x="column1", y="column2")
2. Customizing plots:
   - df.plot(kind="bar", title="My Title", xlabel="X-Axis", ylabel="Y-Axis", colormap="viridis")
3. Integrating with Matplotlib:
   - import matplotlib.pyplot as plt to use more advanced settings

4.5.2 Matplotlib:

Matplotlib is a versatile, low-level library that serves as the foundation for many other visualization libraries in Python. It provides extensive control over plot customization, making it suitable for creating visualizations across different domains. The core component of Matplotlib is the `pyplot` module, which is a collection of functions that provide an interface similar to MATLAB's plotting functions. The `pyplot` module simplifies the process of creating and customizing plots, making it easier for users to generate a wide range of visualizations such as line plots, scatter plots, bar plots, histograms, 3D plots, and more. It's highly customizable, allowing control over figure size, colors, labels, and axes.

The primary focus of this chapter is on Pandas' plotting capabilities. We will explore deeper into Matplotlib and other advanced Python visualization libraries at the end of this chapter.

4.5.3 Plotting Exercises using Pandas and Matplotlib¶

Now, let's use the read_excel() method to import the "Invoice" sheet from the "Bookstore-Ch04.xlsx" file into a Pandas DataFrame:

```
In[#]:

import pandas as pd

filepath = "/Users/chi2019/Desktop/Book/Excel Files/Bookstore-Ch04.
xlsx" # Change the path according to your file location

# For Windows users, prefix r is added:
# filepath = r"C:\Users\chi2019\Desktop\Book\Excel Files\Bookstore-
Ch04.xlsx"

sales = pd.read_excel(filepath, sheet_name = "Invoice", header = 0,
usecols = "A:R", nrows = 2016)
print(sales.head(5))
```

Out[#]:

	Invoice Number	Date	Item Number	Item	Quantity	Discount	\
0	1	2023-01-01	PI-003	Jacket	3	0.00	
1	1	2023-01-01	PI-012	Pen	3	0.15	
2	2	2023-01-01	PI-012	Pen	3	0.10	
3	3	2023-01-01	PI-011	Stuffed Mascot	1	0.15	
4	3	2023-01-01	PI-007	Baseball Cap	3	0.15	

	Cost	List Price	Extension - Discounted	Margin	Quantity in Stock	\
0	25.87	43.12	129.3600	51.7500	44	
1	25.07	41.79	106.5645	31.3545	32	
2	25.07	41.79	112.8330	37.6230	32	
3	1.55	2.59	2.2015	0.6515	22	
4	4.21	7.02	17.9010	5.2710	14	

	Emp ID	Name	Start Date	Weekly Payment	Store ID	Store Name	\
0	EMP-003	Daniel Marquez	2023-02-08	1139	ST-003	North	
1	EMP-003	Daniel Marquez	2023-02-08	1139	ST-003	North	
2	EMP-006	Kristin Lee	2022-01-05	1013	ST-002	West	
3	EMP-002	Valerie Gibson	2022-04-09	1115	ST-002	West	
4	EMP-002	Valerie Gibson	2022-04-09	1115	ST-002	West	

	Address
0	078 Cindy Shore, Los Angeles, CA 96017
1	078 Cindy Shore, Los Angeles, CA 96017
2	845 Lloyd Walk Apt. 693, Los Angeles, CA 91326
3	845 Lloyd Walk Apt. 693, Los Angeles, CA 91326
4	845 Lloyd Walk Apt. 693, Los Angeles, CA 91326

Q1: Identify the top 10 invoices with the highest total amounts.

In Chapter 3, we explored how to use Pandas' pivot_table() to summarize and reorganize data from an original DataFrame. To address Q1, we can create a pivot table with "Invoice Number" as the index, aggregating the data by the "Extension - Discounted" amount for each invoice:

In[#]:

```
q1 = pd.pivot_table(sales, values="Extension - Discounted", index=
"Invoice Number", aggfunc="sum")
q1
```

Out[#]:

	Invoice Number	Extension - Discounted
1		235.9245
2		112.8330
3		20.1025
4		196.5795
5		193.6960
...		...
996		50.8860
997		102.4190
998		180.0580
999		72.6480
1000		55.8000

1000 rows × 1 columns

You may change the column label to more accurately reflect the context of Q1, as shown below. For more details of rename() and other DataFrame operations, please refer to the Complementary Note on page 157.

In[#]:

```
q1.rename(columns = {"Extension - Discounted": "Amount"}, inplace
= True)
q1
```

Out[#]:

		Amount
	Invoice Number	
1		235.9245
2		112.8330
3		20.1025
4		196.5795
5		193.6960
...		...
996		50.8860
997		102.4190
998		180.0580
999		72.6480
1000		55.8000

1000 rows × 1 columns

To retrieve the top 10 records with the highest values in a specific column of a Pandas DataFrame, you can use the `nlargest()` function. This method allows you to efficiently get the rows with the largest values (and sorted in the descending order) from a specific column.

In[#]:

```
# Retrieve the top 10 records with the highest sales
top_10_sales = q1.nlargest(10, "Amount")
top_10_sales
```

Out[#]:

Invoice Number	Amount
601	299.1730
840	294.8900
218	291.5145
489	281.1000
180	275.2080
643	262.0310
743	260.2600
11	259.8605
468	259.4025
260	257.3760

For the lowest values, you can use `nsmallest()` function instead:

In[#]:

```
# Retrieve the bottom 10 records with the lowest sales
bottom_10_sales = q1.nsmallest(10, "Amount")
bottom_10_sales
```

Out[#]:

Invoice Number	Amount
203	2.0720
422	2.0720
168	2.2015
406	2.2015
663	2.2015
600	2.3310
247	2.5900
924	2.5900
269	4.0480
547	4.0480

• Complementary Note – Basic Operations in Pandas DataFrame

Pandas provides a set of fundamental operations that are very useful when working with data in DataFrames as summarized and illustrated below:

1. Accessing: Use loc[] and iloc[] for accessing data.
2. Renaming: Use rename() to rename rows and columns.
3. Dropping: Use drop() to remove rows or columns.
4. Reindexing: Use reindex() to change or add indexes.
5. Adding columns and rows: Simply assign a new column (or row) to df["new_column"] or df.loc["new_row"].
6. Sorting: Use sort_values() to sort by specific columns.
7. Filtering: Use condition-based filtering to select specific rows.

In[#]:

```
# Create a Sample 5x5 DataFrame
df = pd.DataFrame({
    "A": [1, 2, 3, 4, 5],
    "B": [6, 7, 8, 9, 10],
    "C": [11, 12, 13, 14, 15],
    "D": [16, 17, 18, 19, 20],
    "E": [21, 22, 23, 24, 25],
}, index=["row1", "row2", "row3", "row4", "row5"])
# Display the DataFrame
df
```

Out[#]:

	A	B	C	D	E
row1	1	6	11	16	21
row2	2	7	12	17	22
row3	3	8	13	18	23
row4	4	9	14	19	24
row5	5	10	15	20	25

1. Accessing columns and rows:
You may use a couple of ways to access specific columns or rows in a DataFrame: 1) by the direct [] accessor with named labels to return specified columns (not for row retrieval), 2) using the loc indexer (or accessor) along with named labels to return the specified columns or rows, and 3) using the iloc indexer (or accessor) along with index numbers to return the specified columns or rows:

Direct [] Accessor

```
In[#]:
print(df["A"], "\n") # Using named label to access a column,
returning a new Series
print(df[["A", "C"]]) # Using named labels to access multiple
columns, returning a new DataFrame

Out[#]:
row1    1
row2    2
row3    3
row4    4
row5    5
Name: A, dtype: int64
        A   C
row1    1   11
row2    2   12
row3    3   13
row4    4   14
row5    5   15
```

The df["A"] method is simple and direct, allowing you to access a single column by specifying its label and return a Pandas Series. To access multiple columns, you need to enclose the column labels in an additional set of brackets, essentially passing a list of column labels like ["A", "C"] to the df[] accessor, and return a new DataFrame with columns "A" and "C".

The direct [] accessor is reserved for column retrieval in Pandas, meaning you cannot use it to access rows directly it. To access rows, you need to use indexers like loc[] or iloc[].

The loc[] Indexer

The loc[] indexer works with row labels. For accessing multiple rows, enclose the row labels in an additional set of brackets, similar to how df[] is used to access multiple columns:

```
In[#]:
print(df.loc["row1"], "\n") # Using loc indexer to access a row by
its label, return a Series
print(df.loc[["row1", "row3"]]) # using loc indexer to access
multiple rows by specified labels, return a DataFrame

Out[#]:
A    1
B    6
C    11
D    16
E    21
```

```
Name: row1, dtype: int64

      A  B   C   D   E
row1  1  6  11  16  21
row3  3  8  13  18  23
```

Fancy Indexing

In fact, the full syntax of loc[] consists of two parts: loc[row indexing, column indexing], where the column indexing is optional. This flexibility allows us to access both specific rows and columns. This is referred to as `fancy indexing`, also known as advanced indexing. Fancy indexing refers to selecting elements using a list of explicit labels or indices. Let's see a few examples:

```
In[#]:
print(df.loc["row1", ["A", "C"]], "\n") # Using fancy indexing to
pick non-adjacent columns "A" and "C" from row1

Out[#]:
A     1
C    11
Name: row1, dtype: int64

In[#]:
print(df.loc[["row1", "row3"], ["A", "C"]]) # Using fancy indexing to
pick non-adjacent columns "A" and "C" from row1 and row3

Out[#]:
      A   C
row1  1  11
row3  3  13
```

As you may have noticed, fancy indexing allows you to arbitrarily select non-adjacent rows and columns based on a list of specific labels or positions.

The iloc[] Indexer

Pandas offers another indexer, iloc[], which uses positional index numbers instead of named labels to access rows and columns. The syntax of iloc[] is similar to loc[], but it operates based on index positions:

```
In[#]:
print(df.iloc[0], "\n") # using iloc indexer to access a row by its
index, return a Series
print(df.iloc[[0, 2]]) # using iloc indexer to access multiple rows
by specified indices, return a DataFrame
```

```
Out[#]:
A        1
B        6
C       11
D       16
E       21
Name: row1, dtype: int64

         A   B    C    D    E
row1     1   6   11   16   21
row3     3   8   13   18   23
```

The iloc[] indexer also supports fancy indexing:

```
In[#]:
print(df.iloc[[0, 2], [0, 2]]) # Using fancy indexing to pick non-
adjacent columns and rows using indices

Out[#]:
         A    C
row1     1   11
row3     3   13
```

Slicing with loc[] and iloc[]

Sometimes, we need to select a range of rows or columns using start and end points, similar to how we select ranges in Excel. Python provides a similar notation for this, called data slicing. In Pandas, data slicing can be performed using the loc[] and iloc[] indexers. The syntax is straightforward: for loc[], use loc[row slicing, column slicing], where row slicing is represented as "start row label":"end row label". For iloc[], use "start row index":"end row index" instead. The notation: should be familiar, as it is also used in Excel's range selection when specifying a range like "A1:C10".

Note: One small clarification is, in iloc[], the end index is exclusive, meaning the last row/column in the specified range is not included, whereas in loc[], the end label is inclusive.

```
In[#]:
print(df.loc["row1":"row3", "A":"C"]) # Slicing the range for columns
from "A" to "C" and rows from row1 to row3

Out[#]:
         A   B    C
row1     1   6   11
row2     2   7   12
row3     3   8   13
```

```
In[#]:

print(df.iloc[0:3, 0:3]) # Slicing the range for columns from "A" to
"C" and rows from row1 to row3

Out[#]:

        A  B   C
row1    1  6  11
row2    2  7  12
row3    3  8  13
```

Keep in mind that when using iloc[], the end index is excluded. This is why we increase the end index to 3 in order to select the same range as loc[].

A comparison between indexing and slicing
Indexing and slicing are both powerful methods for retrieving data, but they are used in different contexts. In indexing, you explicitly select specific rows and columns by their labels (e.g., "row1" and "row3" for rows, and "A" and "C" for columns) or by their index positions (e.g., [0, 2]). Slicing, on the other hand, typically refers to selecting a continuous range of rows or columns using start and end points (e.g., 0:3), covering a sequential section of the data.

The following figures illustrate the difference:
The result of fancy indexing with iloc[[0, 2], [0, 2]]:

The result of slicing with iloc[0:3, 0:3]:

2. Renaming Columns or Rows

You can rename columns or rows using the `rename()` method by specifying the columns or index parameters. The syntax is {"old name": "new name", ...}:

In[#]:
```
# Rename columns
df_renamed_cols = df.rename(columns={"A": "Col_A", "B": "Col_B"}) #
rename columns A and B

# Rename rows
df_renamed_rows = df.rename(index={"row1": "First", "row2":
"Second"}) # rename rows row1 and row2

print(df_renamed_cols, "\n") # Add an "\n" to print a new line
print(df_renamed_rows)
```
Out[#]:
```
        Col_A  Col_B   C   D   E
row1        1      6  11  16  21
row2        2      7  12  17  22
row3        3      8  13  18  23
row4        4      9  14  19  24
row5        5     10  15  20  25

         A   B   C   D   E
First    1   6  11  16  21
Second   2   7  12  17  22
row3     3   8  13  18  23
row4     4   9  14  19  24
row5     5  10  15  20  25
```

3. Dropping Rows or Columns

You can delete rows or columns using the `drop()` method by specifying the axis parameter (zero for rows, one for columns):

In[#]:
```
# Drop a column
df_drop_col = df.drop("B", axis=1)

# Drop a row
df_drop_row = df.drop("row2", axis=0) # For row dropping, you may
omit axis = 0 since it's the default value

print(df_drop_col, "\n")
print(df_drop_row)
```

```
Out[#]:

        A    C    D    E
row1    1   11   16   21
row2    2   12   17   22
row3    3   13   18   23
row4    4   14   19   24
row5    5   15   20   25


        A    B    C    D    E
row1    1    6   11   16   21
row3    3    8   13   18   23
row4    4    9   14   19   24
row5    5   10   15   20   25
```

In this example, we drop the "C" column from the result DataFrame by specifying axis=1. If you don't provide the axis parameter or set it to 0 (default value), Pandas will try to remove rows with the specified label(s) and may raise an error if the labels don't match any row index.

4. Reindexing

Reindexing allows you to change the index of a DataFrame. It can be used to change the order of rows or columns.

```
In[#]:

# Reindex rows
df_reindexed_rows = df.reindex(["row3", "row1", "row2", "row4",
"row5"]) # For row reindexing, you may omit index = [] since it's the
default value

# Reindex columns
df_reindexed_cols = df.reindex(columns = ["B", "A", "C", "D", "E"]) #
For column reindexing, you need to specify columns = []

print(df_reindexed_rows, "\n")
print(df_reindexed_cols)

Out[#]:

        A    B    C    D    E
row3    3    8   13   18   23
row1    1    6   11   16   21
row2    2    7   12   17   22
row4    4    9   14   19   24
row5    5   10   15   20   25


        B    A    C    D    E
row1    6    1   11   16   21
row2    7    2   12   17   22
row3    8    3   13   18   23
row4    9    4   14   19   24
row5   10    5   15   20   25
```

5. Adding New Columns and Rows

You can add a new column (or row) by assigning a value or performing an operation on existing columns (rows), or just None for a blank column or row.

```
In[#]:

# Make a copy of df DataFrame
df_c = df.copy()

# Add a new column based on existing columns
df_c["F"] = df_c["A"] + df_c["B"]

print(df_c)
```

Out[#]:

```
      A   B   C   D   E   F
row1  1   6   11  16  21  7
row2  2   7   12  17  22  9
row3  3   8   13  18  23  11
row4  4   9   14  19  24  13
row5  5   10  15  20  25  15
```

```
In[#]:

# Add a new row based on existing rows
df_c.loc["row6"] = df_c.loc["row1"] + df_c.loc["row2"]

print(df_c)
```

Out[#]:

```
      A   B   C   D   E   F
row1  1   6   11  16  21  7
row2  2   7   12  17  22  9
row3  3   8   13  18  23  11
row4  4   9   14  19  24  13
row5  5   10  15  20  25  15
row6  3   13  23  33  43  16
```

```
In[#]:

# Add a new blank row with None
df_c.loc["row7"] = None

print(df_c)
```

Out[#]:

```
        A      B      C      D      E      F
row1   1.0    6.0    11.0   16.0   21.0   7.0
row2   2.0    7.0    12.0   17.0   22.0   9.0
row3   3.0    8.0    13.0   18.0   23.0   11.0
row4   4.0    9.0    14.0   19.0   24.0   13.0
row5   5.0    10.0   15.0   20.0   25.0   15.0
row6   3.0    13.0   23.0   33.0   43.0   16.0
row7   NaN    NaN    NaN    NaN    NaN    NaN
```

```
In[#]:
df
Out[#]:
```

	A	B	C	D	E
row1	1	6	11	16	21
row2	2	7	12	17	22
row3	3	8	13	18	23
row4	4	9	14	19	24
row5	5	10	15	20	25

6. Sorting Data

You can sort DataFrame rows by values in one or more columns:

```
In[#]:
# Sort by column "A"
df_sorted = df.sort_values(by="A", ascending=False)

print(df_sorted)
Out[#]:
      A   B   C   D   E
row5  5  10  15  20  25
row4  4   9  14  19  24
row3  3   8  13  18  23
row2  2   7  12  17  22
row1  1   6  11  16  21
```

7. Filtering Data

You can filter rows based on conditions, a technique known as `Boolean indexing`. We have seen it once in Chapter 1 and we will explore this in more detail in Chapter 7.

```
In[#]:
# Filter rows where values in column "A" are greater than 3
filtered_df = df[df["A"] > 3]

print(filtered_df)
Out[#]:
      A   B   C   D   E
row4  4   9  14  19  24
row5  5  10  15  20  25
```

As introduced in this Note, Pandas offers a wide array of powerful and user-friendly functions, extending beyond those introduced above. In the Introduction Chapter, we have emphasized that this book adopts a **Teachable Moment** approach. This strategy introduces concepts within the context of their application. We will explore additional functionalities in upcoming chapters to make your learning journey more relevant and practical.

Q2: Which product is the most popular? What are the top 3 most popular products? Does your answer change when using different measures of "popularity", such as the number of transactions, quantity sold, or total sales?

To address Q2, we first create a pivot table with "Item" as the index, using both "count" and "sum" to aggregate the data by "Quantity" and "Extension - Discounted" for each item:

In[#]:

```
q2 = pd.pivot_table(sales, values=["Quantity", "Extension -
Discounted"], index="Item", aggfunc=["count","sum"])
q2
```

Out[#]:

	count		sum	
	Extension - Discounted	Quantity	Extension - Discounted	Quantity
Item				
Backpack	127	127	9567.285	254
Baseball Cap	125	125	1575.639	249
Gloves	132	132	5312.460	271
Greeting Card	131	131	1240.206	273
Handbag	106	106	3549.762	223
Hat	125	125	7205.256	242
Hoodie	130	130	9372.275	243
Jacket	126	126	9428.188	246
Keychain	118	118	3794.944	230
Magnet	105	105	3286.710	188
Mug	130	130	10041.984	247
Notebook	131	131	11408.120	278
Pen	133	133	10079.748	271
Scarf	128	128	2721.328	273
Stuffed Mascot	148	148	680.652	293
T-Shirt	121	121	3158.735	246

Despite its conciseness, the two-by-two combination of values and aggfunc creates three minor issues: 1) the creation of undesired hierarchical indexes (also called `MultiIndex`) in the columns of q2; 2) counting functions are invoked twice, resulting in duplicate columns; and 3) level 1 indices (the second level) contain duplicate column labels.

1. Remove the MultiIndex:

To remove the unnecessary level 0 indices, we can use the `droplevel(n)` function, where n specifies the level of the MultiIndex to drop. In this case, we want to remove the level 0 indices:

In[#]:

```
q2.columns = q2.columns.droplevel(0)
q2
```

Out[#]:

	Extension - Discounted	Quantity	Extension - Discounted	Quantity
Item				
Backpack	127	127	9567.285	254
Baseball Cap	125	125	1575.639	249
Gloves	132	132	5312.460	271
Greeting Card	131	131	1240.206	273
Handbag	106	106	3549.762	223
Hat	125	125	7205.256	242
Hoodie	130	130	9372.275	243
Jacket	126	126	9428.188	246
Keychain	118	118	3794.944	230
Magnet	105	105	3286.710	188
Mug	130	130	10041.984	247
Notebook	131	131	11408.120	278
Pen	133	133	10079.748	271
Scarf	128	128	2721.328	273
Stuffed Mascot	148	148	680.652	293
T-Shirt	121	121	3158.735	246

2. Rename column labels:

When dealing with duplicate column labels, you cannot use rename() to change just one specific column, as it will modify all columns with the same label. Instead, use the column's position (index) to target it directly. For example, if you want to rename the second column (with an index of one) in q2, you can assign the new label like this:

In[#]:

```
q2.columns.values[1] = "Count"
q2
```

Out[#]:

	Extension – Discounted	Count	Extension – Discounted	Quantity
Item				
Backpack	127	127	9567.285	254
Baseball Cap	125	125	1575.639	249
Gloves	132	132	5312.460	271
Greeting Card	131	131	1240.206	273
Handbag	106	106	3549.762	223
Hat	125	125	7205.256	242
Hoodie	130	130	9372.275	243
Jacket	126	126	9428.188	246
Keychain	118	118	3794.944	230
Magnet	105	105	3286.710	188
Mug	130	130	10041.984	247
Notebook	131	131	11408.120	278
Pen	133	133	10079.748	271
Scarf	128	128	2721.328	273
Stuffed Mascot	148	148	680.652	293
T-Shirt	121	121	3158.735	246

Using the same approach, we rename the first column to "Redundant", the third column to "Total Sales", and the fourth column to "Quantity Sold":

In[#]:

```
q2.columns.values[0] = "Redundant"
q2.columns.values[2] = "Total Sales"
q2.columns.values[3] = "Quantity Sold"
q2
```

Out[#]:

	Redundant	Count	Total Sales	Quantity Sold
Item				
Backpack	127	127	9567.285	254
Baseball Cap	125	125	1575.639	249
Gloves	132	132	5312.460	271
Greeting Card	131	131	1240.206	273
Handbag	106	106	3549.762	223
Hat	125	125	7205.256	242
Hoodie	130	130	9372.275	243
Jacket	126	126	9428.188	246
Keychain	118	118	3794.944	230
Magnet	105	105	3286.710	188
Mug	130	130	10041.984	247
Notebook	131	131	11408.120	278
Pen	133	133	10079.748	271
Scarf	128	128	2721.328	273
Stuffed Mascot	148	148	680.652	293
T-Shirt	121	121	3158.735	246

3. Delete the "Redundant" column:

Now we can delete the "Redundant" column using drop(). We have demonstrated the reassignment approach to apply the modification and save it to the original DataFrame itself, like q2 = q2.drop(). Alternatively, you can set the `inplace` parameter to True in the drop() method to modify the original DataFrame in place:

In[#]:

```
q2.drop(columns = "Redundant", inplace = True)
q2
```

Out[#]:

Item	Count	Total Sales	Quantity Sold
Backpack	127	9567.285	254
Baseball Cap	125	1575.639	249
Gloves	132	5312.460	271
Greeting Card	131	1240.206	273
Handbag	106	3549.762	223
Hat	125	7205.256	242
Hoodie	130	9372.275	243
Jacket	126	9428.188	246
Keychain	118	3794.944	230
Magnet	105	3286.710	188
Mug	130	10041.984	247
Notebook	131	11408.120	278
Pen	133	10079.748	271
Scarf	128	2721.328	273
Stuffed Mascot	148	680.652	293
T-Shirt	121	3158.735	246

• **Side Note – The** `inplace` **Parameter**

In Pandas, the inplace parameter is used in several methods to control whether the operation should modify the original DataFrame or Series, or return a new object with the modifications. When `inplace=True`, the operation is performed in-place, meaning the original object is modified directly. When `inplace=False` (which is the default), the method returns a new object with the modifications, and the original object remains unchanged.

Below are some examples of Pandas methods that use the inplace parameter:

1. rename(): Alters axes labels (index or columns) of the DataFrame.
2. drop(): Drops specified labels from rows or columns.
3. reindex(): Resets the index of the DataFrame.
4. sort_values(): Sorts a DataFrame or Series by values.
5. fillna(): Fills missing values (NaN) in the DataFrame or Series.
6. drop_duplicates(): Removes duplicate rows from the DataFrame.

Please note that there have been discussions in the Pandas community about deprecating the inplace parameter due to its issues with code clarity and consistency concerns. In general, it is recommended to use the default behavior (inplace=False) and assign the result to a new variable or overwrite the original variable, if necessary.

Now, we can simply use `sort_values()` along with `nlargest()` to answer Q2:

In[#]:

```
# Sort by column "Count" and take the top 3
q2 = q2.sort_values(by="Count", ascending=False)
q2_top3_count = q2.nlargest(3, "Count")
print(q2_top3_count)
```

Out[#]:

```
                Count   Total Sales   Quantity Sold
Item
Stuffed Mascot   148       680.652             293
Pen              133     10079.748             271
Gloves           132      5312.460             271
```

In[#]:

```
# Sort by column "Total Sales" and take the top 3
q2 = q2.sort_values(by="Total Sales", ascending=False)
q2_top3_sales = q2.nlargest(3, "Total Sales")
print(q2_top3_sales)
```

Out[#]:

```
            Count   Total Sales   Quantity Sold
Item
Notebook     131     11408.120             278
Pen          133     10079.748             271
Mug          130     10041.984             247
```

In[#]:

```
# Sort by column "Quantity Sold" and take the top 3
q2 = q2.sort_values(by="Quantity Sold", ascending=False)
q2_top3_quantity = q2.nlargest(3, "Quantity Sold")
print(q2_top3_quantity)
```

Out[#]:

```
                Count   Total Sales   Quantity Sold
Item
Stuffed Mascot   148       680.652             293
Notebook         131     11408.120             278
Scarf            128      2721.328             273
```

Q3: Create a pie chart displaying the top 10 products with the highest total amounts.

To address Q3, we can slightly modify the code that finds the top 3 products with highest sales:

```
In[#]:

# Drop columns "Count" and "Quantity Sold"
q3 = q2.drop(columns = ["Count", "Quantity Sold"])
q3.columns

Out[#]:

Index(["Total Sales"], dtype="object")

In[#]:

# Sort by column "Total Sales" and take the top 10

q3 = q3.sort_values(by="Total Sales", ascending=False)
q3 = q3.nlargest(10, "Total Sales")
print(q3)

Out[#]:

                Total Sales
Item
Notebook         11408.120
Pen              10079.748
Mug              10041.984
Backpack          9567.285
Jacket            9428.188
Hoodie            9372.275
Hat               7205.256
Gloves            5312.460
Keychain          3794.944
Handbag           3549.762
```

Now, you may use Pandas' plot() function to quickly generate a pie chart. Pandas' plot() provides different parameters for each chart type, similar to Excel's chart formatting panel. Only you will need to assign appropriate values to those parameters. To create a pie chart with shadow effect, slice explosion and data label in percentages, you will need to use the follow parameters:

1. kind = "pie": Using the kind parameter, you can use plot() to create many different chart types, including line (default), pie, bar, barh (horizontal bar), hist, box, scatter, etc.

2. figsize = (5, 5): Defines the size of the figure in inches. Here, it creates a chart with both width and height of five inches.

3. title = "Sales by Product": Adds a title to the plot. In this case, the title will be "Sales by Product".

4. autopct="%1.1f%%": Formats the percentage labels on the pie chart. The format string "%1.1f%%" uses %-formatting (also called

printf-style formatting). It means it will display the percentages with one decimal place, followed by a percentage sign.

5. shadow = True: Adds a shadow effect to the pie chart, giving it a 3D appearance and making the slices more visually distinct.

6. explode = explode: This is used to "explode" slice(s) of the pie chart for emphasis. The explode parameter is typically a list of values where each value corresponds to how much a specific slice should be pulled away from the center. For example, explode = [0, 0.1, 0, 0] would pull the second slice slightly (10% of the slice length) away from the pie.

7. ylabel = "": Removes the y-axis label (the default label is the column label, but pie charts usually don't need it) by setting it to an empty string. This makes the chart cleaner without unnecessary labels.

- **Side Note – %-formatting**

Breakdown of "%1.1f%%":

1. %: This is the placeholder that tells Python you're about to insert a value or a variable.

2. 1.1: The 1 before the decimal point is the minimum width of the output field. In this case, it means the number will take at least one character space before the decimal point. However, if the number is larger, more space will automatically be used. The .1 after the decimal specifies precision, meaning there will be one digit after the decimal point.

3. f: This means floating-point number, specifying that the number will be formatted as a float (a number with a decimal point).

4. %%: The double %% is used to display a literal percent sign (%). If you used a single %, Python would interpret it as part of the format string (the placeholder of a variable or a value). The double percent escapes it, meaning the output will show a single % symbol.

While Python now offers more modern ways to handle string formatting (str.format() and f-strings), %-formatting style is still widely used, especially in function parameters that require formatting of numbers or strings, like charts. We will explore str.format() and f-strings in the following chapters when the appropriate learning opportunity comes.

```
In[#]:

explode = [0] * 10
explode[2] = 0.2
q3["Total Sales"].plot(kind = "pie", figsize = (5, 5), title = "Sales
by Product", autopct="%1.1f%%", shadow = True, explode = explode)

Out[#]:

<Axes: title={"center": "Sales by Product"}, ylabel="Total Sales">
```

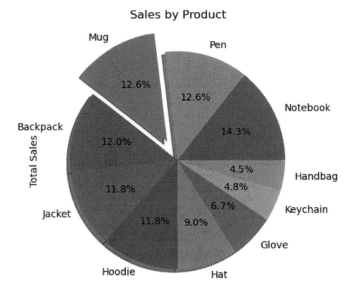

Q4: Create a bar chart comparing the margin and sales for each store.
To address Q4, we first create a pivot table with "Store Name" as the index, using "sum" to aggregate the data by "Margin" and "Extension - Discounted" for each store:

```
In[#]:

q4 = pd.pivot_table(sales, values=["Margin", "Extension -
Discounted"], index="Store Name", aggfunc="sum")

q4

Out[#]:
```

	Extension – Discounted	Margin
Store Name		
East	23126.8215	7599.3715
North	21546.2335	6943.7035
South	24775.2655	8043.5455
West	22974.9715	7475.4115

Then, we rename columns to more accurately reflect Q4's context:

```
In[#]:

q4 = q4.rename(columns = {"Extension - Discounted": "Sales"})
q4

Out[#]:
```

	Sales	Margin
Store Name		
East	23126.8215	7599.3715
North	21546.2335	6943.7035
South	24775.2655	8043.5455
West	22974.9715	7475.4115

A bar chart typically requires fewer special parameters because Pandas' plot() automatically uses the index as the x-axis and numerical columns as y-values. However, if you need more control – such as plotting specific columns – you can specify the x= or y= parameters to customize the chart.

```
In[#]:

q4.plot(kind = "bar", figsize = (5, 5), title = "Sales and Margin by
Store")

Out[#]:

<Axes: title={"center": "Sales and Margin by Store"}, xlabel=
"Store Name">
```

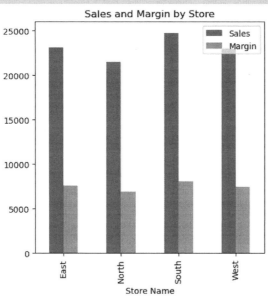

```
In[#]:

# To specify only column Margin for y-values
q4.plot(kind = "bar", y = "Margin", figsize = (5, 5), title = "Sales
and Margin by Store")

Out[#]:

<Axes: title={"center": "Sales and Margin by Store"}, xlabel=
"Store Name">
```

You may create a horizontal bar chart by assigning `barh` to the `kind` parameter:

```
In[#]:

q4.plot(kind = "barh", figsize = (5, 5), title = "Sales and Margin by
Store")

Out[#]:

<Axes: title={"center": "Sales and Margin by Store"}, ylabel=
"Store Name">
```

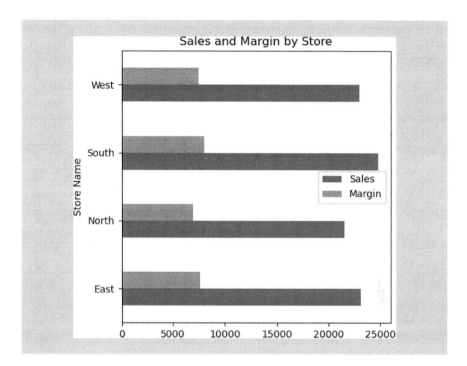

Q5: Create a line chart comparing the sales made by each store in the past three months.

Handling date and time data is essential for businesses to make informed decisions based on trends. While Python doesn't have built-in data types for dates and times, Pandas provides the dt accessor for DataFrame columns (or Series) containing datetime data. This accessor enables easy access to various datetime attributes and methods. For instance, dt.day, dt.month, and dt.year return the day, month, and year numbers directly:

In[#]:

```
sales["Date"].dt.day, sales["Date"].dt.month, sales["Date"].dt.year
```

Out[#]:

```
(0       1
 1       1
 2       1
 3       1
 4       1
        ..
 2011   31
 2012   31
 2013   31
 2014   31
 2015   31
```

```
Name: Date, Length: 2016, dtype: int32,
0        1
1        1
2        1
3        1
4        1
        ..
2011     3
2012     3
2013     3
2014     3
2015     3
Name: Date, Length: 2016, dtype: int32,
0        2023
1        2023
2        2023
3        2023
4        2023
        ...
2011     2023
2012     2023
2013     2023
2014     2023
2015     2023
Name: Date, Length: 2016, dtype: int32)
```

Accordingly, we can get the month numbers from the "Date" column using dt.month and save the results to a Series as below:

In[#]:

```
month = sales["Date"].dt.month
month
```

Out[#]:

```
0        1
1        1
2        1
3        1
4        1
        ..
2011     3
2012     3
2013     3
2014     3
2015     3
Name: Date, Length: 2016, dtype: int32
```

Since the month Series shares the same index as the sales DataFrame, we can create a pivot table with month as the index, using "sum" to aggregate the data by "Extension - Discounted" for each store:

In[#]:

```python
q5 = pd.pivot_table(sales, values="Extension - Discounted", index=
month, columns = "Store Name", aggfunc="sum")
q5
```

Out[#]:

Store Name	East	North	South	West
Date				
1	7558.5825	7108.6790	8971.0660	7043.7110
2	7033.2535	6441.9285	7490.5355	8162.8765
3	8534.9855	7995.6260	8313.6640	7768.3840

Apparently, the current name of the index column, "Date", is not appropriate. You can rename it using `index.name`:

In[#]:

```python
q5.index.name = "Month"
q5
```

Out[#]:

Store Name	East	North	South	West
Month				
1	7558.5825	7108.6790	8971.0660	7043.7110
2	7033.2535	6441.9285	7490.5355	8162.8765
3	8534.9855	7995.6260	8313.6640	7768.3840

For date representation, it's uncommon to use integers. Instead, people typically prefer to see month names. A common approach is to use a dictionary to map the integer codes to their corresponding month names:

In[#]:

```python
# Dictionary to map month numbers to names
month_map = {
    1: "January", 2: "February", 3: "March", 4: "April", 5: "May", 6:
"June",
    7: "July", 8: "August", 9: "September", 10: "October", 11:
"November", 12: "December"
}
```

Then, with Pandas' map() function, you can map the integers in q5.index to month names defined in the month_map dictionary:

```
In[#]:
q5.index = q5.index.map(month_map)
q5
Out[#]:
```

Store Name	East	North	South	West
Month				
January	7558.5825	7108.6790	8971.0660	7043.7110
February	7033.2535	6441.9285	7490.5355	8162.8765
March	8534.9855	7995.6260	8313.6640	7768.3840

• Side Note – Pandas' map()

In Pandas, map() is a Series method used to map values from a Series (or a DataFrame column) to new values based on a dictionary, function, or another Series. It is often used to transform or replace values in a column by applying a dictionary or a function for mapping. We will see more map() examples in upcoming chapters.

Now, with the modified q5, we can call plot() to quickly create a line chart as below:

```
In[#]:
q5.plot(kind = "line", title="Monthly Sales", marker="o")
Out[#]:
<Axes: title={"center": "Monthly Sales"}, xlabel="Month">
057
```

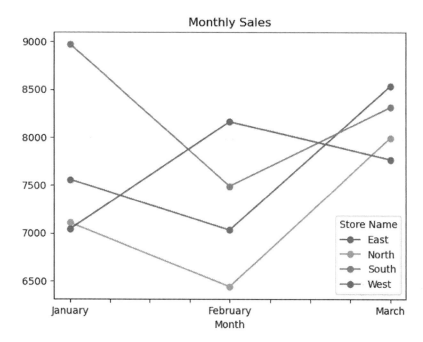

The last parameter `marker` specifies each data point along the line, making it useful for distinguishing data points or clusters. In Pandas, you can use several common marker options. In Pandas, you have the following common marker options:

```
"o": Circle
"^": Triangle up
"v": Triangle down
"s": Square
"D": Diamond
"*": Star
"x": X
```

You are encouraged to try them out yourself.

Q6: Develop a heat map to analyze the sales performance of each store over the past three months.

Pandas' plot() method does not include a built-in heatmap function, but you can use Seaborn (which is built on top of Matplotlib) to create heatmaps.

• **Side Note – Matplotlib and Seaborn**
Seaborn is a popular Python library for data visualization that is built on top of Matplotlib, the foundational plotting library in Python. Seaborn improves on Matplotlib by providing a more high-level interface, more visually appealing default themes, and easy-to-use functions for common plot types. For example, Seaborn's heatmap() function makes it easy to generate advanced heatmaps. You can easily add annotations to each cell, or use different color maps.

Install Matplotlib and Seaborn
If it's your first time using Matplotlib and Seaborn, you will need to install them using pip before importing the libraries. Both Matplotlib and Seaborn are not part of the standard Python library, so they must be installed separately:

In[#]:

```
pip install matplotlib seaborn
```

Out[#]:

```
Requirement already satisfied: matplotlib in /opt/anaconda3/lib/
python3.12/site-packages (3.9.2)
Requirement already satisfied: seaborn in /opt/anaconda3/lib/
python3.12/site-packages (0.13.2)
Requirement already satisfied: contourpy>=1.0.1 in /opt/anaconda3/lib/
python3.12/site-packages (from matplotlib) (1.2.0)
Requirement already satisfied: cycler>=0.10 in /opt/anaconda3/lib/
python3.12/site-packages (from matplotlib) (0.11.0)
Requirement already satisfied: fonttools>=4.22.0 in /opt/anaconda3/
lib/python3.12/site-packages (from matplotlib) (4.51.0)
Requirement already satisfied: kiwisolver>=1.3.1 in /opt/anaconda3/
lib/python3.12/site-packages (from matplotlib) (1.4.4)
Requirement already satisfied: numpy>=1.23 in /opt/anaconda3/lib/
python3.12/site-packages (from matplotlib) (1.26.4)
Requirement already satisfied: packaging>=20.0 in /opt/anaconda3/lib/
python3.12/site-packages (from matplotlib) (24.1)
Requirement already satisfied: pillow>=8 in /opt/anaconda3/lib/
python3.12/site-packages (from matplotlib) (10.4.0)
Requirement already satisfied: pyparsing>=2.3.1 in /opt/anaconda3/lib/
python3.12/site-packages (from matplotlib) (3.1.2)
Requirement already satisfied: python-dateutil>=2.7 in /opt/anaconda3/
lib/python3.12/site-packages (from matplotlib) (2.9.0.post0)
Requirement already satisfied: pandas>=1.2 in /opt/anaconda3/lib/
python3.12/site-packages (from seaborn) (2.2.2)
Requirement already satisfied: pytz>=2020.1 in /opt/anaconda3/lib/
python3.12/site-packages (from pandas>=1.2->seaborn) (2024.1)
```

```
Requirement already satisfied: tzdata>=2022.7 in /opt/anaconda3/lib/
python3.12/site-packages (from pandas>=1.2->seaborn) (2023.3)
Requirement already satisfied: six>=1.5 in /opt/anaconda3/lib/
python3.12/site-packages (from python-dateutil>=2.7->matplotlib)
(1.16.0)
Note: you may need to restart the kernel to use updated packages.
```

Now, you can import both libraries. For Matplotlib, we'll import only its pyplot module, which contains the essential functions for plotting, instead of importing the entire library.

In[#]:

```
import matplotlib.pyplot as plt
import seaborn as sns
```

Note: If the library does not import successfully after installation, you might need to restart the kernel to reload all modules using the `restart` image icon on the Jupyter ribbon or go to the "Kernel" menu in Jupyter and select "Restart".

In the example below, we use hot, `viridis,  coolwarm` to generate various colormaps (cmap parameter). Some other colormap options include "cool", "magma", "plasma", "inferno", "cubehelix", "Blues", "Greens", etc. You are welcome to try them out. We also use `annot=True` to add annotations (i.e., "data labels" in Excel's term) to each `square` cell in the heatmaps. Each annotation indicates the value of the cell is formatted as a floating number with two decimal places by `fmt=".2f"`:

In[#]:

```
sns.heatmap(q5, cmap="hot", square=True, annot=True, fmt=".2f")
plt.show()
sns.heatmap(q5, cmap="viridis", square=True, annot=True, fmt=".2f")
plt.show()
sns.heatmap(q5, cmap="coolwarm", square=True, annot=True, fmt=".2f")
plt.show()
```

Out[#]:

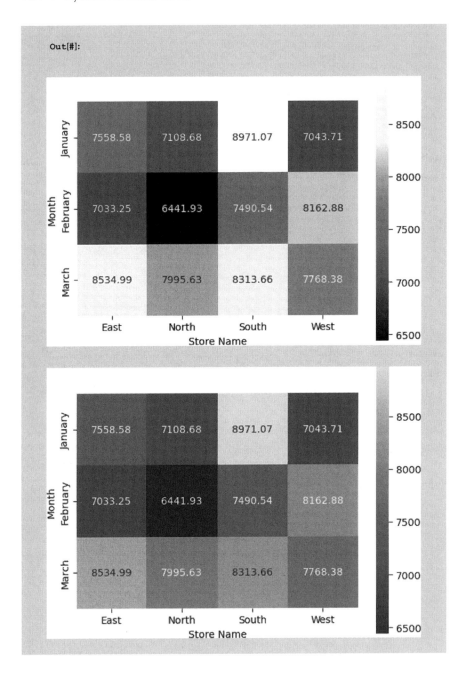

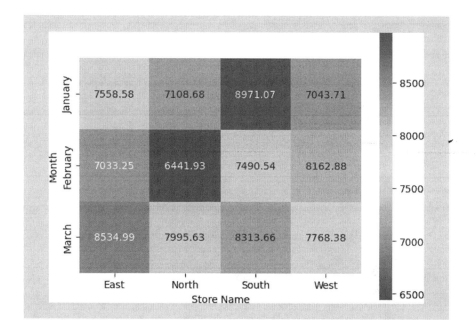

• **Side Note – show() or not show()?**

You have seen plt.show() appears in the above snippet. When you call plt.show(), it displays all figures and their associated plots that you've defined prior to calling it. It's worth noting that in interactive environments like Jupyter Notebooks the plotting behaves a bit differently: plots are displayed as soon as they are created, so plt.show() isn't always necessary.

In these environments, when you create a plot, it is automatically displayed without the need to call plt.show(). This is often called inline plotting, as the plots appear in-place within the notebook.

However, if you want to create multiple plots in a single Jupyter cell, like in the above snippet, you should call plt.show() after each plot to display it immediately. Otherwise, the plots would overlap in a single figure, leading to unexpected results. In the example below, only the final "coolwarm" heatmap is displayed because the first two plots are overwritten by it:

In[#]:

```
sns.heatmap(q5, cmap="hot", square=True, annot=True, fmt=".2f")
sns.heatmap(q5, cmap="viridis", square=True, annot=True, fmt=".2f")
sns.heatmap(q5, cmap="coolwarm", square=True, annot=True, fmt=".2f")
```

Out[#]:

```
<Axes: xlabel="Store Name", ylabel="Month">
```

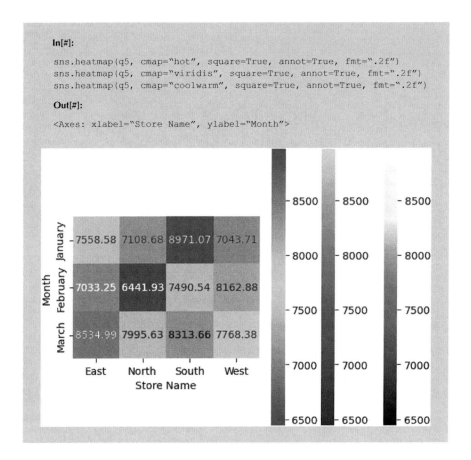

If you would like to switch the rows and columns in a plot, you can leverage either the transpose() method or Pandas' T property. In Pandas, the T property is short for transpose(). It's used to transpose a DataFrame, which means it swaps the rows and columns. This operation can be particularly useful when you need to change the orientation of your data for further processing. Note that the T property is equivalent to calling the transpose() method on the DataFrame:

In[#]:

```
sns.heatmap(q5.T, cmap="viridis", square=True, annot=True, fmt=
".2f") # adds annotations to each cell and uses a different
color map
plt.show()
```

Out[#]:

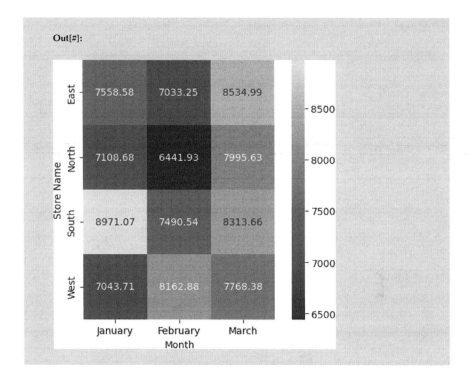

4.5.4 The Power of Modular Programming

We'd like to use the final example in this chapter to demonstrate the power of Python's modular programming. Most programming languages support (and actually recommend) programmers to develop applications using a modular approach. Modular programming means to separate a program into independent pieces or building blocks, each containing all the parts needed to execute a reusable functionality.

In Python, a module can be thought of as a reusable piece of code that can be imported and used in other Python programs. Specifically, a module is a file containing Python code that defines functions, classes, and other objects that can be used in a Python program. Please note that the file can have any name, but it must end with the .py extension.

For example, you can open the `piechart.py` file in the supplementary materials. This file defines a function called `pie_plotting()` that generates a pie chart using three parameters: (df, dim, value):

```
import pandas as pd
import matplotlib.pyplot as plt

def pie_plotting(df, dim, value):
    pivot = pd.pivot_table(df, values=value, index=dim, aggfunc=
"sum")
    pivot[value].plot(kind = "pie", figsize = (5, 5), title = value +
" - " + dim, autopct = "%1.1f%%",
                             shadow = True, ylabel = "")
    plt.show()
```

Create and Call a Function

In Python, the building block in a module (or a .py) is a function that starts with the keyword def followed by a function name and/or a few parameters, as illustrated in the pie_plotting example. Once a function is built, you may run it by calling its name and passing necessary arguments (values you assign to parameters) into it. Then the function will execute the code inside it or return some data as a result. If you have some experience in using Excel functions, you probably know how a function takes input arguments and return results. In Excel, we use functions as blackboxes since we don't need to know the design details of a function. But in Python, you can use Python statements to define your own function.

The pie_plotting function takes three parameters and uses them to: 1) create a pivot table, 2) generate a pie chart based on the numerical column specified by the value parameter, and 3) call plt.show() to display the chart. Now, the module is ready to be imported.

Below we import the `piechart` module that resides in the local piechart.py file with an additional proposition from, and import its only function: pie_plotting:

```
In[#]:

from piechart import pie_plotting
```

Now, we can call pie_plotting() as it is a locally defined function. First, we define two lists: the first contains three dimensional column names ["Store Name", "Name", "Item"] that can be used as indexes in pivot tables, and the second contains two numerical column names ["Margin", "Extension - Discounted"] to be used as values in the pivot tables. Next, we create a nested for-loop to pass the 6 (3×2) combinations of indexes and values, along with the sales DataFrame, to pie_plotting() to automate the creation of all possible pie charts:

In[#]:

```
dimensions = ["Store Name", "Name", "Item"]
values = ["Margin", "Extension - Discounted"]
for dim in dimensions:
    for value in values:
        pie_plotting(sales, dim, value)
```

Out[#]:

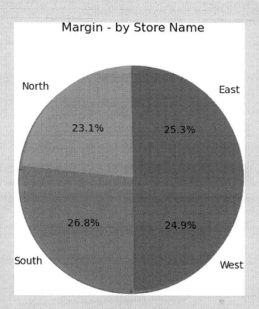

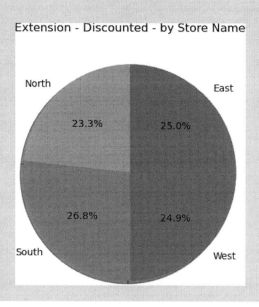

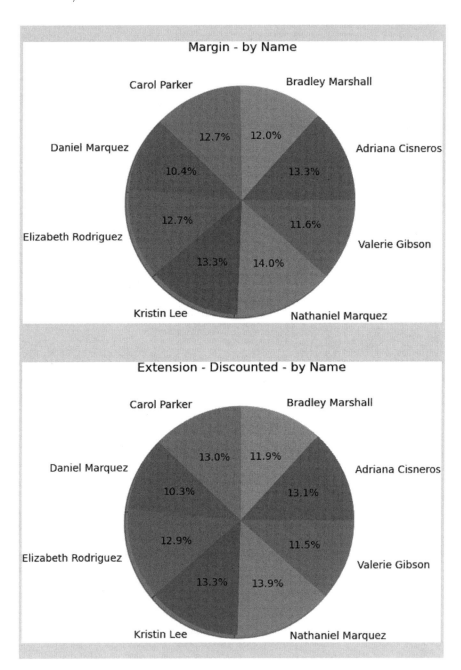

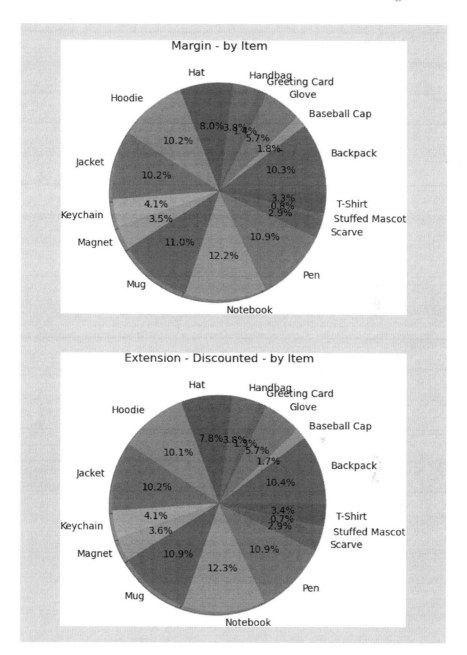

4.6 DISCUSSIONS

In this chapter, you have learned how to use Excel's charting function-ality and Pandas' plotting methods. Some of the key comparisons are summarized as follows:

1. Ease of Use:
   1) Excel: Excel is highly user-friendly with a point-and-click interface. Charts such as pie, bar, and line can be created quickly by selecting data and choosing the chart type from a menu. However, creating complex or repetitive charts requires manual steps for each chart, which can become cumbersome.
   2) Pandas: Pandas' plotting methods are code-based and less intuitive for beginners compared to Excel's graphical interface. However, once mastered, they allow for much faster chart creation, especially when dealing with larger datasets or automating repetitive tasks.

2. Automation and Reusability:
   1) Excel: Excel requires manual steps to create each chart. While you can copy-paste similar charts or use templates, automating repetitive chart creation is limited without complex VBA scripting. Reproducing the same chart for updated datasets also requires manual intervention.
   2) Pandas: Python's automation capability is a major advantage. With loops and reusable functions, you can generate dozens or hundreds of charts with ease. Once you write a function, you can rerun it on new data, ensuring consistency and saving significant time. In addition, combined with libraries like Seaborn and Matplotlib, Pandas' plotting enables complex visualizations that would require extensive manual effort in Excel.

3. Scalability:
   1) Excel: Excel handles small to moderately-sized datasets well, but performance degrades with large datasets. Charts become slower to update and can crash when dealing with very large data.
   2) Pandas: Pandas is designed to work with large datasets efficiently. It can handle millions of rows of data, perform transformations, and generate charts quickly.

4. Customization and Control:
   1) Excel: Excel provides a rich set of formatting and chart customization options via its UI. Users can customize colors, labels, data points, and legends with a few clicks.
   2) Pandas: Pandas offers basic customization, but for more control, you can integrate with Matplotlib. This gives you fine-grained control over every element of a chart, such as labels,

gridlines, tick marks, and more, allowing for far greater flexibility than Excel.

In sum, Excel's user-friendly charting is ideal for quick, one-time visualizations with small datasets. On the other hand, Pandas's plotting excels in automation and handling large datasets, making it more efficient for repetitive plotting tasks. Python's powerful automation with loops, functions, and integration with libraries like Seaborn and Matplotlib gives you far greater flexibility and control, especially for large or complex visualization tasks.

4.7 EXERCISES

Using the concepts covered in this chapter, complete the following exercises with "Exercise-Ch04.xlsx" as your dataset.

E1: **Create a bar chart displaying the top five suppliers with the highest purchase amounts.**

E2: **Excel: Generate two pie charts displaying products ranked from highest to lowest, one based on order quantities and the other based on order frequencies.**

Python: Use a for-loop to generate a series of pie charts ranking products, suppliers, and stores from highest to lowest, based on purchase amounts and order quantities.

(*Hint: Import the pie_plotting function from the piechart module, which is located in the local piechart.py file.*)

E3: **Develop a line chart and a heat map to visualize and compare the purchase amounts by each store over time, grouped by month.**

## CHAPTER 5

Conditional Functions and What-if Analysis

I N PROGRAMMING, THERE ARE three primary control flow structures that dictate how a program executes its instructions:

1. **Sequential Flow**

   This is the simplest flow where instructions are executed in the order they appear, one after the other. Each line of code runs sequentially from the top to the bottom. This flow is foundational and is used unless directed otherwise by loops or conditions.

2. **Looping (or Iterative) Flow**

   Looping enables the repeated execution of a set of instructions as long as a specific condition is true. This flow is useful for tasks requiring repetitive processing, such as iterating over lists or performing repeated calculations, until a certain condition or endpoint is reached. Common loops include for and while loops. You have learned how to use for loops in Chapter 3.

3. **Conditional Flow**

   Also known as decision flow or control flow, conditional flow allows a program to choose between different paths based on specified

DOI: 10.1201/9781003567103-6

conditions. if, else if, and else statements (or similar constructs in other languages) enable the program to execute certain parts of the code only if certain conditions are met. This is the primary focus of this chapter.

In addition to forming the foundation of logic in computer programming languages like Python, the use of sequence, selection, and iteration enables the creation of various functions or scripts that power many analytics tools (e.g., Excel, Tableau, Power BI). These logic flows facilitate complex analytical tasks, including the decision-making processes using conditionals and partial automation of workflows within applications. In this chapter, we will explore how to leverage conditional flows for decision-making in both Excel and Python.

5.1 CONDITIONAL FLOWS WITH BOOKSTORE DATASET

We will use the "Bookstore-Ch05.xlsx" file to demonstrate how to create conditional flows in both Excel and Python. For simplicity, this workbook includes two small worksheets, "Item" and "Employee", extracted from the original "Invoice" sheet. Before starting the exercises, take a moment to review these two sheets.

Q1: For employees working in the East store (using Store="ST-001"), increase their weekly payment by 5%.

Q2: For employees whose current weekly pay is between $1,050 and $1,100, increase their salary by 3%. For all others, apply a 5% raise.

Q3: For employees whose weekly pay is between $1,050 and $1,100, increase their salary by 3%. For those earning below $1,050, apply a 5% raise. For everyone else, apply a 1% raise.

Q4: Add a new column labeled "Store Name" to match store IDs with their corresponding store names using the table below:

Store	Store Name
ST-001	East
ST-002	West
ST-003	North
ST-004	South

Q5: The gross margin ratio (GMR) for the Hoodie is 40.01%. Calculate the required List Price to achieve a 42% GMR, assuming the unit cost remains unchanged.

5.2 EXCEL

Excel's control flow functionality is implemented through functions such as **AND()**, **OR()**, **NOT()**, and **IF()**. These functions together provide a robust foundation for logical operations and control flow in Excel.

1. **Logical Operators: AND(), OR(), and NOT()**
   The three functions have intuitive names:

   - **AND()** and **OR()** enable you to combine up to 255 conditions.
   - **NOT()** simply negates a given condition.

   These functions, when used alongside comparison operators like =, >, and <, form the basis for creating logical tests in Excel.

2. **Control Flow: IF()**
   The **IF()** function extends control flow by executing specific actions based on the outcome of a logical test. Its syntax includes three key components, separated by commas:

   - **Logical Test**: A condition to evaluate, which may incorporate **AND()**, **OR()**, **NOT()**, and logical operators such as =, >, and <.
   - **Value (or Action) if True**: The return value, or action to execute, if the logical test evaluates to **TRUE**. In more complex cases, this can include additional tests or calculations.
   - **Value (or Action) if False**: The return value, or action to execute, if the logical test evaluates to **FALSE**.

   The general syntax of the **IF()** function is as follows:

   IF(logical_test, value_or_action_if_true, value_or_action_if_false)

Q1: For employees working in the East store, increase their weekly payment by 5%.

Q1 illustrates a basic control flow where specific values are returned directly based on the outcome of the logical test.

1. In cell G5, type "=IF(" and launch the formula builder by clicking "*fx*" in the formula bar:

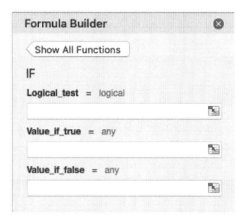

2. Fill in the three parameters:

- **Logical test**: Check if the "Store Name" is "East."
- **Value_if_true**: Calculate the weekly pay with a 5% increase.
- **Value_if_false**: Use the original weekly pay.

   The completed formula will look as follows:

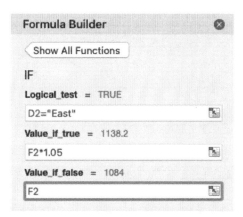

3. You may verify your answers with the screenshot below:

F
Q1
$1,138.20
$1,115.00
$1,139.00
$1,144.00
$1,207.50
$1,013.00
$1,175.00
$1,072.00

Q2: For employees whose current weekly pay is between $1,050 and $1,100, increase their salary by 3%. For all others, apply a 5% raise.

Q2 demonstrates a test with multiple conditions, demanding the insertion of AND() within the logical test of the IF() function. This requires creating a nested function. In Excel, to switch between the main function and its embedded functions in the formula builder, simply click on the desired function name within the formula bar and click "*fx*". This allows you to edit or review the specific function's parameters directly.

1. Insert AND() within the logical test of IF():

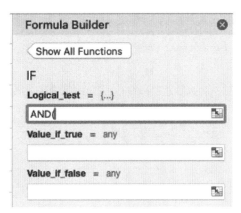

2. Click on the AND() function name in the formula bar (you might need to further click "*fx*" in some operating systems) to switch between the main IF() function and its embedded AND():

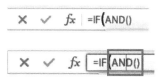

3. Complete the conditions in AND() according to the requirements:

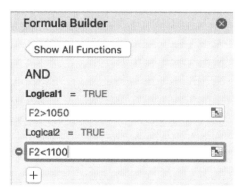

4. Switch back to main IF() to complete the two actions:

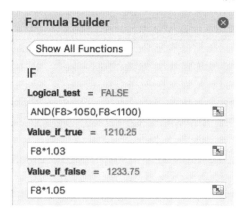

5. You can confirm your answers with the screenshot below:

G
Q2
$1,116.52
$1,170.75
$1,195.95
$1,201.20
$1,207.50
$1,063.65
$1,233.75
$1,104.16

Q3: For employees whose weekly pay is between $1,050 and $1,100, increase their salary by 3%. For those earning below $1,050, apply a 5% raise. For everyone else, apply a 1% raise.

Q3 builds on the conditions in Q2 by adding complexity to handle cases where the weekly pay falls outside the range of $1,050 to $1,100. This requires the use of nested IF statements.

1. Start by completing the first two parameters as you did in Q2:

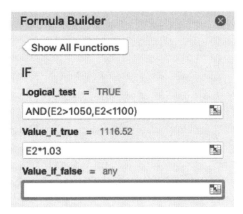

2. For **value_if_false**, add another **IF()** to check whether the earning is below $1,050 or above $1,100, and define the corresponding actions for each scenario. The embedded **IF()** will look like this:

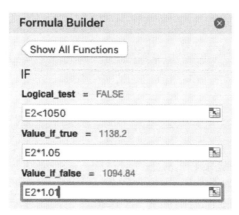

3. Switch back to main IF() to double check the setting:

4. You can confirm your answers with the screenshot below:

H
Q3
$1,116.52
$1,126.15
$1,150.39
$1,155.44
$1,161.50
$1,063.65
$1,186.75
$1,104.16

Q4: Add a new column labeled "Store Name" to match store IDs with their corresponding store names.

Using nested **IF** statements for Q4 involves multiple layers, making the conditions difficult to maintain and reuse. For matching scenarios like this, Excel supports the **SWITCH()** function, which behaves similarly to **Switch** or **Case** statements in programming languages. It allows you to evaluate one expression against multiple possible values and return a corresponding result. Its general syntax function is as follows:

SWITCH(expression, value1, result1, [value2, result2], ..., [default_result])

- **expression**: The value to be evaluated.
- **value1, result1**: The first value to match and its corresponding result.
- **value2, result2**, etc.: Additional value-result pairs (optional).
- **default_result**: The result to return if no match is found (optional).

1. In cell I2, type "=SWITCH(" and click "fx" to open the formula builder for SWITCH(). Then, fill in the parameters as shown below based on the reference table:

2. You can confirm your answers with the screenshot below:

COMPLEMENTARY NOTE – IFS() AND VLOOKUP()

In addition to **SWITCH()**, **IFS()** and **VLOOKUP()** can also be used for similar purposes as **SWITCH()** but they are structured differently.

1. IFS()

IFS() follows the similar [test, value] pattern as **SWITCH()**, but lacks the "default" functionality. The general syntax is as follows:

IFS(logical_test1, value_if_true1, [logical_test2, value_if_true2], ...)

- **logical_test1, logical_test2, ...**: Conditions to evaluate. These are logical expressions that return either **TRUE** or **FALSE**.
- **value_if_true1, value_if_true2, ...**: The values or actions to return when the corresponding logical test evaluates to **TRUE**.
  Below are the formula settings for using **IFS()** to solve **Q4**. The results for "**Store Name**" will be identical to those obtained with **SWITCH()**.

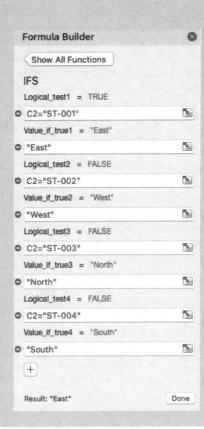

2. VLOOKUP()

The **VLOOKUP()** function in Excel is a powerful tool for looking up and retrieving data from a table. By default, it performs an approximate match, but you can enable an exact match test by specifying the 4th argument ([range_lookup]) as FALSE or 0. Its syntax is as follows:

VLOOKUP(lookup_value, table_array, col_index_num, [range_lookup])

- **lookup_value**: The key value you want to search for, typically a referenced cell.
- **table_array**: The range of cells containing the dataset, including the lookup key and the related data.
- **col_index_num**: The column number relative to the key column (index of one) in the table_array, from which to retrieve the desired data.
- **range_lookup**: FALSE or 0 for an exact match, TRUE or omitted for an approximate match, or range test.

For **Q4**, start by preparing the table array as shown below:

M	N
1	2
Store	Store Name
ST-001	East
ST-002	West
ST-003	North
ST-004	South

Then, in cell **K2**, create a **VLOOKUP()** formula and use the formula builder to set up the four parameters as follows:

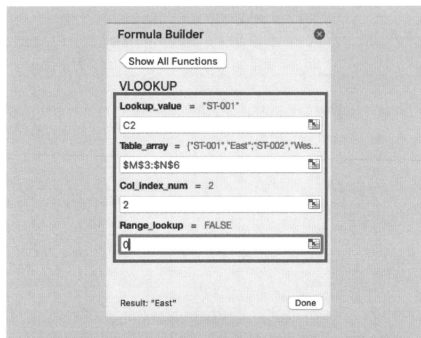

1) Reference **C2**, which contains "ST-001", as the **lookup_value**.
2) Select the reference table array **$M$3:$N$6**. Note that the range must use absolute references ($) to ensure the formula works when filled down to other rows.
3) Assign **2** for the third parameter, as the "Store Name" column (the target data) is the second column relative to the key column in the table array.
4) For the last parameter, select **0** (or FALSE) to specify an **exact match test**.

Once the formula is complete, you can copy it down to populate the other rows. The results of **IFS()** and **VLOOKUP()** are placed in columns **J** and **K**, respectively.

Please note that **SWITCH()** in Excel does not work for range tests. It is designed for exact matches only, meaning it cannot evaluate whether a value falls within a range like <, >, or BETWEEN. For range-based conditions, you should use **IFS()** or **VLOOKUP()** functions instead. We will explore range tests using either **VLOOKUP()** or **IFS()** in Chapter 7.

Q5: The gross margin ratio (GMR) for the Hoodie is 40.01%. Calculate the required List Price to achieve a 42% GMR, assuming the unit cost remains unchanged.

Q5 is a "what-if" scenario rather than a typical conditional question. Excel's **"What-If Analysis"** tools offer several options for handling such scenarios. For Q5, we can utilize the **"Goal Seek"** functionality:

1. In the "Item" sheet, calculate the Hoodie's gross margin ratio (GMR) using the following formula:

   GMR by unit = (List Price – Cost) / List Price x 100%

   Using this formula, you can compute Hoodie's GMR in cell E2 as shown below:

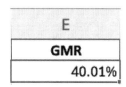

2. To use Excel's **"What-If Analysis"** tools, go to the "Data" tab and open the **"What-If Analysis"** menu:

3. From the menu, select "Goal Seek":

4. In the **Goal Seek** settings window, enter the following parameters:
   - **Set cell**: E2 (current GMR for Hoodie)
   - **To value**: 42% (target GMR value)
   - **By changing cell**: $D$2 (Hoodie's List Price)

	B	C	D	E	Goal Seek
	Item	**Cost**	**List Price**	**GMR**	Set cell: E2
	Hoodie	B1 $26.00	$43.34	40.01%	To value: 42%
	T-Shirt	$8.75	$14.59		By changing cell: $D$2
	Jacket	$25.87	$43.12		Cancel OK
	Scarve	$6.79	$11.32		

5. Click **OK**, and Goal Seek will calculate the List Price required to achieve a GMR of 42%:

	B	C	D	E	Goal Seek Status
	Item	**Cost**	**List Price**	**GMR**	Goal Seeking with Cell E2 OK
	Hoodie	$26.00	$44.79	41.95%	found a solution. Cancel
	T-Shirt	$8.75	$14.59		Target value: 0.42
	Jacket	$25.87	$43.12		Current value: 41.95% Step
	Scarve	$6.79	$11.32		Pause

However, you may notice a slight deviation from the target GMR. This often occurs due to rounding or the iterative nature of the tool, which stops as soon as it finds a solution close enough to the target before it reaches a better result. We will address this issue using Python's computational libraries, which offer higher precision for calculations.

5.3 PYTHON

Please refer to the Jupyter notebook file "Bookstore-Ch05.ipynb" to access the code, or view the "Bookstore-Ch05.html" file to see the outputs of all code.

5.3.1 Control Flow

The `control flow` is the order in which a computer executes statements in a script. Most of the time, code is run in a `sequential` order: from the first line in the script to the last line, unless the script specifies certain structures that change the sequential flow, such as conditionals (`if`, `elif`, else in Python) and loops (for, while in Python). As mentioned at the beginning of this chapter, the 1) sequential flow, 2) conditional flow, and 3) iterative flow (loops) are the three types of control flow in computer programming. We have frequently seen how the sequential flow works in many of the previous examples. We also used for in some previous examples. So they are not new to you.

Conditionals – if Statements

You already have experience in using the IF function in Excel. To build an if statement, Python adopts the similar three-part structure: 1) a logical test (or condition), 2) actions when the logical test returns True, 3) actions when the logical test returns False. Let's start from a simple example:

```
In[#]:

a=0;  b=4
if (a>b):  # The logical test. Given a=0 and b=4, the test result
is False.
    print("Not possible.")   # Will not be executed since the
    condition is not True.
else:  # The following indented statements will be executed since the
condition is False.
    print("It's simple math:")
    print("0 must be less than 4.")

Out[#]:

It's simple math:
0 must be less than 4.
```

The Indentation Prompt ":"

In the if and else example above, you should have noticed we added a colon at the end of each if or else. The colon is also required at the end of for, while, elif, and other Python keywords that leads to a block of indented code (e.g., try, except, a function, a class, etc.). This required label: prompts Python to execute code in the scope that follows it. In the if and else example above, the colon at the end of if tells Python that the next line of indented code should only be run if the test condition is True, and the colon at the end of else means the next two lines of indented code will only be run if the test condition is False.

The if-elif-else Block

In some more complicated scenarios, we may need to conduct more logical tests to trigger more precise actions. For example, the if example below will print out one of the three customized messages according to the results of two different conditional tests. The first condition tests if a==b and prints the "equal" message if True. In logical expressions, == is used to test for equality. If not, we further test if a<b using elif and print the "less than" message if True. If still not, it means a must be greater than b (else), so the "greater than" message will be printed out. You may change the values of a and b to test the if-elif-else block.

```
In[#]:

a=0; b=4
if (a==b):
    print("a and b are equal.")
elif (a<b):
    print("a is less than b.")
else:
    print("a is greater than b.")

Out[#]:

a is less than b.
```

Combining if with and, or, and not

In Python, the logical operators and (logical AND), or (logical OR), and not (logical NOT) are used to combine multiple conditions or modify them. They are commonly used in if-else-elif statements, loops, and other conditional flows. You can also combine these operators to create more complex conditional logic. Keep in mind, not is evaluated first, followed by and, then or. Use parentheses to clarify and control the order of evaluation.

Here is an example of combining different logical operators for a loan approval scenario: A loan is approved if the applicant's age is greater than 22, and either their income exceeds 30,000 or their credit score is above 650, and they have no late payment records:

```
In[#]:

age = 25
income = 40000
credit_score = 700
late_payment_rec = False

if age > 22 and (income > 30000 or credit_score > 650) and not late_
payment_rec:
    print("Loan approved")
else:
    print("Loan denied")

Out[#]:

Loan approved
```

In Python, you may also check if the condition is `True` or `False` by quickly printing the value out:

```
In[#]:
print(age > 22)
Out[#]:
True
```

• Side Note – Boolean Data Type

Boolean data type (`bool`) is particularly important when we need Python to make a decision according to a given condition. For example, in the snippet above, the first condition shows: `if age > 22`. Here we ask Python to evaluate if the current value of `age` is greater than 22. If it is, then Python will return `True` to the evaluation.

Basically, Python's `bool` type has only two values: `True` and `False`. Note that they are case-sensitive (i.e., they must be capitalized). In fact, Python's bool type is a subclass of the int type, meaning `True` is internally represented as one and `False` as zero. You can verify this behavior with the following examples:

```
In[#]:
print(True + 1)    # Output: 2 (True acts as 1)
print(False * 10)  # Output: 0 (False acts as 0)
Out[#]:
2
0
```

Please also note that Python considers many objects as `True` or `False` beyond the normal `True`/`False` Boolean values. For example, non-zero numbers, non-empty strings, lists, etc., are considered `True`, whereas zero, None, and empty collections (e.g., lists, strings, etc.) are considered `False`:

```
In[#]:

name = "" # name is an empty string
z = 0

if not z: # not z returns True
    print("z is zero")  # This will execute

if not name: # not name returns True
    print("Name is empty")  # This will execute

Out[#]:

z is zero
Name is empty
```

The if-elif-else Is Not a Good Choice for Vectorized Conditional Operations

Please note that the `if-elif-else` block is primarily used for control flow to handle conditional logic. It operates on scalar values (single elements) or iterable elements via a loop. It also allows for complex, nested, and sequential logic with multiple conditions.

However, it does not work very efficiently on element-wise computations in DataFrames such as the Bookstore dataset. It is because, for large datasets, you'd need a loop to process element-wise, which is slower compared to the vectorized operations we have introduced in Chapter 3.

For element-wise conditional computations, we can utilize the `np.where()` function from the NumPy (commonly abbreviated as `np`) library.

5.3.2 np.where()

The `np.where()` function from NumPy is very useful when working with Pandas DataFrames for performing `element-wise` conditional computations. It allows you to efficiently apply conditions across columns or rows and assign values based on whether the condition is `True` or `False`, similar to Excel's IF() function, but more versatile and powerful.

The general syntax for np.where() is:

np.where(condition, value_if_true, value_if_false)

The syntax is similar to Excel's IF() function, but it allows the use of defined variables for the `condition`, `value_if_true`, and `value_if_false`. This offers a more concise and maintainable approach for handling complex conditions and actions. We will use the Bookstore dataset to demonstrate its superiority.

5.3.3 Data Import

As in previous chapters, we can separately use the read_excel() method to import both the "Item" and "Employee" sheets from the "Bookstore-Ch05. xlsx" file into Pandas DataFrames. This time, however, we will attempt to read all sheets at once by assigning sheet_name = None:

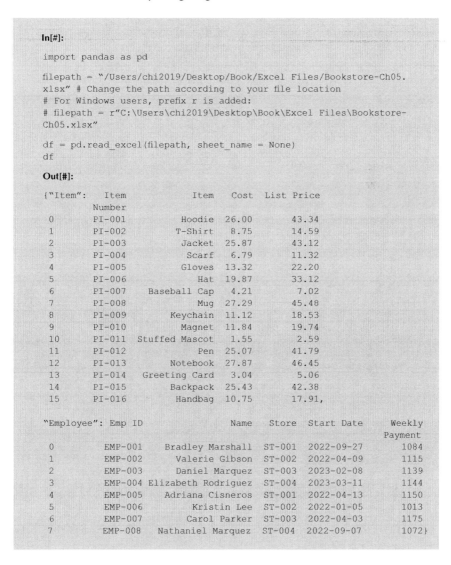

```
In[#]:

import pandas as pd

filepath = "/Users/chi2019/Desktop/Book/Excel Files/Bookstore-Ch05.
xlsx" # Change the path according to your file location
# For Windows users, prefix r is added:
# filepath = r"C:\Users\chi2019\Desktop\Book\Excel Files\Bookstore-
Ch05.xlsx"

df = pd.read_excel(filepath, sheet_name = None)
df
```

Out[#]:

```
{"Item":    Item                Item   Cost  List Price
            Number
0           PI-001           Hoodie   26.00      43.34
1           PI-002          T-Shirt    8.75      14.59
2           PI-003           Jacket   25.87      43.12
3           PI-004            Scarf    6.79      11.32
4           PI-005           Gloves   13.32      22.20
5           PI-006              Hat   19.87      33.12
6           PI-007     Baseball Cap    4.21       7.02
7           PI-008              Mug   27.29      45.48
8           PI-009         Keychain   11.12      18.53
9           PI-010           Magnet   11.84      19.74
10          PI-011   Stuffed Mascot    1.55       2.59
11          PI-012              Pen   25.07      41.79
12          PI-013         Notebook   27.87      46.45
13          PI-014    Greeting Card    3.04       5.06
14          PI-015         Backpack   25.43      42.38
15          PI-016          Handbag   10.75      17.91,

"Employee": Emp ID                 Name  Store  Start Date   Weekly
                                                            Payment
0           EMP-001   Bradley Marshall  ST-001  2022-09-27     1084
1           EMP-002     Valerie Gibson  ST-002  2022-04-09     1115
2           EMP-003     Daniel Marquez  ST-003  2023-02-08     1139
3           EMP-004 Elizabeth Rodriguez ST-004  2023-03-11     1144
4           EMP-005    Adriana Cisneros ST-001  2022-04-13     1150
5           EMP-006       Kristin Lee   ST-002  2022-01-05     1013
6           EMP-007      Carol Parker   ST-003  2022-04-03     1175
7           EMP-008  Nathaniel Marquez  ST-004  2022-09-07     1072}
```

The result may appear to combine both sheets, but in reality, df is a dictionary containing the "Item" and "Employee" sheets:

In[#]:
```
type(df)
```
Out[#]:
```
dict
```

The keys for the two sheets are their original sheet names in Excel:

In[#]:
```
df.keys()
```
Out[#]:
```
dict_keys(["Item", "Employee"])
```

This means we can call their keys to retrieve "Item" and "Employee" respectively:

In[#]:
```
df["Item"]
```
Out[#]:

	Item Number	Item	Cost	List Price
0	PI-001	Hoodie	26.00	43.34
1	PI-002	T-Shirt	8.75	14.59
2	PI-003	Jacket	25.87	43.12
3	PI-004	Scarf	6.79	11.32
4	PI-005	Gloves	13.32	22.20
5	PI-006	Hat	19.87	33.12
6	PI-007	Baseball Cap	4.21	7.02
7	PI-008	Mug	27.29	45.48
8	PI-009	Keychain	11.12	18.53
9	PI-010	Magnet	11.84	19.74
10	PI-011	Stuffed Mascot	1.55	2.59
11	PI-012	Pen	25.07	41.79
12	PI-013	Notebook	27.87	46.45
13	PI-014	Greeting Card	3.04	5.06
14	PI-015	Backpack	25.43	42.38
15	PI-016	Handbag	10.75	17.91

In[#]:

```
df["Employee"]
```

Out[#]:

	Emp ID	Name	Store	Start Date	Weekly Payment
0	EMP-001	Bradley Marshall	ST-001	2022-09-27	1084
1	EMP-002	Valerie Gibson	ST-002	2022-04-09	1115
2	EMP-003	Daniel Marquez	ST-003	2023-02-08	1139
3	EMP-004	Elizabeth Rodriguez	ST-004	2023-03-11	1144
4	EMP-005	Adriana Cisneros	ST-001	2022-04-13	1150
5	EMP-006	Kristin Lee	ST-002	2022-01-05	1013
6	EMP-007	Carol Parker	ST-003	2022-04-03	1175
7	EMP-008	Nathaniel Marquez	ST-004	2022-09-07	1072

This approach is particularly efficient for reading all sheets from an Excel file at once, as long as all sheets are in tabular form (i.e., an m×n matrix). We can now assign each dictionary entry to more descriptive DataFrame names:

In[#]:

```
item = df["Item"]
emp = df["Employee"]
item, emp
```

Out[#]:

```
(   Item Number           Item   Cost  List Price
0        PI-001         Hoodie  26.00       43.34
1        PI-002        T-Shirt   8.75       14.59
2        PI-003         Jacket  25.87       43.12
3        PI-004          Scarf   6.79       11.32
4        PI-005         Gloves  13.32       22.20
5        PI-006            Hat  19.87       33.12
6        PI-007   Baseball Cap   4.21        7.02
7        PI-008            Mug  27.29       45.48
8        PI-009       Keychain  11.12       18.53
9        PI-010         Magnet  11.84       19.74
10       PI-011 Stuffed Mascot   1.55        2.59
11       PI-012            Pen  25.07       41.79
12       PI-013       Notebook  27.87       46.45
13       PI-014  Greeting Card   3.04        5.06
```

```
14        PI-015       Backpack  25.43      42.38
15        PI-016        Handbag  10.75      17.91,
      Emp ID                  Name   Store Start Date  Weekly Payment
0    EMP-001     Bradley Marshall  ST-001 2022-09-27            1084
1    EMP-002       Valerie Gibson  ST-002 2022-04-09            1115
2    EMP-003       Daniel Marquez  ST-003 2023-02-08            1139
3    EMP-004  Elizabeth Rodriquez  ST-004 2023-03-11            1144
4    EMP-005     Adriana Cisneros  ST-001 2022-04-13            1150
5    EMP-006         Kristin Lee   ST-002 2022-01-05            1013
6    EMP-007         Carol Parker  ST-003 2022-04-03            1175
7    EMP-008    Nathaniel Marquez  ST-004 2022-09-07           1072)
```

5.3.4 Control Flow Exercises with np.where()

Q1: For employees working in the East store (using Store="ST-001"), increase their weekly payment by 5%.

To use np.where(), we first need to import the NumPy library:

```
In[#]:

import numpy as np
```

As mentioned earlier, one of the key advantages of Python's conditional statements (such as if-elif-else blocks, np.where, loops, etc.) is the ability to define both conditions and actions as variables. This flexibility significantly enhances code readability and maintainability. For instance, deeply nested IF formulas in Excel can be challenging to develop, debug, and maintain. In contrast, Python's approach to defining conditions and actions makes the code more concise, structured, and easier to work with, particularly for handling complex logic. For instance, based on Q1's requirements, we can first define the `condition` and the actions for `value_if_true` and `value_if_false` as callable variables. These variables can then be passed as parameters to `np.where()` in the subsequent steps:

```
In[#]:

# Define condition
cond_q1 = (emp["Store"] == "ST-001")

# Define actions for value_if_true (yes) and value_if_false (no)
yes_q1 = emp["Weekly Payment"] * 1.05
no_q1 = emp["Weekly Payment"]

emp["Q1"] = np.where(cond_q1, yes_q1, no_q1)
emp
```

Out[#]:

	Emp ID	Name	Store	Start Date	Weekly Payment	Q1
0	EMP-001	Bradley Marshall	ST-001	2022-09-27	1084	1138.2
1	EMP-002	Valerie Gibson	ST-002	2022-04-09	1115	1115.0
2	EMP-003	Daniel Marquez	ST-003	2023-02-08	1139	1139.0
3	EMP-004	Elizabeth Rodriguez	ST-004	2023-03-11	1144	1144.0
4	EMP-005	Adriana Cisneros	ST-001	2022-04-13	1150	1207.5
5	EMP-006	Kristin Lee	ST-002	2022-01-05	1013	1013.0
6	EMP-007	Carol Parker	ST-003	2022-04-03	1175	1175.0
7	EMP-008	Nathaniel Marquez	ST-004	2022-09-07	1072	1072.0

As you may have noticed, predefining conditions and their corresponding actions enhances the flexibility of maintaining control flows while making the structure of np.where() significantly more concise.

Q2: For employees whose current weekly pay is between $1,050 and $1,100, increase their salary by 3%. For all others, apply a 5% raise.
To address Q2, we can use a similar approach from Q1 to predefine conditions and actions and use them in np.where():

In[#]:

```
# Define condition
cond_q2 = (emp["Weekly Payment"] >= 1050) & (emp["Weekly Payment"] <=
1100) # See explanation below for the `&` operator

# Define actions for value_if_true (yes) and value_if_false (no)
yes_q2 = emp["Weekly Payment"] * 1.03
no_q2 = emp["Weekly Payment"] * 1.05
```

In Python, logical operators such as and, or, and not are used to combine conditional statements for controlling program flow. For example: if a > 5 and b < 10. However, when performing element-wise logical operations on Pandas DataFrames or NumPy arrays, you must use &, |, and ~ instead. These operators are designed to handle vectorized operands and return

Boolean values of the same shape as the input arrays. For instance: result = (col_a > 5) & (col_b < 10). This is why the & operator is used to combine the two conditions in cond_q2 in the previous example. Note that & requires parentheses around each condition to ensure proper evaluation, whereas and does not.

In[#]:

```
emp["Q2"] = np.where(cond_q2, yes_q2, no_q2)
emp
```

Out[#]:

	Emp ID	Name	Store	Start Date	Weekly Payment	Q1	Q2
0	EMP-001	Bradley Marshall	ST-001	2022-09-27	1084	1138.2	1116.52
1	EMP-002	Valerie Gibson	ST-002	2022-04-09	1115	1115.0	1170.75
2	EMP-003	Daniel Marquez	ST-003	2023-02-08	1139	1139.0	1195.95
3	EMP-004	Elizabeth Rodriguez	ST-004	2023-03-11	1144	1144.0	1201.20
4	EMP-005	Adriana Cisneros	ST-001	2022-04-13	1150	1207.5	1207.50
5	EMP-006	Kristin Lee	ST-002	2022-01-05	1013	1013.0	1063.65
6	EMP-007	Carol Parker	ST-003	2022-04-03	1175	1175.0	1233.75
7	EMP-008	Nathaniel Marquez	ST-004	2022-09-07	1072	1072.0	1104.16

Q3: For employees whose weekly pay is between $1,050 and $1,100, increase their salary by 3%. For those earning below $1,050, apply a 5% raise. For everyone else, apply a 1% raise.

To address Q3, we would need to develop a nested np.where() by slightly modifying the predefinitions from Q2:

In[#]:

```
# Define condition
cond_q3_1 = (emp["Weekly Payment"] >= 1050) & (emp["Weekly Payment"]
<= 1100)
cond_q3_2 = (emp["Weekly Payment"] < 1050)

# Define actions for value_if_true (yes) and value_if_false (no)
yes_q3 = emp["Weekly Payment"] * 1.03
no_q3 = np.where(cond_q3_2, emp["Weekly Payment"] * 1.05, emp["Weekly
Payment"] * 1.01)
```

Since it is essential to determine the specific range each employee's weekly pay falls into, a second np.where() is required for an additional condition check, as demonstrated in no_q3 above.

In[#]:

```
emp["Q3"] = np.where(cond_q3_1, yes_q3, no_q3)
emp
```

Out[#]:

	Emp ID	Name	Store	Start Date	Weekly Payment	Q1	Q2	Q3
0	EMP-001	Bradley Marshall	ST-001	2022-09-27	1084	1138.2	1116.52	1116.52
1	EMP-002	Valerie Gibson	ST-002	2022-04-09	1115	1115.0	1170.75	1126.15
2	EMP-003	Daniel Marquez	ST-003	2023-02-08	1139	1139.0	1195.95	1150.39
3	EMP-004	Elizabeth Rodriguez	ST-004	2023-03-11	1144	1144.0	1201.20	1155.44
4	EMP-005	Adriana Cisneros	ST-001	2022-04-13	1150	1207.5	1207.50	1161.50
5	EMP-006	Kristin Lee	ST-002	2022-01-05	1013	1013.0	1063.65	1063.65
6	EMP-007	Carol Parker	ST-003	2022-04-03	1175	1175.0	1233.75	1186.75
7	EMP-008	Nathaniel Marquez	ST-004	2022-09-07	1072	1072.0	1104.16	1104.16

Q4: Add a new column labeled "Store Name" to match store IDs with their corresponding store names.

Dictionary and map()

In Chapter 4, we demonstrated how to use a dictionary to map integer codes to their corresponding month names. To address Q4, we can apply the same approach:

In[#]:

```
# Dictionary to map Store IDs to Names
store_map = {
    "ST-001": "East", "ST-002": "West", "ST-003": "North", "ST-004": "South"
}

emp["Store Name"] = emp["Store"].map(store_map)
emp
```

Out[#]:

	Emp ID	Name	Store	Start Date	Weekly Payment	Q1	Q2	Q3	Store Name
0	EMP-001	Bradley Marshall	ST-001	2022-09-27	1084	1138.2	1116.52	1116.52	East
1	EMP-002	Valerie Gibson	ST-002	2022-04-09	1115	1115.0	1170.75	1126.15	West
2	EMP-003	Daniel Marquez	ST-003	2023-02-08	1139	1139.0	1195.95	1150.39	North
3	EMP-004	Elizabeth Rodriguez	ST-004	2023-03-11	1144	1144.0	1201.20	1155.44	South
4	EMP-005	Adriana Cisneros	ST-001	2022-04-13	1150	1207.5	1207.50	1161.50	East
5	EMP-006	Kristin Lee	ST-002	2022-01-05	1013	1013.0	1063.65	1063.65	West
6	EMP-007	Carol Parker	ST-003	2022-04-03	1175	1175.0	1233.75	1186.75	North
7	EMP-008	Nathaniel Marquez	ST-004	2022-09-07	1072	1072.0	1104.16	1104.16	South

match-case and map()

Alternatively, we can also use Python's `match-case` statement. This serves as a structured way to handle multiple conditions, similar to a switch-case in other computer languages. Using Python's `match-case` for an exact match case is straightforward and intuitive. The `map_store` function defined below is how it works in scenarios where you want to map specific values directly to corresponding outputs. The match statement evaluates an expression or variable (in this case, id). It compares the variable against the values or patterns defined in the case statements and returns the predefined value corresponding to the matching case. The _ is a wildcard, acting as a default case when no other patterns match.

In[#]:

```
# Function using match-case
def map_store(id):
    match id:
        case "ST-001":
            return "East"
        case "ST-002":
            return "West"
        case "ST-003":
            return "North"
        case "ST-004":
            return "South"
```

```
            case _:
                return "Unknown"  # Default case

# Map the function to the DataFrame
emp["Store Name 2"] = emp["Store"].map(map_store) # Add the second
Store Name for match-case
emp
```

Out[#]:

	Emp ID	Name	Store	Start Date	Weekly Payment	Q1	Q2	Q3	Store Name	Store Name 2
0	EMP-001	Bradley Marshall	ST-001	2022-09-27	1084	1138.2	1116.52	1116.52	East	East
1	EMP-002	Valerie Gibson	ST-002	2022-04-09	1115	1115.0	1170.75	1126.15	West	West
2	EMP-003	Daniel Marquez	ST-003	2023-02-08	1139	1139.0	1195.95	1150.39	North	North
3	EMP-004	Elizabeth Rodriguez	ST-004	2023-03-11	1144	1144.0	1201.20	1155.44	South	South
4	EMP-005	Adriana Cisneros	ST-001	2022-04-13	1150	1207.5	1207.50	1161.50	East	East
5	EMP-006	Kristin Lee	ST-002	2022-01-05	1013	1013.0	1063.65	1063.65	West	West
6	EMP-007	Carol Parker	ST-003	2022-04-03	1175	1175.0	1233.75	1186.75	North	North
7	EMP-008	Nathaniel Marquez	ST-004	2022-09-07	1072	1072.0	1104.16	1104.16	South	South

As illustrated in the example above, Python's `match-case` construct can be used to determine the values of a new column in a pandas DataFrame based on the values from an existing column. However, since match-case is typically applied row by row, you would integrate it with pandas' row-wise operations using `map()` or other row iteration methods like `apply()`.

Q5: Calculate the required List Price to achieve a 42% GMR, assuming the unit cost remains unchanged.

To solve Q5 using Python, we simply need to develop a formula to calculate the list price required to achieve a 42% GMR. Before doing so, let's explore the concept of Boolean indexing in Python. Boolean indexing allows you to filter a DataFrame based on specific conditions applied to its columns. For example, if we want to extract only the row corresponding to the item "Hoodie", we can achieve this using Boolean indexing as shown below:

In[#]:

```
cond_q5 = item["Item"] == "Hoodie" # when there is only one
condition, parenthese can be omitted
hoodie = item[cond_q5]
hoodie
```

Out[#]:

	Item Number	Item	Cost	List Price
0	PI-001	Hoodie	26.0	43.34

Now, we can come up with the target list price to achieve a GMR of 42% by solving the equation manually:

In[#]:

```
cost = hoodie.iloc[0, 2] # Retrieve the unit cost using iloc[]
GMR = .42
target_price = cost/(1 - GMR)
print(target_price)
```

Out[#]:

```
44.82758620689655
```

Using Python's Equation Solver
Alternatively, you can utilize Python's versatile equation solvers. For a symbolic computation (or algebraic in a more specific sense) like Q5, the sympy library is an excellent choice. It enables you to define equations symbolically and solve them algebraically. Using the snippet below, you don't need to solve the equation manually; simply provide the equation for the desired GMR, and the library will handle the solution for you.

In[#]:

```
from sympy import symbols, Eq, solve # import necessary classes
from sympy

# Define symbols
x = symbols("x")

# Define the equation
equation = Eq((x - cost)/x, GMR)

# Solve for x
target_price = solve(equation, x)
print(target_price)
```

Out[#]:

```
[44.8275862068966]
```

You can compare these results with Excel's "What-If" analysis. The outcomes from the two methods above are both more precise than those obtained using Excel.

5.4 DISCUSSIONS

Excel's logical functions (e.g., IF, AND, OR) and Python's `np.where()` both allow conditional computations, but they differ significantly in how they handle vectorized datasets:

1. Vectorized Operations
   1) Excel: Excel's logical functions operate on cell-by-cell basis. You must write formulas for each cell or use drag-and-fill to apply the logic across a range of data. Operations aren't inherently vectorized and require manual repetition.
   2) Python (np.where): np.where() is inherently vectorized, applying the condition across entire datasets (e.g., Pandas DataFrames or NumPy arrays) at once. This makes it more efficient for large datasets.

2. Performance
   1) Excel: Performance can degrade with large datasets, especially when using complex or nested formulas across many cells.
   2) Python (np.where): Optimized for handling large datasets efficiently, leveraging NumPy's underlying C implementation.

3. Readability
   1) Excel: Nested IF functions can become difficult to read and maintain, especially for complex conditions.
   2) Python (np.where): Conditions and actions can be predefined and reused, leading to more concise and maintainable code.

4. Scalability
   1) Excel: Suitable for small to medium datasets but less practical for large-scale data processing.
   2) Python (np.where): Scales well for large datasets and integrates with other data processing libraries.

In sum, while Excel is user-friendly and accessible for small-scale operations, Python's `np.where()` is far more powerful, efficient, and scalable for handling vectorized datasets programmatically.

5.5 EXERCISES

Using the concepts covered in this chapter, complete the following exercises using "Exercise-Ch05.xlsx" as your dataset. This file contains current item details in the "Item" sheet and a "New Suppliers" sheet listing price quotes for each item from three potential new suppliers.

E1: **In the "Item" dataset, apply an 8% cost increase to all items containing "coffee" in their names due to rising raw coffee bean prices.**

E2: **In the "New Suppliers" dataset, identify the lowest quoted price for each item.**

E3: **Determine which supplier offers the lowest price for each item.**

E4: **Compare the adjusted current costs (after the 8% increase) with the lowest supplier quotes. If the adjusted cost is higher than the lowest quote, print "Better price!", otherwise print "Stay."**

## CHAPTER 6

Record Lookup and Data Segmentation

R ECORD LOOKUP AND DATA segmentation are essential tasks in data management and analysis. They allow you to extract relevant data from large datasets efficiently, based on specific criteria. These techniques are foundational to any data-driven decision-making process, as they simplify complex datasets and provide targeted, more precise insights.

1. **Record Lookup**
   This involves identifying specific data points or rows in a dataset based on a unique key or matching criteria. For example, finding a customer's purchase history using their ID or retrieving a product's details from a catalog based on its SKU (stock keeping unit).

2. **Data Segmentation**
   It allows you to isolate subsets of data that meet particular conditions, such as sales records from a specific region, transactions within a date range, or products within a specified price range.

Efficient record lookup and data segmentation become increasingly important as datasets grow in size and complexity. Both Excel and Python

DOI: 10.1201/9781003567103-7

offer powerful tools to perform these tasks. Whether using Excel for small, interactive datasets or Python for automating large-scale analysis, understanding both tools allows you to choose the method that best fits your data analytics needs.

6.1 DATA SEGMENTATION AND RECORD LOOKUP WITH BOOKSTORE DATASET

We will use the "Bookstore-Ch06.xlsx" file to demonstrate how to utilize data visualization tools in both Excel and Python. The "Invoice" worksheet in "Bookstore-Ch06.xlsx" has already been formatted as an Excel Table named "sales". Before proceeding with the exercises below, please take a moment to familiarize yourself with the fundamental operations of Excel Tables.

Q1: Create a pivot table grouped by **Employee**, including two summarized fields: "**Sum of Extension – Discounted**" and "**Sum of Margin**", as demonstrated in Chapter 3's Q2. Add a new column to the pivot table labeled "**Bonus Rate**" by referring to the reference table below. Finally, calculate each employee's bonus by adding another column labeled "**Bonus Amount**".

Sum of Extension – Discounted	Bonus Rate
0	1%
$10,000	3%
$11,000	5%
$12,000	8%

Q2: Use the **by-Employee** pivot table, add a new column to the pivot table labeled "**Performance Level**" by referring to the reference table below.

Sum of Margin	Performance Level
0	Unsatisfied
$2,000	Developing
$3,000	Adequate
$3,500	Commendable
$4,000	Outstanding

Q3: Pull out the records of "Baseball Cap" sales on 1/3/2023, and find the employee's name for that transaction.

Q4: List the transaction details that meet either of the following criteria: 1) **Hoodies** sold by **Daniel Marquez Elizabeth** with a quantity of at least two units, or 2) **Handbags** sold by **Rodriguez** with **no discount**.

Q5: With Q4's conditions, instead of displaying the records, calculate the following statistics: 1) the record **count**, 2) the **total** and 3) **average** sales (**Sum and Average of Extension – Discounted**), 4) the latest **date** of sale, and 5) the minimum **quantity** sold.

6.2 EXCEL

In Chapter 5, we have used the **VLOOKUP()** function for exact match tests when specifying 0 (or False) for the 4th parameter. Now, we are going to use its second application: range test by selecting 1 (or True) for the 4th parameter. Let's recap its syntax as follows:

VLOOKUP(lookup_value, table_array, col_index_num, [range_lookup])

- **lookup_value**: The key value you want to search for, typically a referenced cell.
- **table_array**: The range of cells containing the dataset, including the lookup key and the related data.
- **col_index_num**: The column number relative to the key column (index of 1) in the table_array, from which to retrieve the desired data.
- **range_lookup**: FALSE or for an exact match, TRUE or omitted for an approximate match, or range test.

For **Q1** and **Q2**, begin by preparing a pivot table with "**Name**" as the rows and "**Sum of Extension – Discounted**" and "**Sum of Margin**" as the values, following the example in Chapter 3's Q2:

	A	B	C
1			
2			
3	Row Labels ▼	Sum of Extension - Discounted	Sum of Margin
4	Adriana Cisneros	$12,138.66	$3,988.65
5	Bradley Marshall	$10,988.16	$3,610.72
6	Carol Parker	$12,011.55	$3,815.39
7	Daniel Marquez	$9,534.69	$3,128.32
8	Elizabeth Rodriguez	$11,908.40	$3,819.89
9	Kristin Lee	$12,333.53	$4,002.86
10	Nathaniel Marquez	$12,866.87	$4,223.66
11	Valerie Gibson	$10,641.44	$3,472.55
12	Grand Total	$92,423.29	$30,062.03

Q1: Add "**Bonus Rate**" column by referring to **Q1's** reference table and calculate each employee's bonus in "**Bonus Amount**" column.

1. First, create the reference table (**$H$3:$I$6**) as below:

H	I
Sum of Extension - Discounted	**Bonus Rate**
0	1%
10000	3%
11000	5%
12000	8%

2. In cell **D4**, create a **VLOOKUP()** formula and use the formula builder to set up the four parameters as follows:

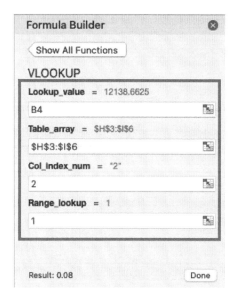

1) Reference B4, the sum of extension for the first employee, as the **lookup_value**.

2) Select the reference table array **$H$3:$I$6**.

3) Assign **2** for the third parameter, as the "**Bonus Rate**" column (the target data) is the second column relative to the key column (the sum of extension) in the table array.

4) For the last parameter, select **1** (or True) to specify a **range test**.

3. Calculate the bonus amount by multiplying "**Sum of Extension – Discounted**" by "**Bonus Rate**" (the lookup result from step 2). Then, copy the formulas (**D4** and **E4**) down to the remaining rows. Verify your results using the screenshot provided below:

	A	B	C	D	E
1					
2					
3	**Row Labels** ▾	Sum of Extension - Discounted	Sum of Margin	**Bonus Rate**	**Bonus Amount**
4	Adriana Cisneros	$12,138.66	$3,988.65	0.08	$971.09
5	Bradley Marshall	$10,988.16	$3,610.72	0.03	$329.64
6	Carol Parker	$12,011.55	$3,815.39	0.08	$960.92
7	Daniel Marquez	$9,534.69	$3,128.32	0.01	$95.35
8	Elizabeth Rodriguez	$11,908.40	$3,819.89	0.05	$595.42
9	Kristin Lee	$12,333.53	$4,002.86	0.08	$986.68
10	Nathaniel Marquez	$12,866.87	$4,223.66	0.08	$1,029.35
11	Valerie Gibson	$10,641.44	$3,472.55	0.03	$319.24
12	**Grand Total**	**$92,423.29**	**$30,062.03**		

Q2: Add "**Performance Level**" column by referring to **Q2's** reference table.

Q2 is another example of range test. Simply follow the same steps outlined in **Q1** to complete it:

1. First, create the reference table (**$H$10:$I$14**) as below:

Sum of Margin	Performance Level
0	Unsatisfied
2000	Developing
3000	Adequate
3500	Commendable
4000	Outstanding

2. In cell **F4**, create a **VLOOKUP()** formula and use the formula builder to set up the four parameters as follows:

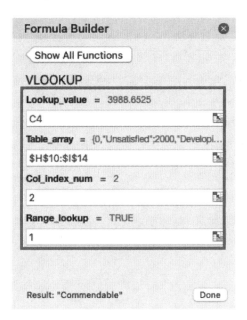

3. After copying the formula in **F4** down to other rows, you may verify your results using the screenshot below:

	A	B	C	D	E	F
1						
2						
3	Row Labels ▾	Sum of Extension - Discounted	Sum of Margin	Bonus Rate	Bonus Amount	Performance Level
4	Adriana Cisneros	$12,138.66	$3,988.65	0.08	$971.09	Commendable
5	Bradley Marshall	$10,988.16	$3,610.72	0.03	$329.64	Commendable
6	Carol Parker	$12,011.55	$3,815.39	0.08	$960.92	Commendable
7	Daniel Marquez	$9,534.69	$3,128.32	0.01	$95.35	Adequate
8	Elizabeth Rodriguez	$11,908.40	$3,819.89	0.05	$595.42	Commendable
9	Kristin Lee	$12,333.53	$4,002.86	0.08	$986.68	Outstanding
10	Nathaniel Marquez	$12,866.87	$4,223.66	0.08	$1,029.35	Outstanding
11	Valerie Gibson	$10,641.44	$3,472.55	0.03	$319.24	Adequate
12	Grand Total	$92,423.29	$30,062.03			

SIDE NOTE – VLOOKUP'S RULES

As demonstrated in Chapter 5 and this chapter, **VLOOKUP** is a versatile function that can handle two key applications: **exact match** and **range tests**. However, there are specific rules and limitations to consider when using it for record lookup:

1. Position of the Key Column

VLOOKUP can only retrieve data from columns to the **right** of the key column within the table array. It cannot access columns located to the left of the key column. For instance, in Q1, if **"Sum of Extension – Discounted"** is positioned as the second column and **"Bonus Rate"** as the first, VLOOKUP will be unable to retrieve the desired data. To maximize the usability of the function, ensure the potential key columns are placed as the first few columns when structuring your table array. This approach allows for greater flexibility in retrieving additional data columns. An alternative is to use **XLOOKUP**, available in newer versions of Excel. This function overcomes VLOOKUP's limitation regarding the position of the key column, allowing lookups in any direction. However, its syntax is slightly more complex compared to VLOOKUP. You are encouraged to explore XLOOKUP further to understand its features and benefits.

2. The Order of the Range Numbers

When using **VLOOKUP** for a range test in Excel, the range numbers must be listed in **ascending order**. It is because the function searches for the closest match **less than or equal to** the lookup value when performing an approximate match. If the range numbers are not in ascending order, VLOOKUP may return incorrect results or fail to locate the appropriate range, as it relies on the sequence to determine the correct boundary.

3. Numbers of Bin Edges and Labels

In VLOOKUP's range tests, as seen in Q1 and Q2, the number of bin edges (or range boundaries) matches the number of labels (the data to be retrieved). However, this differs from how Pandas' **cut()** function operates. In cut(), the number of bin edges must always be greater than the number of labels, following mathematical conventions. This is because bin edges represent the "boundaries of intervals", and one additional boundary is needed to enclose all intervals properly. You will learn how to use cut() in the Python part.

SIDE NOTE – USING IFS() FOR RANGE TESTS

You can also use **IFS()** for range tests. Refer to the general syntax of IFS introduced in Chapter 5. Unlike VLOOKUP, the **[test, value]** pattern in **IFS** requires the conditions to be structured in **reverse order**. This means you must place the largest boundary number as the first test, followed by smaller boundaries, because IFS returns the value for the **first condition that evaluates to TRUE**.

You can follow the general syntax to explore how to use **IFS** to solve Q1 and Q2. However, keep in mind that for larger datasets or scenarios involving repeated range checks, **VLOOKUP** is generally more efficient than using multiple IFS statements.

Q3: Pull out the records of "Baseball Cap" sales on 1/3/2023, and find the employee's name for that transaction.

Excel offers a convenient "**what-you-see-is-what-you-get**" (WYSIWYG) interface for quick filtering, as seen in Q3. This process becomes even easier when working with Excel Tables, as filter icons are automatically added to the header row.

1. Click the filter icon on the "**Date**" column label to open the filter builder:

2. Deselect all default selections, expand "**January**", and select "**03**" to filter transactions that occurred on **1/3/2023**. Then click "**Apply Filter**":

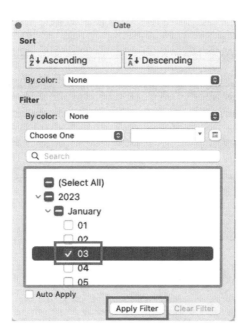

3. Then Click the filter icon on the "**Item**" column, deselect all default selections, select "**Baseball Cap**", and click "**Apply Filter**":

4. You can confirm your answers with the screenshot below:

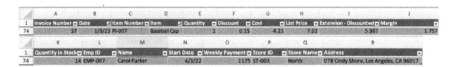

Now, we know the employee who handled this transaction is Carol Parker.

5. Before you move forward to the next question, remember to clear both the **Date** and **Item** filters:

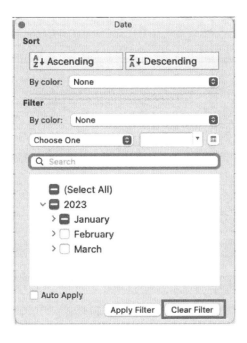

Q4: List the transaction details that meet either of the following criteria: 1) **Hoodies** sold by **Daniel Marquez** with a quantity of at least two units, or 2) **Handbags** sold by **Elizabeth Rodriguez** with **no discount**.

The filtering method used in Q3 works well for straightforward criteria that can be applied to a single column or a combination of "AND" conditions. However, when "**OR**" conditions are introduced, as Q4 requires, standard filters become insufficient. Instead, we would need to use Excel's **Advanced Filter**. The **Advanced Filter** provides the flexibility needed for compound conditions (e.g., multi-column conditions that includes both "AND" and "OR") by allowing users to define complex criteria in a separate range of cells.

1. We begin by creating a new sheet named "**Queries**". Set up the criteria range for Q4 and define this range as "**Criteria**" using the name box, as shown below:

Criteria		f_x	Item	
	A	B	C	D
1	**Q4:**			
2	Item	Quantity	Discount	Name
3	Hoodie	>=2		Daniel Marquez
4	Handbag		0	Elizabeth Rodriguez

The details of the "**Criteria**" range are as follows:

- **Column Headers (Row 2):**
  These headers (Item, Quantity, Discount, Name) **must** exactly match the dataset's column headers to ensure proper filtering. This is the most important rule when performing Advanced Filter.

- **Hoodies Condition (Row 3):**
  1) **Item (Hoodie):** Filters records where the "Item" is **Hoodie**.
  2) **Quantity (>=2):** Includes Hoodie records where the "Quantity" is greater than or equal to 2.
  3) **Name (Daniel Marquez):** Ensures the employee is **Daniel Marquez**.

  Remember, in Advanced Filter, conditions in one same row applies **AND** logic. Therefore, this row will filter records with all three conditions satisfied.

- **Handbags Condition (Row 4):**
  1) **Item (Handbag):** Filters records where the "Item" is **Handbag**.
  2) **Discount (0):** Includes only records with **no discount**.
  3) **Name (Elizabeth Rodriguez):** Ensures the employee is **Elizabeth Rodriguez**.

  Again, this row applies **AND** logic to records with all three conditions satisfied.

- **Overall Logic:**
  Each row in the criteria range represents an **OR** condition. This means the filter will include records that meet **either** the Hoodie conditions (Row 3) **or** the Handbag conditions (Row 4).

This setup ensures the filter retrieves the desired records efficiently, presenting **AND** and **OR** logic in a better visualizable way.

2. In the "**Queries**" sheet, go to the "Data" tab and select "Advanced" under the Filter group:

3. Follow the following steps to complete the three parameters in the Advanced Filter builder:

   1) Select "Copy to another location":

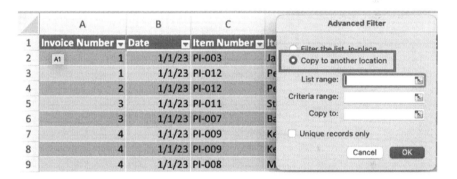

   2) Switch to the "Invoice" sheet. In the "**List range**" field, move the cursor to the top-left corner of cell **A1** in the sales table. When the cursor changes to a solid arrow pointing diagonally to the bottom-right, double-click until the "**List range**" field displays "**sales[#All]**". Then, press **OK** to select the entire table:

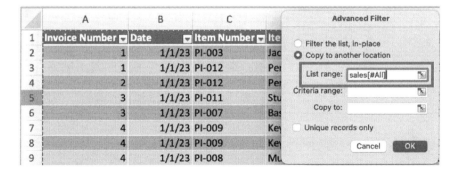

3) In the "Criteria range" box, select the range named "**Criteria**":

	A	B	C	D
1	Q4:			
2	Item	Quantity	Discount	Name
3	Hoodie	>=2		Daniel Marquez
4	Handbag		0	Elizabeth Rodriguez
5				
6				
7				
8				

Advanced Filter

○ Filter the list, in-place
● Copy to another location

List range: sales[#All]
Criteria range: Queries!Criteria
Copy to:

☐ Unique records only

Cancel   OK

4) In the "Copy to" box, select cell A7 as the location to display the filtered results. Then, press OK:

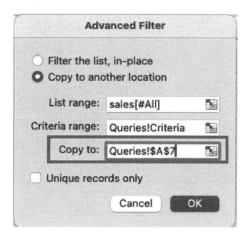

Advanced Filter

○ Filter the list, in-place
● Copy to another location

List range: sales[#All]

Criteria range: Queries!Criteria

Copy to: Queries!$A$7

☐ Unique records only

Cancel   OK

5) At cell **A7,** you should see six rows that meet the criteria. You can verify your results using the screenshot below:

	Invoice Number	Date	Item Number	Item	Quantity	Discount	Cost	List Price
7								
8	161	1/15/23	PI-016	Handbag	2	0	10.75	17.91
9	345	1/31/23	PI-001	Hoodie	2	0.15	26	43.34
10	580	2/21/23	PI-001	Hoodie	2	0.2	26	43.34
11	738	3/7/23	PI-001	Hoodie	2	0	26	43.34
12	801	3/13/23	PI-016	Handbag	2	0	10.75	17.91
13	805	3/13/23	PI-016	Handbag	3	0	10.75	17.91

Q5: With Q4's conditions, calculate: 1) the record **count**, 2) the **total** and 3) **average** sales (**Sum and Average of Extension − Discounted**), 4) the latest **date** of sale, and 5) the minimum **quantity** sold.

Excel provides a set of **Database Functions** – such as **DSUM**, **DAVERAGE**, **DCOUNT**, and others – that enable users to perform calculations or aggregations on subsets of data based on specific criteria. These functions work similarly to **Advanced Filtering**, as both utilize a **criteria range** to define the conditions for querying data. This approach aligns with the concept of **Query by Example (QBE)**, where users define desired outputs through structured examples. Below are the explanations of some key database functions:

- **DCOUNT/DCOUNTA:** Counts the number of entries that meet the criteria. **DCOUNTA** counts any nonblank cells in a column, while **DCOUNT** counts only cells containing numbers. We recommend using **DCOUNTA** because it is more flexible and can handle a wider variety of data types.
- **DSUM:** Calculates the sum of values in a specified column that meet the given criteria.
- **DAVERAGE:** Computes the average of values in a specified column that meet the criteria.
- **DMAX/DMIN:** Finds the maximum or minimum value in a column based on the criteria.

1. On the "**Queries**" sheet, select Row 18 as the header for Q5, with the answers to be placed in Row 19. Since the criteria range from **Q4** has already been defined as "**Criteria**", it can be reused for all parts of **Q5**.

17	Q5:				
18	Record Count	Total Sales Amount	Average Sales Amount	Latest Date of Sale	Minimum Quantity Sold
19					

2. To calculate the record count, we can quickly use **DCOUNTA** in cell **A19**, as shown below. You'll notice that the parameters are very similar to those used in Q4's Advanced Filter. The key difference is the inclusion of the "**Field**" parameter. Unlike Advanced Filter, database functions perform aggregations based on the "**Criteria**". That's why we need to specify "**Field**" to indicate the column to be used for the calculation. In the case of **DCOUNTA**, you can select any column since it simply counts.

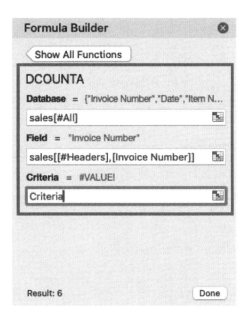

3. To calculate the total sales, use **DSUM** in cell **B19**, as shown below. For the "**Field**" parameter, select "**Sum and Average of Extension – Discounted**", as the aggregation will sum the values in this column based on the specified "**Criteria**".

4. For the average sales, use **DAVERAGE** in cell **C19**, as shown below. The three parameters are identical to those used in **DSUM**:

5. To determine the latest date of sale based on the "**Criteria**", use **DMAX** in cell **D19**, as shown below. Set "**Date**" as the "**Field**" parameter, and **DMAX** will return the most recent date since it corresponds to the largest numerical value in the column.

6. To find the minimum quantity sold, use **DMIN** in cell **E19**, as shown below. Simply set "**Quantity**" as the "**Field**" parameter, and you will obtain the result.

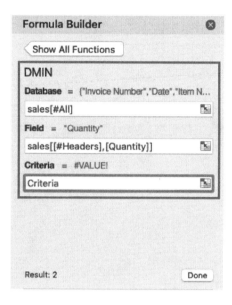

7. The results in the screenshot below appear correct, except for the **Latest Date of Sale**, which is displayed as a large integer instead of a date:

17	Q5:				
18	Record Count	Total Sales Amount	Average Sales Amount	Latest Date of Sale	Minimum Quantity Sold
19	6	$355.07	$59.18	44998	2

This occurs because Excel stores dates as numerical values. To fix this, simply reformat the cell to the "**Date**" format, and it will display the correct date:

17	Q5:				
18	Record Count	Total Sales Amount	Average Sales Amount	Latest Date of Sale	Minimum Quantity Sold
19	6	$355.07	$59.18	3/13/23	2

Excel's **Database Functions** and **Advanced Filtering** offer an intuitive, database-like querying experience for users who work extensively with structured data in spreadsheets. They empower both record lookup and filtering, serving as a bridge between spreadsheet tools and database systems.

6.3 PYTHON

Please refer to the Jupyter notebook file "Bookstore-Ch06.ipynb" to access the code, or view the "Bookstore-Ch06.html" file to see the outputs of all code.

6.3.1 Python's Record Lookup

In Chapter 5, you learned how to utilize Pandas' `Boolean indexing` to effectively access, and filter data based on various logical conditions. Given Python's capability to handle logical operations like and, or, and not, coupled with the ability to define these conditions as reusable variables, Boolean indexing offers significant advantages over Excel's lookup and database functions for data retrieval and filtering. This functionality is particularly powerful when dealing with large datasets or complex data transformations that require automated workflows.

6.3.2 Python's Data Segmentation

Additionally, Pandas excels in data segmentation, akin to performing range tests in Excel. The `cut()` function is a standout feature for dividing continuous numerical data into discrete intervals, or "buckets". This capability is invaluable for organizing data into categories, which simplifies subsequent analysis and is especially beneficial in large-scale data environments.

However, it's important to note that while Pandas is optimized for extensive data manipulation and automated processing, Excel is also highly effective for interactive data manipulation, particularly with smaller datasets.

Key Features of pd.cut():
1. Binning Data: pd.cut() allows you to divide the data into intervals of your choosing, either by specifying the number of bins or the exact bin edges. This can help in grouping data into a set number of categories based on the data distribution.
2. Customizable Bins: You can define the exact breakpoints of the bins or let Pandas calculate these from the data to have equal-sized bins in terms of the range of values.

3. Labels: Optionally, you can label the bins with meaningful names instead of numeric intervals.

4. Including or Excluding Edges: You can specify whether the bins should include the rightmost edge or the leftmost edge, allowing for finer control over bin definitions.

pd.cut()'s Parameters:

The general syntax of pd.cut() is as follows:

pd.cut(x, bins, labels = None, right = True)

1. x: The input array-like object you want to bin. This could be a Pandas Series.

2. bins: This can be an integer specifying the number of equally spaced bins, or a sequence of bin edges.

3. labels: Optional array of strings providing labels for the bins.

4. right: Boolean value that indicates whether the bins include the right-most edge. Default is True.

Here's an example showing how to use `pd.cut ()` to categorize a series of ages into groups according to the settings of bins and labels:

```
In[#]:

import pandas as pd

# Sample data
ages = pd.Series([22, 55, 14, 42, 85, 18, 33, 61, 45, 41])

# Define number of bins to equally divide the range of the minimum and
maximum ages into four segments
bins = 4

# Customized labels for bins; if omitted, return the bin edges of
each range
labels=["Child", "Young Adult", "Adult", "Senior"]

# Bin data
age_groups = pd.cut(ages, bins = bins, labels = labels)

print(age_groups)
```

```
Out[#]:
0              Child
1              Adult
2              Child
3        Young Adult
4             Senior
5              Child
6        Young Adult
7              Adult
8        Young Adult
9        Young Adult
dtype: category
Categories (4, object): ["Child" < "Young Adult" < "Adult" < "Senior"]
```

In the example above, specifying `bins=4` in `pd.cut()` instructs the function to automatically segment the data range between the minimum and maximum values of your dataset (ages in this case) into four equally divided intervals or bins. Labels are assigned meaningful names rather than numerical intervals, enhancing readability. Additionally, you have the option to define a sequence of `bin edges` to customize the bin intervals. When customizing bin edges, ensure that the number of bin edges provided exceeds the number of labels (or segments) by one to accommodate the range properly.

```
In[#]:
# Define bins
bins = [0, 18, 35, 60, 100]

# Bin data
age_groups = pd.cut(ages, bins = bins, labels = labels)

print(age_groups)
```

```
Out[#]:
0        Young Adult
1              Adult
2              Child
3              Adult
4             Senior
5              Child
6        Young Adult
7             Senior
8              Adult
9              Adult
dtype: category
Categories (4, object): ["Child" < "Young Adult" < "Adult" <
  "Senior"]
```

The results differ from the previous example due to the use of different bins.

6.3.3 Data Import

As in previous chapters, we use the read_excel() method to import both the "Invoice" sheet from the "Bookstore-Ch06.xlsx" file into Pandas DataFrames:

```
In[#]:

import pandas as pd

filepath = "/Users/chi2019/Desktop/Book/Excel Files/Bookstore-Ch06.
xlsx" # Change the path according to your file location

# For Windows users, prefix r is added:
# filepath = r"C:\Users\chi2019\Desktop\Book\Excel Files\Bookstore-
Ch06.xlsx"

sales = pd.read_excel(filepath, sheet_name = "Invoice", header = 0,
usecols = "A:R", nrows = 2016)
print(sales.tail())
```

```
Out[#]:

        Invoice        Date        Item          Item Quantity  Discount  \
        Number                     Number
2011       998  2023-03-31    PI-007  Baseball Cap         1       0.0
2012       999  2023-03-31    PI-004         Scarf         3       0.2
2013       999  2023-03-31    PI-008           Mug         1       0.0
2014      1000  2023-03-31    PI-005        Gloves         1       0.1
2015      1000  2023-03-31    PI-016       Handbag         2       0.0

        Cost    List  Extension - Margin  Quantity in Stock  \
                Price  Discounted
2011    4.21    7.02       7.020   2.810                 14
2012    6.79   11.32      27.168   6.798                 39
2013   27.29   45.48      45.480  18.190                 38
2014   13.32   22.20      19.980   6.660                 17
2015   10.75   17.91      35.820  14.320                 16

         Emp ID          Name Start        Date  Weekly Payment Store ID  \
2011   EMP-008  Nathaniel Marquez  2022-09-07            1072   ST-004
2012   EMP-007       Carol Parker  2022-04-03            1175   ST-003
2013   EMP-007       Carol Parker  2022-04-03            1175   ST-003
2014   EMP-001   Bradley Marshall  2022-09-27            1084   ST-001
2015   EMP-001   Bradley Marshall  2022-09-27            1084   ST-001

       Store Name                                      Address
2011        South  2320 Saunders Square Suite 940, Los Angeles, C...
2012        North          078 Cindy Shore, Los Angeles, CA 96017
2013        North          078 Cindy Shore, Los Angeles, CA 96017
2014         East  98982 Adam Ports Suite 231, Los Angeles, CA 91696
2015         East  98982 Adam Ports Suite 231, Los Angeles, CA 91696
```

Q1: Add "Bonus Rate" column by referring to Q1's reference table and calculate each employee's bonus in "Bonus Amount" column.

First, we follow the method illustrated in Chapter 3 to create a pivot table summarizing sales, as well as margin, by employee:

In[#]:

```
by_emp_sales = pd.pivot_table(sales, index="Name", values=["Extension -
Discounted", "Margin"], aggfunc="sum")
by_emp_sales
```

Out[#]:

Name	Extension - Discounted	Margin
Adriana Cisneros	12138.6625	3988.6525
Bradley Marshall	10988.1590	3610.7190
Carol Parker	12011.5450	3815.3850
Daniel Marquez	9534.6885	3128.3185
Elizabeth Rodriguez	11908.3985	3819.8885
Kristin Lee	12333.5345	4002.8645
Nathaniel Marquez	12866.8670	4223.6570
Valerie Gibson	10641.4370	3472.5470

With the understanding of how pd.cut() works, we can efficiently create bins and labels to address Q1. It's important to note that we include an extra bin edge by using max(by_emp_sales["Extension - Discounted"]) to set the highest value as the upper limit. This approach adheres to the principle that the number of bin edges must be one more than the number of labels:

In[#]:

```
# Define bins; include an extra bin edge using the highest value
q1_bins = [0, 10000, 11000, 12000, max(by_emp_sales["Extension -
Discounted"])]

# Customized labels for bins according to Q1
q1_labels=[0.01, 0.03, 0.05, 0.08]

# Bin data
bonus_rates = pd.cut(by_emp_sales["Extension - Discounted"], bins =
q1_bins, labels = q1_labels)
bonus_rates
```

```
Out[#]:

Name
Adriana Cisneros        0.08
Bradley Marshall        0.03
Carol Parker            0.08
Daniel Marquez          0.01
Elizabeth Rodriguez     0.05
Kristin Lee             0.08
Nathaniel Marquez       0.08
Valerie Gibson          0.03
Name: Extension - Discounted, dtype: category
Categories (4, float64): [0.01 < 0.03 < 0.05 < 0.08]
```

The astype() Function

When you use the labels parameter in Pandas' cut() function, the resulting object is of type Categorical. By default, labels are often provided as strings or can be inferred as such, but you can assign numerical values (like bonus rates in Q1) as labels directly. However, even if you use numbers (floats or integers) as labels, the resulting Categorical data type does not change to float or int; it remains categorical, but with categories that are numerical values.

Since we need the resulting series for further calculations of bonus amount, we need to call Pandas' astype() function to convert the categorical result into a float type after the binning.

```
In[#]:

# Using astype(float) to convert categorical values into a float type
by_emp_sales["Bonus Rate"] = bonus_rates.astype(float)
```

Now, we can calculate the bonus amount:

```
In[#]:

by_emp_sales["Bonus Amount"] = by_emp_sales["Extension - Discounted"]
* by_emp_sales["Bonus Rate"]
by_emp_sales
```

Out[#]:

Name	Extension - Discounted	Margin	Bonus Rate	Bonus Amount
Adriana Cisneros	12138.6625	3988.6525	0.08	971.093000
Bradley Marshall	10988.1590	3610.7190	0.03	329.644770
Carol Parker	12011.5450	3815.3850	0.08	960.923600
Daniel Marquez	9534.6885	3128.3185	0.01	95.346885
Elizabeth Rodriguez	11908.3985	3819.8885	0.05	595.419925
Kristin Lee	12333.5345	4002.8645	0.08	986.682760
Nathaniel Marquez	12866.8670	4223.6570	0.08	1029.349360
Valerie Gibson	10641.4370	3472.5470	0.03	319.243110

Q2: Add "Performance Level" column by referring to Q2's reference table.

To address Q2, we can use a similar approach to Q1 to segment the by_emp_sales dataset:

In[#]:

```
# Define bins; include an extra bin edge using the highest value
q2_bins = [0, 2000, 3000, 3500, 4000, max(by_emp_sales["Margin"])]

# Customized labels for bins according to Q1
q2_labels=["Unsatisfied", "Developing", "Adequate", "Commendable",
"Outstanding"]

# Bin data
performance = pd.cut(by_emp_sales["Margin"], bins = q2_bins, labels =
q2_labels)
performance
```

Out[#]:

```
Name
Adriana Cisneros        Commendable
Bradley Marshall        Commendable
Carol Parker            Commendable
Daniel Marquez             Adequate
Elizabeth Rodriguez     Commendable
Kristin Lee             Outstanding
Nathaniel Marquez       Outstanding
Valerie Gibson             Adequate
Name: Margin, dtype: category
Categories (5, object): ["Unsatisfied" < "Developing" < "Adequate" <
"Commendable" < "Outstanding"]
```

In[#]:

```
by_emp_sales["Performance level"] = performance
by_emp_sales
```

Out[#]:

Name	Extension – Discounted	Margin	Bonus Rate	Bonus Amount	Performance level
Adriana Cisneros	12138.6625	3988.6525	0.08	971.093000	Commendable
Bradley Marshall	10988.1590	3610.7190	0.03	329.644770	Commendable
Carol Parker	12011.5450	3815.3850	0.08	960.923600	Commendable
Daniel Marquez	9534.6885	3128.3185	0.01	95.346885	Adequate
Elizabeth Rodriguez	11908.3985	3819.8885	0.05	595.419925	Commendable
Kristin Lee	12333.5345	4002.8645	0.08	986.682760	Outstanding
Nathaniel Marquez	12866.8670	4223.6570	0.08	1029.349360	Outstanding
Valerie Gibson	10641.4370	3472.5470	0.03	319.243110	Adequate

From Q1 and Q2, we know that the `pd.cut()` function in Pandas is used to segment and sort data values into bins or categories. This function is especially useful for converting a continuous variable into a categorical variable by categorizing data into specified intervals (bins) for further analysis, such as age groups, score ranges, or other quantitative intervals as illustrated in Q1 and Q2.

Q3: Pull out the records of "Baseball Cap" sales on 1/3/2023, and find the employee's name for that transaction.

To address Q3, we would develop a Boolean indexing to look up the records that satisfy the conditions:

In[#]:

```
# Define condition
cond_q3 = (sales["Item"] == "Baseball Cap") & (sales["Date"] == "1/
3/2023")

# Using boolean indexing for record lookups
q3 = sales[cond_q3]
print(q3)
```

```
Out[#]:

      Invoice Number      Date Item Number      Item  Quantity  Discount  \
72                37 2023-01-03      PI-007  Baseball Cap       1      0.15

      Cost  List Price  Extension - Discounted  Margin  Quantity in Stock  \
72   4.21        7.02                   5.967   1.757                 14

      Emp ID          Name Start Date  Weekly Payment Store ID Store Name  \
72   EMP-007  Carol Parker 2022-04-03           1175   ST-003       North

                                    Address
72   078 Cindy Shore, Los Angeles, CA 96017
```

To find employee's name, you can further retrieve it by the column label:

In[#]:

```
print(q3["Name"])
```

Out[#]:

```
72      Carol Parker
Name: Name, dtype: object
```

Q4: List the transaction details that meet either of the following criteria: 1) Hoodies sold by Daniel Marquez with a quantity of at least two units, or 2) Handbags sold by Elizabeth Rodriguez with no discount.

As shown below, we develop a lengthier compound condition to look up the records that satisfy the Q4 requirements:

In[#]:

```
# Define condition
cond_q4 = ((sales["Item"] == "Hoodie") & (sales["Name"] == "Daniel
Marquez") & (sales["Quantity"] >= 2)) | (
        (sales["Item"] == "Handbag") & (sales["Name"] ==
"Elizabeth Rodriguez") & (sales["Discount"] == 0))

# Using boolean indexing for record lookups
q4 = sales[cond_q4]
print(q4)
```

Out[#]:

```
      Invoice         Date Item Number    Item  Quantity  Discount  \
       Number
312       161 2023-01-15      PI-016  Handbag       2      0.00
670       345 2023-01-31      PI-001   Hoodie       2      0.15
1146      580 2023-02-21      PI-001   Hoodie       2      0.20
1473      738 2023-03-07      PI-001   Hoodie       2      0.00
1606      801 2023-03-13      PI-016  Handbag       2      0.00
1616      805 2023-03-13      PI-016  Handbag       3      0.00
```

```
          Cost    List    Extension -  Margin  Quantity in Stock  \
                  Price   Discounted
   312    10.75   17.91        35.820  14.320                  16
   670    26.00   43.34        73.678  21.678                  45
  1146    26.00   43.34        69.344  17.344                  45
  1473    26.00   43.34        86.680  34.680                  45
  1606    10.75   17.91        35.820  14.320                  16
  1616    10.75   17.91        53.730  21.480                  16

          Emp ID                 Name Start Date  Weekly  Store ID  \
                                                  Payment
   312    EMP-004  Elizabeth Rodriguez 2023-03-11    1144   ST-004
   670    EMP-003       Daniel Marquez 2023-02-08    1139   ST-003
  1146    EMP-003       Daniel Marquez 2023-02-08    1139   ST-003
  1473    EMP-003       Daniel Marquez 2023-02-08    1139   ST-003
  1606    EMP-004  Elizabeth Rodriguez 2023-03-11    1144   ST-004
  1616    EMP-004  Elizabeth Rodriguez 2023-03-11    1144   ST-004

        Store Name                                          Address
   312       South  2320 Saunders Square Suite 940, Los Angeles, C...
   670       North         078 Cindy Shore, Los Angeles, CA 96017
  1146       North         078 Cindy Shore, Los Angeles, CA 96017
  1473       North         078 Cindy Shore, Los Angeles, CA 96017
  1606       South  2320 Saunders Square Suite 940, Los Angeles, C...
  1616       South  2320 Saunders Square Suite 940, Los Angeles, C...
```

Remember, when using & and | in Python, ensure that individual conditions are wrapped in parentheses to avoid errors. If a compound condition is lengthy, you can use line breaks within an open parenthesis, as shown in cond_q4 above. Python allows line breaks within parentheses, square brackets, and curly braces for better readability, but avoid line breaks outside these enclosures unless explicitly continued with a backslash (\), which specifies that the statement continues on the next line.

Q5: With Q4's conditions, calculate: 1) the record count, 2) the total and 3) average sales (Sum and Average of Extension – Discounted), 4) the latest date of sale, and 5) the minimum quantity sold.

To address Question 5, we employ the aggregation functions – count, sum, mean, max, and min – that were introduced in Chapter 3. We start by creating an empty Series object and then sequentially assign the results of each aggregation, as each element demands a different aggregation function:

In[#]:

```
q5 = pd.Series()
q5
```

Out[#]:

```
Series([], dtype: object)
```

In[#]:

```
q5["Record Count"] = q4["Name"].count()
q5["Total Sales"] = q4["Extension - Discounted"].sum()
q5["Average Sales"] = q4["Extension - Discounted"].mean()
q5["Latest Date of Sale"] = q4["Date"].max()
q5["Minimum Quantity Sold"] = q4["Quantity"].min()
print(q5)
```

Out[#]:

```
Record Count                              6.0
Total Sales                           355.072
Average Sales                       59.178667
Latest Date of Sale       2023-03-13 00:00:00
Minimum Quantity Sold                       2
dtype: object
```

6.4 DISCUSSIONS

Record lookup and data segmentation are indispensable in data science, each serving distinct purposes – data segmentation for categorizing continuous data into bins and record lookup for querying or further manipulating data based on conditions. Python's `pd.cut()` and Pandas' `Boolean indexing` offer more programmatic flexibility and are better suited for automated, large-scale data manipulations than Excel's VLOOKUP and database functions:

1. Data Segmentation:
   1) Python's pd.cut() is specifically designed for segmenting continuous numerical data into defined intervals (bins), making it perfect for categorical grouping and data analysis. It allows for precise definition of bin edges, either manually or automatically, and can apply descriptive labels to each bin for clarity and ease of analysis. It also supports complex configurations like inclusion or exclusion of bin edges and handling the lowest data values specially to ensure accurate categorization.
   2) Excel's VLOOKUP is often used for range lookups, where it finds the closest match to a specified value in a sorted column, returning a corresponding value from another column. This can be used for categorizing data into predefined ranges. It requires the data to be sorted for approximate matches and is less flexible due to its certain rules or limitations. However, VLOOKUP's approximate

match can be easier for users familiar with Excel and not proficient in programming.

2. Record Lookup:

1) Python's Boolean indexing allows for filtering and manipulating data frames based on complex logical conditions applied across multiple columns. It supports immediate and interactive data querying and modification directly in the script. It is highly efficient with large datasets, allowing complex queries and operations without significant performance issues. It also offers the flexibility to create complex conditions and immediately apply changes to the dataset, facilitating advanced data manipulation and cleaning.

2) Excel's database functions like DSUM, DAVERAGE, and others allow for performing calculations on subsets of data defined by specific criteria. These are analogous to performing conditional aggregations. They might be more accessible for users without programming skills, as they use a formula-based approach within Excel's GUI. However, setting up complex criteria ranges can be less intuitive than Boolean indexing in Python. Additionally, despite it being well-suited for smaller datasets or isolated tasks, as the data size and complexity of queries increase, performance can become a limiting factor.

In sum, while Excel provides a user-friendly interface and is sufficient for smaller datasets or simpler tasks, Pandas is more robust for complex data segmentation and record lookup, especially when dealing with large volumes of data.

6.5 EXERCISES

Using the concepts covered in this chapter, complete the following exercises using "Exercise-Ch06.xlsx" as your dataset.

E1: Create a pivot table grouped by **Supplier**, add a new column to the pivot table labeled "**Category**" by referring to the reference table below.

Purchase Amount	Category
0	Basic
$2,000	Moderate
$5,500	Preferred
$7,000	Premium

E2: List the transaction details that meet either of the following criteria: 1) **Ground Coffee** sold by **JavaFlow Packaging** with a quantity of at least 10 units, or 2) **Coffee Beans** sold by **JavaFlow Packaging** with a discount no less than 10%.

E3: With E2's conditions, instead of displaying the records, calculate the following statistics: 1) the record **count**, 2) the **total** and 3) **average** purchase amounts (**Sum and Average of**), 4) the latest **date** of purchase, and 5) the minimum **quantity** purchased.

## CHAPTER 7

Text Processing

TEXT PROCESSING PLAYS A crucial role in helping businesses extract insights from textual data, which is abundant in sources like customer reviews, emails, social media, and internal reports. By analyzing text, organizations can uncover patterns, identify customer sentiment, and detect emerging trends that inform strategic decisions. For example, businesses can refine their marketing strategies based on feedback analysis, improve customer satisfaction by addressing common complaints, or obtain the technological frontier by tracking industry-related keywords. Whether applied to small-scale tasks or large datasets, text analytics empowers businesses to transform unstructured information into valuable intelligence. However, unlike structured data, which you have analyzed in previous chapters using tools like formulas, pivot tables, or aggregation functions, text lacks a machine-readable format. As a result, it requires additional processing to extract structure and meaning before it can be effectively analyzed.

Both Excel and Python offer effective tools for handling textual data. Excel provides a suite of text functions designed primarily for character-based processing. These functions enable users to manipulate, extract, and transform text in a straightforward, formula-driven approach, making them accessible for a wide range of tasks such as cleaning and formatting

 DOI: 10.1201/9781003567103-8

data. Python, on the other hand, provides similar capabilities through its string methods, which are equally intuitive but offer more flexibility. Python's approach allows users to manipulate text with methods well-suited for tasks like trimming spaces, splitting strings into parts, or replacing specific characters.

In addition to character-based methods, Python extends the capabilities of text processing through its specialized libraries. While Python's built-in string methods excel in character-based manipulation similar to Excel, its additional libraries, like NLTK (Natural Language Toolkit), enable more advanced, term-based text analytics, such as tokenization, sentiment analysis, and natural language understanding. This difference highlights how Excel's approach caters to simpler, formulaic tasks, whereas Python provides a scalable solution for more complex text analytics.

In this chapter, we will compare Excel's text functions with Python's string-related methods, emphasizing their similarities and differences. Additionally, we will briefly discuss how Python's libraries broaden the scope of text processing, making it suitable for tasks that go beyond Excel's capabilities.

7.1 TEXT PROCESSING WITH BOOKSTORE DATASET

We will use the "Bookstore-Ch07.xlsx" file to explore data visualization tools in both Excel and Python. For simplicity, the workbook contains three small worksheets: "Text", "Employee", and "Store". The "Text" sheet is designed for practicing fundamental character-based functions in both Excel and Python. It features the widely recognized pangram, "The quick brown fox jumps over the lazy dog", often used as a test sentence because it contains all the letters of the English alphabet. The "Employee" and "Store" sheets are derived from the original "Invoice" sheet and serve as examples for applying text functions in the Bookstore scenario. Before beginning the exercises, take a moment to familiarize yourself with these sheets.

Q1: On the "Text" sheet, complete the tasks specified in columns B through L using fundamental character-based text functions.

Q2: On the "Employee" sheet, create new columns for each employee's first name, last name, and email address. The email address follows the format: Lastname_Firstname@bk.com.

Q3: On the "Store" sheet, extract the street, city, and zip code from the store address.

Q4: For stores where the street address contains "Suite" or "Apt.", return "Complex Building". Otherwise, return "Standalone Unit".

7.2 EXCEL

Excel offers a variety of character-based text functions to solve the questions outlined above. These functions form the foundation for manipulating text in Excel and are essential for cleaning and organizing data efficiently:

- **LEN**: Calculates the total number of characters in a text string, including spaces and punctuation marks. It's useful for understanding the length of a string.
  Example: =LEN("Excel") returns 5.
- **SEARCH**: Finds the position of a specific character or substring within a text string. Note that it's case insensitive.
  Example: =SEARCH("x", "Excel") returns 2.
- **LEFT**: Extracts a specified number of characters from the leftmost character of a string.
  Example: =LEFT("Excel", 2) returns "Ex".
- **RIGHT**: Extracts a specified number of characters from the rightmost character of a string.
  Example: =RIGHT("Excel", 2) returns "el".
- **MID**: Extracts a specified number of characters from a text string, starting at a given position.
  Example: =MID("Excel", 2, 2) returns "xc".
- **CONCAT**: Concatenates multiple strings into one. Alternatively, you can use the & operator to achieve the same result.
  Example: =CONCAT("Hello", " ", "World") returns "Hello World", or ="Hello" & " " & "World" produces the same result.
- **SUBSTITUTE**: Replaces a specified text within a string with another text.
  Example: =SUBSTITUTE("Excel is fun", "fun", "useful") returns "Excel is useful".
- **UPPER**: Converts all characters in a string to uppercase.
  Example: =UPPER("Excel") returns "EXCEL".
- **LOWER**: Converts all characters in a string to lowercase.
  Example: =LOWER("Excel") returns "excel".
- **PROPER**: Capitalizes the first letter of each word in a string and converts the rest to lowercase.

Example: =PROPER("excel functions") returns "Excel Functions".

- **TEXTSPLIT**: Splits a text string into an array based on specified delimiters to return the split words respectively.

  Example: =TEXTSPLIT("Excel,Text,Functions", ",") returns "Excel", "Text", "Functions" in separate columns.

Q1: On the "Text" sheet, complete the tasks specified in columns B through L using fundamental character-based text functions.

1. In cell **B2**, use the **LEN()** function with the following formula:

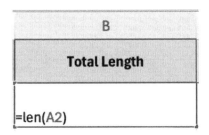

The result will be 44.

2. In cell **C2**, create a **SEARCH()** formula and use the formula builder to set up the first two parameters as follows:

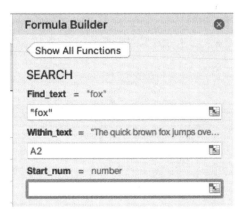

The result will be 17.

3. In cell **D2**, create a **LEFT()** formula and use the formula builder to set up the two parameters as follows:

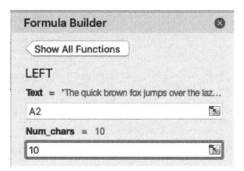

The result will be "The quick ". Note that there is a space after "quick" because the formula retrieves 10 characters from the left side, including the space.

4. In cell **E2**, create a **RIGHT()** formula and use the formula builder to set up the two parameters as follows:

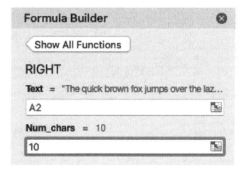

The result will be " lazy dog." with a space before "lazy" and ending with the "." This is because the formula retrieves 10 characters from the right side, including spaces and punctuation.

5. In cell **F2**, create a **MID()** formula and use the formula builder to set up the three parameters as follows:

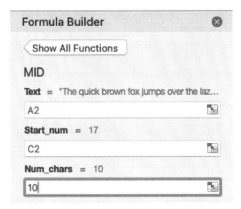

Note that in Start_num, we reference the search result from cell **C2**. This means we create a nested function by embedding SEARCH() inside MID() to dynamically use the search result rather than a fixed number. The result will be "fox jumps ". Once again, note the space after "jumps".

6. In cell **G2**, create a **CONCAT()** formula and use the formula builder to set up the strings to be concatenated as below:

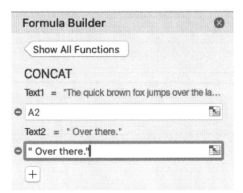

The result will be "The quick brown fox jumps over the lazy dog. Over there." Alternatively, you can use the & operator to combine the two strings directly.

7. In cell **H2**, use the **SUBSTITUTE()** function and use the formula builder to set up the three parameters as follows:

The result will be "The quick brown fox jumps over the funny dog." Alternatively, you can try using the **REPLACE()** function.

8. Cells **I2**, **J2**, and **K2** demonstrate case-changing operations. Use the functions **UPPER()**, **LOWER()**, and **PROPER()** respectively, and verify the results yourself.

9. In cell **L2**, create a **TEXTSPLIT()** formula and use the formula builder to configure the first two parameters. Make sure to set the **Col_delimiter** to " " since the sentence uses spaces as the word delimiter. You may omit other optional parameters as follows:

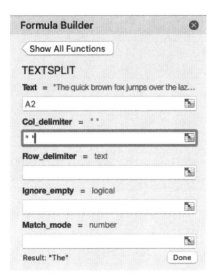

The result will appear as the screenshot below. The sentence is split into an array based on the specified delimiter " ", with each word displayed in a separate column.

L	M	N	O	P	Q	R	S	T
Split Words								
The	quick	brown	fox	jumps	over	the	lazy	dog.

Q2: On the "Employee" sheet, create new columns for each employee's first name, last name, and email address. The email address follows the format: Lastname_Firstname@bk.com.

To address **Q2**, we may use **TEXTSPLIT()** with " " as the delimiter to quickly separate the employee's first name and last name. However, to demonstrate another common approach, we'll use **LEFT()** and **RIGHT()** in combination with **SEARCH()**.

1. The **LEFT()** function can extract the first few characters of a string based on a specified length. However, since each employee's first name varies in length, we'll need to use the **SEARCH()** function within the **Num_chars** parameter to determine the position of the delimiter " ". By further subtracting 1 from the position of " ", we can obtain the exact length of the first name. In cell **F2**, we create the nested **LEFT()** function as shown in the screenshots below:

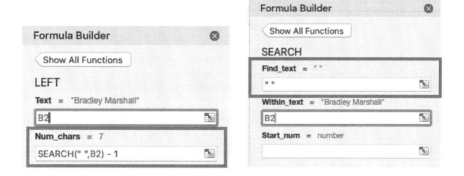

The results, after filling the formula down, are shown below:

2. The **RIGHT**() function extracts the last few characters of a string based on a specified length. Again, since each employee's last name varies in length, we first use the **SEARCH**() function to find the position of the delimiter " ". Next, we use the **LEN**() function to determine the total length of the full name and subtract the delimiter's position from it to calculate the exact length of the last name. In cell **G2**, we create the nested **RIGHT**() function as shown in the screenshots below:

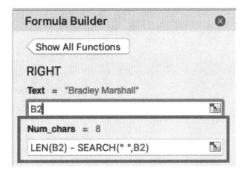

The results are as shown below:

G
Last Name
Marshall
Gibson
Marquez
Rodriguez
Cisneros
Lee
Parker
Marquez

3. After extracting the employee's first and last names, you can use either the **CONCAT**() function or the **&** operator to generate their email addresses. Refer to the screenshot below to verify your results:

H
Email Address
Marshall_Bradley@bk.com
Gibson_Valerie@bk.com
Marquez_Daniel@bk.com
Rodriguez_Elizabeth@bk.com
Cisneros_Adriana@bk.com
Lee_Kristin@bk.com
Parker_Carol@bk.com
Marquez_Nathaniel@bk.com

Q3: On the "Store" sheet, extract the street, city, and zip code from the store address.

To solve **Q3**, we will use **TEXTSPLIT()** with ", " as the delimiter to quickly split the store address into street, city, and zip code.

1. In cell **D2**, create a **TEXTSPLIT()** formula and use the formula builder to configure the first two parameters. Make sure to set the **Col_delimiter** to ", " since the store address uses ", " as the delimiter. You may omit other optional parameters as follows:

2. Add column labels and fill the formula down. The results are as shown below:

D	E	F
Street	**City**	**Zip Code**
98982 Adam Ports Suite 231	Los Angeles	CA 91696
845 Lloyd Walk Apt. 693	Los Angeles	CA 91326
078 Cindy Shore	Los Angeles	CA 96017
2320 Saunders Square Suite 940	Los Angeles	CA 91101

Q4: For stores where the street address contains "Suite" or "Apt.", return "Complex Building". Otherwise, return "Standalone Unit".

Q4 is a typical text search question. However, when the **SEARCH()** function cannot find the specified keyword (like "Suite" or "Apt." in this case) in a text string, it returns an error (**#VALUE!**). This happens because **SEARCH()** expects to locate the keyword and return its position, but if the keyword is absent, no valid position exists. To handle such cases, we generally use the **ISERROR**() function to catch these errors. **ISERROR**() checks if the result of **SEARCH**() is an error and returns **TRUE** if an error occurs (**not found**), or **FALSE** otherwise (**found**). This allows us to build more robust formulas by detecting and responding to errors instead of letting them disrupt the calculation. For example, we can use **IF** in combination with **ISERROR**() to specify alternative actions when a search fails.

1. In cell G2, we first create an IF(), and in its Logical_test parameter, add an AND() function as below:

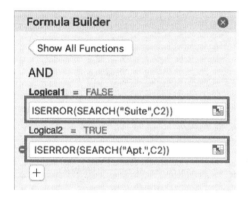

The combined test of the two **ISERROR**() functions returns **TRUE** only when an address does not contain either "Suite" or "Apt."; otherwise, it returns **FALSE**. This indicates that the store is in a "Standalone Unit" rather than a "Complex Building".

2. Based on the logical analysis from Step 1, we determine that "Standalone Unit" should assigned to the Value_if_true parameter, and "Complex Building" to the Value_if_false parameter:

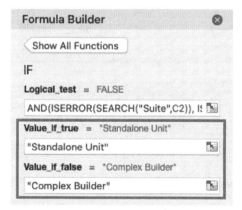

3. Verify your answers with the screenshot below:

G
Q4
Complex Builder
Complex Builder
Standalone Unit
Complex Builder

7.3 PYTHON

Please refer to the Jupyter notebook file "Bookstore-Ch07.ipynb" to access the code, or view the "Bookstore-Ch07.html" file to see the outputs of all code.

7.3.1 Python's String Type

Strings as Lists

Python is an excellent tool for working with text. In Python, strings (`str`) behave similarly to an ordered list of characters. You can think of the `str` type as a specialized form of a `list` because, like lists, strings allow you to access individual elements using indexing. Recall that Python uses `zero-based indexing`, meaning the first character in a string is at index 0, the second at index 1, and so on. Additionally, Python offers `negative indexing`, which lets you access characters starting from the end of the string, where -1 refers to the last character, -2 to the second-to-last, and so forth.

The table below demonstrates how both `zero-based indexing` and `negative indexing` can be used to access characters in the string "Python":

Zero-based Indexing	0	1	2	3	4	5
Content	P	y	t	h	o	n
Negative Indexing	-6	-5	-4	-3	-2	-1

String Indexing

To access a character in a string or string variable, use its index number inside square brackets (e.g., [0]). Below is an example of using `zero-based indexing` to print each character in a string one at a time:

In[#]:

```
s = "Python" # Print each character in s using `zero-based indexing`:
print(s[0])
print(s[1])
print(s[2])
print(s[3])
print(s[4])
print(s[5])
```

Out[#]:

```
P
y
t
h
o
n
```

Now, let's try negative indexing:

In[#]:

```
print(s[-6]) # Print each character using `negative indexing`:
print(s[-5])
print(s[-4])
print(s[-3])
print(s[-2])
print(s[-1])
```

Out[#]:

```
P
y
t
h
o
n
```

In[#]:

```
"create"[1] # You can, actually, use square brackets to access any
part of an undefined string
```

Out[#]:

```
"r"
```

Checking for a Substring

The easiest way to check if a specific sequence of characters is present in a string is by using the `in` keyword.

In[#]:

```
print("thon" in s)
```

Out[#]:

```
True
```

You may also check if a phrase is `not` in a string:

```
In[#]:
print("Path" not in s)
Out[#]:
True
```

Looping through a String

Since strings are lists (thereby iterables), you can use a `for` loop to process each character in a string, as discussed in Chapter 3. The `for` loop is a powerful tool for performing repetitive actions on each element in a data sequence, such as a range of numbers, a string, a list, a dictionary, or an array. When using a `for` loop, you define a `loop` variable (e.g., i, j, x, y, etc.) to represent each element of the sequence during the loop's execution. In the example below, s is the `iterable` (the string), and `char` is the loop variable, representing each character of the string as the loop iterates:

```
In[#]:
for char in s: # a temporary variable or iterator "char" is specified
to represent each character in s
    print(char)
Out[#]:
p
y
t
h
o
n
```

Since each character can be accessed using an index number, we may also print all s[i] in a loop:

```
In[#]:
for i in range(len(s)): # temporary variable "i" represents the index
number from 0 to 5
    print(s[i])     # print all s[i] using a for loop
Out[#]:
p
y
t
h
o
n
```

Slicing a String

Often, you'll need to extract a specific portion of a string for further processing. Python makes this easy with a feature called `slicing`, which allows you to retrieve a substring by specifying a range of indices. To slice a string, provide the start index and the end index, separated by a colon and enclosed in square brackets. Python will return the substring starting at the start index and ending just before the end index (i.e., up to but `not` including the end index). The exclusion of the end index is similar to the `iloc slicing` introduced in Chapter 4.

NOTE: The rule for slicing is straightforward: the start index is always included, while the end index is always excluded (unless it is omitted). If the start index is omitted, slicing begins from the first character. For example, with an end index of 4, the slice returns characters from index 0 to 3 (up to but not including 4), as shown below:

```
In[#]:

s1 = s[:4] # Omitting the start index and with end index of 4
print(s1)

Out[#]:

Pyth

In[#]:

s2 = s[2:4] # start index: 2, end index: 4, this slicing returns
characters from 2 to 3 (4-1)
print(s2)

Out[#]:

Th
```

You can also perform slicing using negative indexing, where the starting index is included:

```
In[#]:

s3 = s[-3:]
print(s3)

In[#]:

hon
```

Modifying a String

Strings in Python are `immutable`, meaning their content cannot be changed once they are created. Each character is considered an integral part of the string, so you cannot directly overwrite any of them. However, you can create a new string by performing operations on the original one and assigning the result to a new variable. For instance, you can use the `replace()` method to substitute a substring with a new one. Keep in mind that the original string remains unchanged unless you explicitly assign the modified string to a new variable:

```
In[#]:

s.replace("y","a") # use replace() to change any "y" to "a" in s

Out[#]:

"Pathon"

In[#]:

print(s) # s remains the same since it is immutable

Out[#]:

Python

In[#]:

ss=s.replace("y","a") # but you may assign the result to a new
variable ss
print(ss)

Out[#]:

Pathon
```

Concatenating Strings

In Python, you can use the + operator to concatenate multiple strings easily. However, keep in mind that while + is used to join strings, the * operator can also be applied to strings for repetition. Other mathematical operators, like − or /, are not valid for string operations.

```
In[#]:

a = "Hello World!"

print(a + " " + s + "!") # string concatenation

Out[#]:

Hello World! Python!

Out[#]:

print(s*5) # string repetition
PythonPythonPythonPythonPython
```

Other String Methods

Python provides several methods to transform strings and create new ones by assigning the result to a new variable. Here are some commonly used methods:

1. upper(): Converts the entire string to uppercase.
2. lower(): Converts the entire string to lowercase.
3. title(): Capitalizes the first letter of each word in the string.
4. strip(): Removes all leading and trailing spaces from the string.
5. split(): Splits the string into a list of substrings based on a specified separator or delimiter.

Note: The default delimiter for the split() method in Python is any whitespace. This includes spaces, tabs (\t), and newlines (\n). Multiple consecutive whitespace characters are treated as a single delimiter. Each of these methods returns a new string while leaving the original string unchanged.

```
In[#]:

a = "Hello, World!"
a1 = a.split(", ") # Split a according to the delimiter to return a
list of segmented words
print(a1)
type(a1) # aa becomes a list

Out[#]:

["Hello", "World!"]
list

In[#]:

a = a + " "*10 # Append 10 spaces to the end of a and assign the
result back to a
a

Out[#]:

"Hello, World!          "

In[#]:

a = a.strip() # Use strip() to remove tailing spaces
a

Out[#]:

"Hello, World!"
```

Q1: Complete the fundamental character-based text processing.
With the string methods, we can solve Q1 as follows:

```
In[#]:
fox = "The quick brown fox jumps over the lazy dog."

len(fox) # Get the length of the test sentence
```
Out[#]:
```
44
```
In[#]:
```
position = fox.find("fox") # Use find() to get the position of "fox"; -
1 if not found
print(position)
```
Out[#]:
```
16
```
In[#]:
```
print(fox[:10]) # Slice the first 10 characters from 0 to 9 (10 is
excluded)
```
Out[#]:
```
The quick
```
In[#]:
```
print(fox[-10:]) # Slice the last 10 characters from -10
(included) to -1
```
Out[#]:
```
lazy dog.
```
In[#]:
```
print(fox[position:(position+10)]) # Slice 10 characters from the
position of "fox"
```
Out[#]:
```
fox jumps
```
In[#]:
```
print(fox + " Over there.") # Use + for string concatenation
```
Out[#]:
```
The quick brown fox jumps over the lazy dog. Over there.
```
In[#]:
```
print(fox.replace("lazy", "funny")) # Use replace() to modify the
test sentence
```
Out[#]:
```
The quick brown fox jumps over the funny dog.
```
In[#]:
```
print(fox.upper())
print(fox.lower())
print(fox.title())
```

```
Out[#]:

THE QUICK BROWN FOX JUMPS OVER THE LAZY DOG.
the quick brown fox jumps over the lazy dog.
The Quick Brown Fox Jumps Over The Lazy Dog.
```

```
In[#]:

print(fox.split()) # Use split() to split the sentence to return a
list of segmented words
```

```
Out[#]:

["The", "quick", "brown", "fox", "jumps", "over", "the", "lazy",
"dog."]
```

Using String Methods in Pandas

Functions like strip(), title(), split() and others are built-in
Python string methods and can be applied to individual strings. However,
when dealing with a textual column in a Pandas DataFrame, these methods
cannot be directly applied to the entire column because the column is
treated as a Pandas Series, not a plain Python string. To apply these string
methods to a column in a DataFrame, you need to use Pandas' .str
accessor, which provides vectorized string operations for Series objects. In
the following questions, we will use the Bookstore data frame to demonstrate how you can use these functions with a DataFrame's textual columns.

7.3.2 Text Processing with Bookstore Data Using Pandas

As in Chapter 5, we use the read_excel() method to import all sheets from
the "Bookstore-Ch07.xlsx" at once:

```
In[#]:

import pandas as pd

filepath = "/Users/chi2019/Desktop/Book/Excel Files/Bookstore-Ch07.
xlsx" # Change the path according to your file location

# For Windows users, prefix r is added:
# filepath = r"C:\Users\chi2019\Desktop\Book\Excel Files\Bookstore-
Ch07.xlsx"

df = pd.read_excel(filepath, sheet_name = None)
df
```

```
Out[#]:

{"Text":                                         Text    Total Length  \
 0   The quick brown fox jumps over the lazy dog          NaN

       Position of "fox"  First 10 Characters  Last 10 Characters  \
 0                  17                    NaN                 NaN
```

```
       10 Characters from "fox"  Add "Over there"  Replace "lazy" with
"funny"  \
0                         NaN                 NaN                    NaN

       Uppercase  Lowercase  Capitalize Words  Split Words
0            NaN        NaN               NaN          NaN  ,
"Employee": Emp ID                 Name  Store         Date       Weekly
                                          Start                  Payment
       0    EMP-001    Bradley Marshall  ST-001  2022-09-27        1084
       1    EMP-002      Valerie Gibson  ST-002  2022-04-09        1115
       2    EMP-003      Daniel Marquez  ST-003  2023-02-08        1139
       3    EMP-004  Elizabeth Rodriguez ST-004  2023-03-11        1144
       4    EMP-005    Adriana Cisneros  ST-001  2022-04-13        1150
       5    EMP-006        Kristin Lee   ST-002  2022-01-05        1013
       6    EMP-007        Carol Parker  ST-003  2022-04-03        1175
       7    EMP-008   Nathaniel Marquez  ST-004  2022-09-07        1072,
"Store":   Store ID Store Name                                   Address
       0    ST-001    East  98982 Adam Ports Suite 231, Los Angeles, CA 91696
       1    ST-002    West      845 Lloyd Walk Apt. 693, Los Angeles, CA 91326
       2    ST-003   North            078 Cindy Shore, Los Angeles, CA 96017
       3    ST-004   South  2320 Saunders Square Suite 940, Los Angeles, C...}
```

We then assign more descriptive DataFrame names to the two dictionary entries:

In[#]:

```
emp = df["Employee"]
store = df["Store"]
emp, store
```

Out[#]:

```
(   Emp ID                 Name   Store  Start Date  Weekly Payment
 0  EMP-001    Bradley Marshall  ST-001  2022-09-27            1084
 1  EMP-002      Valerie Gibson  ST-002  2022-04-09            1115
 2  EMP-003      Daniel Marquez  ST-003  2023-02-08            1139
 3  EMP-004  Elizabeth Rodriguez ST-004  2023-03-11            1144
 4  EMP-005    Adriana Cisneros  ST-001  2022-04-13            1150
 5  EMP-006        Kristin Lee   ST-002  2022-01-05            1013
 6  EMP-007        Carol Parker  ST-003  2022-04-03            1175
 7  EMP-008   Nathaniel Marquez  ST-004  2022-09-07            1072,
   Store ID Store Name                                          Address
 0  ST-001    East  98982 Adam Ports Suite 231, Los Angeles, CA 91696
 1  ST-002    West      845 Lloyd Walk Apt. 693, Los Angeles, CA 91326
 2  ST-003   North            078 Cindy Shore, Los Angeles, CA 96017
 3  ST-004   South  2320 Saunders Square Suite 940, Los Angeles, C...)
```

Q2: On the "Employee" sheet, create new columns for each employee's first name, last name, and email address. The email address follows the format: Lastname_Firstname@bk.com.

To address Q2, we can apply slicing as demonstrated in Q1. However, as previously noted, combining slicing with find() for a textual column in a DataFrame requires row-wise processing, which can be inefficient for larger datasets. In contrast, using `str.split()` is more efficient, concise, and Pythonic, especially when paired with `unpacking` assignments:

In[#]:

```
emp[["First Name", "Last Name"]] = emp["Name"].str.split(expand=True)
emp
```

Out[#]:

	Emp ID	Name	Store	Start Date	Weekly Payment	First Name	Last Name
0	EMP-001	Bradley Marshall	ST-001	2022-09-27	1084	Bradley	Marshall
1	EMP-002	Valerie Gibson	ST-002	2022-04-09	1115	Valerie	Gibson
2	EMP-003	Daniel Marquez	ST-003	2023-02-08	1139	Daniel	Marquez
3	EMP-004	Elizabeth Rodriguez	ST-004	2023-03-11	1144	Elizabeth	Rodriguez
4	EMP-005	Adriana Cisneros	ST-001	2022-04-13	1150	Adriana	Cisneros
5	EMP-006	Kristin Lee	ST-002	2022-01-05	1013	Kristin	Lee
6	EMP-007	Carol Parker	ST-003	2022-04-03	1175	Carol	Parker
7	EMP-008	Nathaniel Marquez	ST-004	2022-09-07	1072	Nathaniel	Marquez

In the snippet above, we accomplished the following tasks in a single line:

- emp["Name"].str: Accesses the string methods for the "Name" column, allowing you to apply string-specific operations to each element of the series.
- .split(): Splits each string in the column at each whitespace delimiter. This separates the first name and last name in this case.
- expand=True: This argument tells Pandas to put the results into separate columns rather than a list. Without expand=True, the split operation would return a Series of lists.
- emp[["First Name", "Last Name"]] = ...: unpacking the split results and assign the resulting series to two new columns respectively.

Now, we can generate the email addresses as required:

```
In[#]:

emp["Email Address"] = emp["Last Name"] + "_" + emp["First Name"] +
"@bk.com"
emp
```

Out[#]:

	Emp ID	Name	Store	Start Date	Weekly Payment	First Name	Last Name	Email Address
0	EMP-001	Bradley Marshall	ST-001	2022-09-27	1084	Bradley	Marshall	Marshall_ Bradley@bk. com
1	EMP-002	Valerie Gibson	ST-002	2022-04-09	1115	Valerie	Gibson	Gibson_ Valerie@bk. com
2	EMP-003	Daniel Marquez	ST-003	2023-02-08	1139	Daniel	Marquez	Marquez_ Daniel@bk. com
3	EMP-004	Elizabeth Rodriguez	ST-004	2023-03-11	1144	Elizabeth	Rodriguez	Rodriguez_ Elizabeth@bk. com
4	EMP-005	Adriana Cisneros	ST-001	2022-04-13	1150	Adriana	Cisneros	Cisneros_ Adriana@bk. com
5	EMP-006	Kristin Lee	ST-002	2022-01-05	1013	Kristin	Lee	Lee_ Kristin@bk. com
6	EMP-007	Carol Parker	ST-003	2022-04-03	1175	Carol	Parker	Parker_ Carol@bk. com
7	EMP-008	Nathaniel Marquez	ST-004	2022-09-07	1072	Nathaniel	Marquez	Marquez_ Nathaniel@bk. com

Q3: On the "Store" sheet, extract the street, city, and zip code from the store address.

We can use Q2's string splitting approach to address Q3:

```
In[#]:

store[["Street", "City", "Zip Code"]] = store["Address"].str.split(",
", expand=True)
store
```

Out[#]:

	Store ID	Store Name	Address	Street	City	Zip Code
0	ST-001	East	98982 Adam Ports Suite 231, Los Angeles, CA 91696	98982 Adam Ports Suite 231	Los Angeles	CA 91696
1	ST-002	West	845 Lloyd Walk Apt. 693, Los Angeles, CA 91326	845 Lloyd Walk Apt. 693	Los Angeles	CA 91326
2	ST-003	North	078 Cindy Shore, Los Angeles, CA 96017	078 Cindy Shore	Los Angeles	CA 96017
3	ST-004	South	2320 Saunders Square Suite 940, Los Angeles, C...	2320 Saunders Square Suite 940	Los Angeles	CA 91101

Q4: For stores where the street address contains "Suite" or "Apt.", return "Complex Building". Otherwise, return "Standalone Unit".

As demonstrated earlier, we use the in keyword to check if a substring exists in a single string or to check for membership in iterable objects like lists. However, when working with a Pandas Series (such as a textual column in a DataFrame), you need to use the .str.contains() method to check if a substring is present in each string of the column.

In[#]:
```
# Check if "East" is in each string of the "Store Name" column
east = store["Store Name"].str.contains("East")
east
```

Out[#]:
```
0    True
1    False
2    False
3    False
Name: Store Name, dtype: bool
```

Now, we can create the conditions and use np.where() to solve Q4. Please review Chapter 5 for the usage of np.where().

```
In[#]:

import numpy as np

cond_q4 = (store["Address"].str.contains("Suite")) |
(store["Address"].str.contains("Apt."))
cond_q4
```

Out[#]:

```
0    True
1    True
2    False
3    True
Name: Address, dtype: bool
```

```
In[#]:

store["Q4"] = np.where(cond_q4, "Complex Building",
"Standalone Unit")
store
```

Out[#]:

	Store ID	Store Name	Address	Street	City	Zip Code	Q4
0	ST-001	East	98982 Adam Ports Suite 231, Los Angeles, CA 91696	98982 Adam Ports Suite 231	Los Angeles	CA 91696	Complex Building
1	ST-002	West	845 Lloyd Walk Apt. 693, Los Angeles, CA 91326	845 Lloyd Walk Apt. 693	Los Angeles	CA 91326	Complex Building
2	ST-003	North	078 Cindy Shore, Los Angeles, CA 96017	078 Cindy Shore	Los Angeles	CA 96017	Standalone Unit
3	ST-004	South	2320 Saunders Square Suite 940, Los Angeles, C...	2320 Saunders Square Suite 940	Los Angeles	CA 91101	Complex Building

Note that the condition we developed differs from Excel's solution for Q4. In Excel, we cannot directly use OR to solve Q4 because ISERROR() returns TRUE only when an error is present. This requires reversing the logical conditions when using ISERROR(). In contrast, Python's `np.where()` supports any logical expressions directly. Additionally, the `.str.contains()` method in Python is more straightforward than Excel's SEARCH() function. As a result, the cond_q4 solution in Python is more concise, readable, and intuitive compared to Excel's approach.

7.4 DISCUSSIONS

1. Functionality and Flexibility
   1) Excel: Offers basic text-processing functions such as LEFT(), RIGHT(), MID(), SEARCH(), and ISERROR(). These are sufficient for straightforward tasks like substring extraction, finding a character, or handling errors. However, these functions can become cumbersome when dealing with complex logic. For instance, combining multiple functions to handle nested logic or error conditions requires creative workarounds, making the formulas lengthy and less readable.
   2) Python: Provides a rich set of string manipulation methods (.split(), .strip(), .replace(), .contains(), etc.) that are both straightforward and versatile. Vectorized operations through Pandas make it possible to process entire columns of text efficiently. Libraries like numpy (np.where) and Pandas enable logical operations directly, simplifying complex conditional statements.

2. Readability and Maintainability
   1) Excel: Complex formulas can quickly become hard to read, debug, or maintain, especially with nested functions and conditional logic.
   2) Python: Python code is more modular and readable, with functions and libraries making even complex tasks clear and concise.

3. Scalability
   1) Excel: Suitable for small to medium-sized datasets but struggles with large volumes of data due to performance constraints.
   2) Python: Ideal for large-scale text processing, with efficient, vectorized operations that can handle millions of rows without significant performance issues.

4. Advanced Capabilities
   1) Excel: Limited to predefined functions; lacks native support for advanced text analysis like tokenization, stemming, or sentiment analysis.
   2) Python: Offers extensive libraries like `nltk` for term-based processing (e.g., tokenization, stemming, stopword removal). Supports more advanced language models and frameworks (e.g., `spaCy`, Hugging Face `Transformers`) for natural language processing tasks such as named entity recognition (NER), text generation, or sentiment analysis.

While Excel is sufficient for simple text-processing tasks and widely accessible for business users, Python offers a far more robust, scalable, and versatile platform for text analysis. Python's ability to handle advanced tasks using libraries like `nltk`, `spaCy` or machine learning-based language models (like `transformers`) makes it the superior choice for those seeking deeper insights or dealing with large datasets, or large language models.

7.5 EXERCISES

Using the concepts covered in this chapter, complete the following exercises using "Exercise-Ch07.xlsx" as your dataset.

E1: On the "Text" sheet, complete the tasks specified in columns B through L using fundamental character-based text functions.

E2: Assuming Bookstore initiates a supplier promotion project to develop brief introduction webpages to their coffee material vendors. On the "Supplier" sheet, retrieve the first word of each supplier's name as "FirstWord", and create a profile page link following the format: "https://bookstore/suppliers/FirstWord".

E3: On the "Supplier" sheet, extract the street, city, and zip code from the address.

## CHAPTER 8

Date Processing

D ATE INFORMATION IS A cornerstone of effective business decision-making, providing temporal context and structure to data. It enables organizations to track trends over time, forecast future performance, and manage schedules efficiently. For instance, sales data tied to specific dates can help businesses identify seasonal patterns, optimize inventory levels, or plan marketing campaigns. Additionally, precise date tracking is critical for compliance with regulatory deadlines, managing employee schedules, and ensuring timely project delivery. By leveraging date information, businesses can make more informed, timely, and strategic decisions that align with their operational and financial goals.

Date information is integral to effective data analysis, and both Excel and Python offer robust capabilities for managing date-related data. Excel, with its user-friendly interface and built-in functions like DATE, YEAR, MONTH, and DAY, simplifies common date manipulations for business users. It is ideal for quickly identifying trends, performing basic calculations, and creating time-based aggregations. Python, on the other hand, offers unparalleled flexibility and scalability through libraries like Pandas and datetime. These tools allow for advanced date parsing, transformations, and integration with larger time-based workflows. By exploring how Excel

DOI: 10.1201/9781003567103-9

and Python handle date data, users can better understand their respective strengths and choose the tool that best aligns with their analytical needs.

In this chapter, we will compare Excel's date functions with Python's methods in Pandas and datetime libraries. You will find Python's broader capabilities, particularly in integration with time-series data-related workflows, surpassing Excel's limits. That makes Python a compelling choice because of its versatility for more complex or large-scale date processing tasks, justifying the journey of transitioning from Excel to Python for advanced business analytics.

8.1 DATE PROCESSING WITH BOOKSTORE DATASET

We will use the "Bookstore-Ch08.xlsx" file to explore data visualization tools in both Excel and Python. The workbook contains two worksheets: "**Date**" and "**Invoice**". The "**Date**" sheet is designed for practicing fundamental date functions in both Excel and Python. The "Invoice" sheet serves as an example for applying date functions in the Bookstore scenario. Keep in mind that the "**Invoice**" dataset contains transaction data from the first quarter. Before beginning the exercises, take a moment to familiarize yourself with these sheets.

> **Q1:** On the "Date" sheet, complete the tasks specified in columns A through E using fundamental date functions or methods.
>
> **Q2:** As a bookstore manager, you may need to create a monthly report using the "Invoice" dataset to show the total and average sales.
>
> **Q3:** Additionally, you might want to create a line chart to depict the weekly sales trend and identify the top three weeks with the highest sales amounts.
>
> **Q4:** Find the busiest weekdays using the number of line items in a transaction as the measure of activity.

8.2 EXCEL

Excel provides several built-in functions to work with date data, making it straightforward to extract, calculate, and manipulate dates:

- **TODAY**: Returns the current date based on the system's clock, automatically updating each day. It's useful for calculating durations.
- **YEAR**: Extracts the year from a given date, helping users analyze data by year or group records based on annual trends.

- **MONTH**: Extracts the month from a date, enabling month-by-month comparisons or identification of seasonal patterns.
- **DAY**: Retrieves the day of the month from a date, useful for daily breakdowns or precise scheduling.
- **DATE**: Constructs a date by combining specific year, month, and day inputs, providing a way to create date values.
- **WEEKNUM**: Returns the week number of a specific date within the year. For example, WEEKNUM("01/10/2024") would return 2 as it is within the second week of the year.
- **WEEKDAY**: Returns the day of the week as a number (e.g., 1 for Sunday, 7 for Saturday). For example, WEEKDAY("01/10/2024") would return 4 for Wednesday.
- **WORKDAY**: Calculates a future or past date by adding or subtracting a specified number of working days, excluding weekends and optionally holidays. For example, WORKDAY("01/10/2024", 5) adds five business days to the date. It's essential for project planning or calculating deadlines.

These functions are intuitive and powerful for common business applications, allowing users to efficiently handle and analyze date data.

Q1: On the "Date" sheet, complete the tasks outlined in columns A through E using basic date functions or methods.

1. In cell **A2**, type "=today()":

	A
1	**Today**
2	=today()

If the result appears as a large integer instead of a proper date, as shown below, don't worry – it's not an error.

	A
1	**Today**
2	45629

This happens because Excel stores dates as integers, with January 1, 1900, represented as 1, and each subsequent day incrementing by 1. You can easily resolve this by applying the appropriate date format using number formatting options on cell A2. In this case, we apply the **dd/mm/yyyy** format, as shown in the screenshot below:

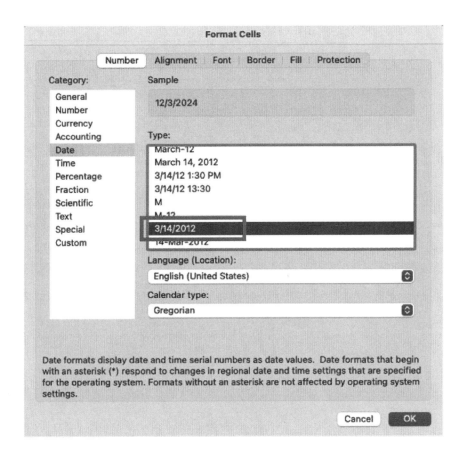

Once applied, you will see the date displayed in the correct format:

2. In cells **B2**, **C2**, and **D2**, enter the following formulas respectively: "=YEAR(A2)", "=MONTH(A2)", "=DAY(A2)". These formulas will extract the year, month, and day from the date in **A2**, producing the results shown below:

B	C	D
Year	**Month**	**Day**
2024	12	3

3. In cell **E2**, create a **DATE()** formula and use the formula builder to reference the three parameters with **B2**, **C2**, and **D2**, respectively, as shown below:

The result will match today's date, as obtained in Step 1.

4. In cell **F2**, type "=WEEKNUM(E2)":

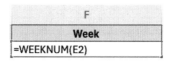

The result will be 49 given that the value in **E2** is "12/3/2024".

5. In cell **G2**, type "=WEEKDAY(E2, 2)":

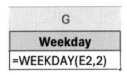

We set the second parameter to 2 to make Monday correspond to 1, and so on. As a result, the output will be 2, given that the value in **E2** is "12/3/2024".

6. In cell **H2**, enter the formula "=E2 + 10", and you will see the result "12/13/2024", as Excel stores dates as integers:

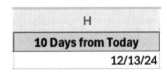

Please note that your result might vary, as we used today as a reference example for **Q1**.

Q2: On the "Invoice" sheet, generate a monthly report showing the total and average sales.

To tackle Q2, we'll utilize pivot tables as introduced in Chapter 3. We've learned that the "**PivotTable Fields**" panel provides drag-and-drop functionality for customizing pivot tables.

1. To create a group-by-month aggregation, drag the "**Date**" field from the list to the "**Rows**" section. The date will initially expand into months, days, and the full date, as shown in the screenshot below. Since we only need the data grouped by month, you can remove the days and full date levels by right-clicking on these items and selecting "Remove".

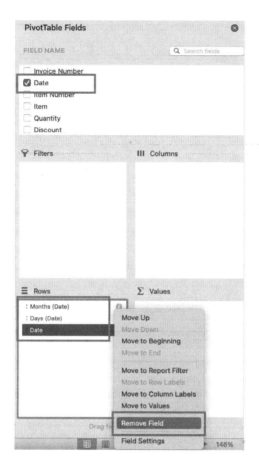

2. Then, further drag the "Extension – Discounted" to the Values section. To include the average amount in the pivot table, simply drag the "Extension – Discounted" field to the Values section once more. Then change its aggregation function by clicking the Φ icon icon located at the end of the item in the Values section:

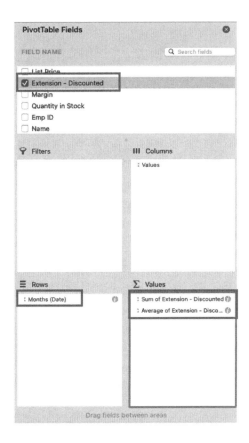

After further formatting, you can view the outcomes of the above drag-and-drop actions as shown below:

	A	B	C
1			
2			
3	**Month** ▼	**Sales Totals**	**Daily Average**
4	Jan	$30,682.04	$45.45
5	Feb	$29,128.59	$44.88
6	Mar	$32,612.66	$47.13
7	**Grand Total**	**$92,423.29**	**$45.84**

Q3: Create a line chart to depict the weekly sales trend and identify the top three weeks with the highest sales amounts.

To solve **Q3**, we first use **WEEKNUM**() to obtain the week number of each transaction in the "**Invoice**" sheet (or the **sales** Table). Then create a group-by-week aggregation using pivot tables.

1. In cell **S2**, enter the label "Week" to add a new column to the sales table. Excel tables will automatically expand to include column **S**, as shown in the screenshot below. This is a key feature of Excel tables: any new columns or rows appended to the table are automatically incorporated into its scope.

2. In cell **S2**, enter "=WEEKNUM(" and reference to the "**Date**" column:

After the formula is accepted, Excel tables will automatically apply it to all rows in the column, as demonstrated in the screenshot below:

3. We then create a group-by-week pivot table by dragging the "**Week**" field to the "**Rows**" section and drag the "Extension – Discounted" to the Values section:

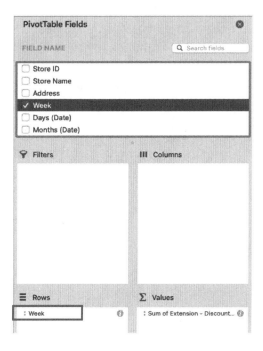

Keep in mind that Excel pivot tables do not always automatically update fields after new columns or rows are added. If the "**Week**" field does not appear, you can use the "**Refresh**" button in the "**PivotTable Analyze**" tab to update the fields:

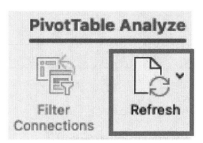

4. Now, you can follow the steps outlined in Chapter 4, **Q5**, to create a line chart that visualizes the trend of weekly sales.

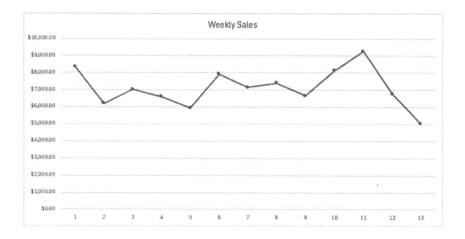

5. To identify the top three weeks with the highest sales amounts, refer to the steps detailed in Chapter 4, **Q1**, under the "**Use Pivot Table's Sorting and Filtering**" section. We encourage you to review and complete these steps independently. You can verify your results (weeks 11, 1, 10) with the screenshot provided below:

	A	B
1		
2		
3	**Week**	**⁺ᵀ Weekly Sales**
4	11	$9,262.94
5	1	$8,346.54
6	10	$8,131.42
7	**Grand Total**	**$25,740.90**

Keep in mind that sorting and filtering the pivot table will also affect the content of the associated pivot chart. To preserve the original pivot chart, you might consider creating a separate pivot table for this task to avoid confusion. Alternatively, you can remove the sorting and filtering effects after identifying the top three weeks.

Q4: Find the busiest weekdays using the number of line items in a transaction as the measure of activity.

To address **Q4**, we can apply similar methods used in **Q3**. Start by using the **WEEKDAY**() function to determine the weekday number for each transaction in the sales table. Then, create a group-by-weekday aggregation using pivot tables. However, weekday numbers can be unclear, so we recommend a quick conversion to more descriptive names (e.g., "Monday", "Tuesday") using **VLOOKUP** before generating the pivot table. This will make the data easier to interpret.

1. In columns **W** and **X**, enter the cell values as shown below:

W	X
Number	Weekday
1	Sunday
2	

Next, select cells **W2** and **W3**, and use the fill handle to extend the series, filling numbers 1 through 7 in column **W**. Then, select cell **X2** and drag the fill handle to fill the corresponding weekdays, from Sunday to Saturday, in column **X**. The completed reference table will look like this:

W	X
Number	Weekday
1	Sunday
2	Monday
3	Tuesday
4	Wednesday
5	Thursday
6	Friday
7	Saturday

2. In cell **T2**, enter "=WEEKDAY(" and reference to the "**Date**" column and accept the formula to fill all rows in the column:

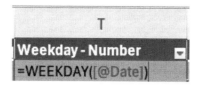

3. In cell **U2**, create a **VLOOKUP()** function to perform an exact match lookup, as illustrated in the screenshot below. Refer to Chapter 5's "**Complementary Note – IFS() and VLOOKUP()**" section for a detailed explanation of the parameter settings required for an exact match.

4. Next, create a group-by-weekday pivot table by dragging the "**Weekday**" field to the "**Rows**" section and any relevant column to the "**Values**" section. Since **Q4** focuses on the number of items in a transaction as the measure, change the aggregation function to "**Count**" by clicking the Φ icon icon at the end of the item.

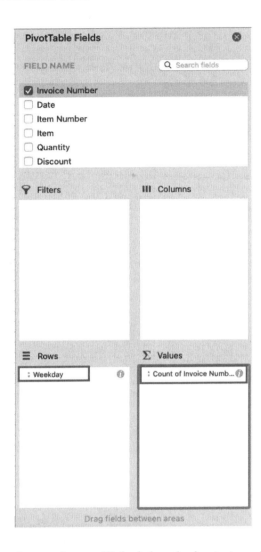

After sorting the results, you'll find that the busiest weekday is **Friday**, with a total of 324 line items:

	A	B
1		
2		
3	**Row Labels** ▾↓	**Count of Invoice Number**
4	Friday	324
5	Wednesday	318
6	Monday	300
7	Thursday	299
8	Sunday	274
9	Tuesday	251
10	Saturday	250
11	**Grand Total**	**2016**

8.3 PYTHON

Please refer to the Jupyter notebook file "Bookstore-Ch08.ipynb" to access the code, or view the "Bookstore-Ch08.html" file to see the outputs of all code.

In Python, date is not a built-in type but is handled through specialized libraries that provide robust functionality for working with date and time data. The primary tools are the `datetime` module and Pandas' `.dt` accessor. Both tools complement each other and can be seamlessly integrated, offering comprehensive solutions for a wide range of date-related tasks. The `datetime` module is suitable for simple and standalone date manipulations in small datasets or individual date operations, whereas Pandas' `.dt` is optimized for handling large datasets and performing complex time-series analyses, making it a better tool for data-intensive tasks.

8.3.1 The `datetime` Module

The `datetime` module is part of the Python standard library and therefore is commonly referred to as a "module", instead of a "library". It offers the following key components for date and time manipulation:

- datetime.date: A class that represents date components (e.g., year, month, day).

- datetime.time: A class that represents time components (e.g., hours, minutes, seconds).

- datetime.datetime: Combines properties of both date and time classes.

- datetime.timedelta: Perform operations like adding or subtracting days, weeks, or other time intervals.
- datetime.strftime: A powerful method as both a versatile formatter and an accessor for date and time.
- datetime.strptime: A method that converts a date/time string into a datetime object.

The following snippets import the four classes from the `datetime` module and use them along with the `strftime` and `strptime` methods as specified in the Q1 requirements.

Q1: Complete the basic date functions or methods.
We begin by using `today()` from the `date` class. Please note that your result might vary, as we used today as a reference example.

```
In[#]:
from datetime import date, time, datetime, timedelta

today = date.today()
print(today)

Out[#]:
2025-03-30
```

• Side Note – strftime's Format Codes
In addition to the default format, you may use `strftime's` versatile format codes to present dates in preferable formats:

Codes for Year, Month, and Day

Year Codes

Format Code	Description	Example Output
%Y	Full year (4 digits)	2024
%y	Two-digit year (last two digits)	24

Month Codes

Format Code	Description	Example Output
%B	Full month name	December
%b	Abbreviated month name	Dec
%m	Zero-padded numeric month	12

Day Codes

Format Code	Description	Example Output
%d	Day of the month (zero-padded)	03
%-d	Day of the month (no leading zero)	3
%A	Full weekday name	Tuesday
%a	Abbreviated weekday name	Tue
%j	Day of the year (zero-padded)	338

Other Format Codes

Format Code	Description	Example Output
%A	Full weekday name	Tuesday
%a	Abbreviated weekday name	Tue
%U	Week number (Sunday as first day, 00-53)	48
%W	Week number (Monday as first day, 00-53)	49
%H	Hour (00-23)	14
%I	Hour (01-12, 12-hour clock)	02
%M	Minute (00-59)	30
%S	Second (00-59)	45
%p	AM/PM	PM

In[#]:

```
print(today.strftime("%Y-%m-%d"))    # Numeric month (zero-padded))
print(today.strftime("%m/%d/%Y"))    # Numeric month (zero-padded))
print(today.strftime("%B %-d, %Y"))   # Full month name (no leading
zero for day))
```

Out[#]:

```
2025-03-30
03/30/2025
March 30, 2025
```

As demonstrated above, you may use different combinations of format codes along with selected separators (such as spaces, commas, etc.) to create custom date formats that suit your specific needs.

You can also access date components using built-in properties as shown below:

```
In[#]:
year = today.year
month = today.month
day = today.day
print(year, month, day)

Out[#]:
2025 3 30
```

The `date` class also allows you to create any custom dates:

```
In[#]:
newdate = date(year, month, day) # Using "date" to generate a date,
zero-padded for month and day
print(newdate)
2025-03-30

Out[#]:
```

To extract week-related data, you can use `strftime()` with its versatile format codes:

```
In[#]:
# Week number (Sunday-based)
week_num_sunday = today.strftime("%U")

# Week number (Monday-based)
week_num_monday = today.strftime("%W")

# Weekday (Full name)
weekday = today.strftime("%A")

print(f"Week Number (Sunday-based): {week_num_sunday}")
print(f"Week Number (Monday-based): {week_num_monday}")
print(f"Weekday: {weekday}")

Out[#]:
Week Number (Sunday-based): 13
Week Number (Monday-based): 12
Weekday: Sunday

In[#]:
print(today + timedelta(days=10))  # Add 10 days to the current date

Out[#]:
2025-04-09
```

Please note that you cannot directly add 10 to today, as it is a date object, not an integer. You need to use `timedelta(days=10)` for date arithmetic in Python.

8.3.2 Pandas .dt Accessor

Pandas extends Python's date-handling capabilities through its `.dt` accessor, which operates on datetime-typed Series. It is ideal for handling time-series data and bulk date manipulations.

1. Date Component Extraction:
   - Extract date components like year, month, day, weekday, quarter, or day of the year.
2. Time-Series Operations:
   - Resampling (e.g., group by month or week).
   - Shifting and lagging dates for time-series analysis.

3. Boolean Flags:
   - Check for properties like leap year (.is_leap_year) or weekend days (.dayofweek > 4).
4. Custom Frequencies:
   - Create custom date ranges using pd.date_range and adjust frequencies for analysis.

The `.dt` accessor in Pandas is conceptually similar to the `.str` accessor for string operations, which we have seen in Chapter 7. Both accessors provide a way to apply operations on an entire Pandas Series or DataFrame column containing specific data types (datetime data for `.dt` and strings for `.str`), enabling `vectorized` operations. The following snippets are some examples showcasing advanced date functionalities using Pandas' `.dt` accessor:

In[#]:

```python
import pandas as pd

# Extract Additional Components (other than year, month, day)

dates = pd.Series(pd.to_datetime(["2024-12-01", "2024-12-03",
"2024-12-05"]))

print(dates.dt.quarter)      # Output: 4, 4, 4
print(dates.dt.dayofweek)    # Output: 6, 1, 3 (Sunday, Tuesday,
Thursday)
print(dates.dt.strftime("%A"))    # Output: Sunday, Tuesday, Thursday
print(dates.dt.strftime("%j"))    # Output: 336, 338, 340
print(dates.dt.is_leap_year) # Output: True, True, True
```

Out[#]:

```
0    4
1    4
2    4
dtype: int32
0    6
1    1
2    3
dtype: int32
0       Sunday
1      Tuesday
2     Thursday
dtype: object
0    336
1    338
2    340
dtype: object
0    True
1    True
2    True
dtype: bool
```

In[#]:

```python
# Check Business Days
print(dates.dt.weekday < 5)  # Output: False, True, True (Mon-Fri
= True)
```

Out[#]:

```
0    False
1     True
2     True
dtype: bool
```

In[#]:

```python
# Custom Formatting using format codes
print(dates.dt.strftime("%A, %B %-d, %Y"))
```

Out[#]:

```
0       Sunday, December 1, 2024
1      Tuesday, December 3, 2024
2     Thursday, December 5, 2024
dtype: object
```

In[#]:

```
# Date Arithmetic and Offsets
from pandas.tseries.offsets import BDay

print(dates + BDay(3))   # Adds 3 business days to each date
```

Out[#]:

```
0    2024-12-04
1    2024-12-06
2    2024-12-10
dtype: datetime64[ns]
```

In[#]:

```
# Resampling and Aggregation
time_series = pd.Series([10, 20, 15, 25], index=pd.to_
datetime(["2024-12-01", "2024-12-13", "2024-12-01", "2024-12-03"]))
print(time_series.resample("D").mean())   # Fills in daily intervals
print(time_series.resample("W").mean())   # Weekly resampling
```

Out[#]:

```
2024-12-01    12.5
2024-12-02    NaN
2024-12-03    25.0
2024-12-04    NaN
2024-12-05    NaN
2024-12-06    NaN
2024-12-07    NaN
2024-12-08    NaN
2024-12-09    NaN
2024-12-10    NaN
2024-12-11    NaN
2024-12-12    NaN
2024-12-13    20.0
Freq: D, dtype: float64
2024-12-01    12.5
2024-12-08    25.0
2024-12-15    20.0
Freq: W-SUN, dtype: float64
```

In[#]:

```
# Generate Date Ranges
date_range = pd.date_range(start="2024-12-01", end="2024-12-10",
freq="B")
print(date_range)   # Business days between the range
```

Out[#]:

```
DatetimeIndex(["2024-12-02", "2024-12-03", "2024-12-04",
               "2024-12-05",
               "2024-12-06", "2024-12-09", "2024-12-10"],
              dtype="datetime64[ns]", freq="B")
```

The examples above illustrate how Pandas' .dt accessor offers advanced time-based data analysis capabilities, enabling scalable operations like date extraction, resampling, and time-series preparation. These features go beyond Excel's formula-driven approach and Python's built-in datetime module, making it a powerful tool for working with large, time-indexed datasets.

8.3.3 Date Processing with Bookstore Data Using Pandas

To solve Q2 to Q4, we use the read_excel() method to import the "Invoice" sheet from the "Bookstore-Ch08.xlsx":

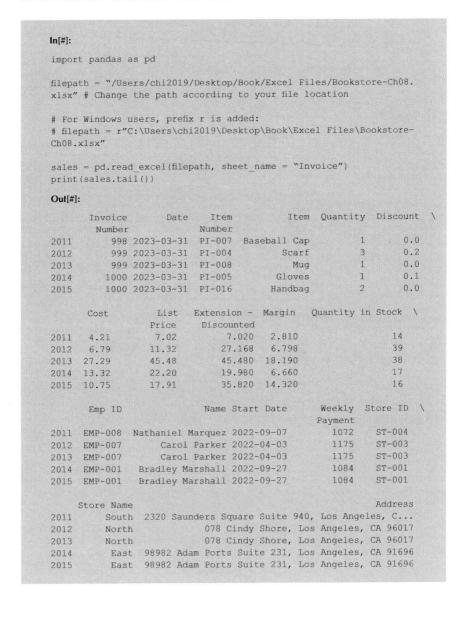

```
In[#]:

import pandas as pd

filepath = "/Users/chi2019/Desktop/Book/Excel Files/Bookstore-Ch08.
xlsx" # Change the path according to your file location

# For Windows users, prefix r is added:
# filepath = r"C:\Users\chi2019\Desktop\Book\Excel Files\Bookstore-
Ch08.xlsx"

sales = pd.read_excel(filepath, sheet_name = "Invoice")
print(sales.tail())
```

Out[#]:

	Invoice Number	Date	Item Number	Item	Quantity	Discount \
2011	998	2023-03-31	PI-007	Baseball Cap	1	0.0
2012	999	2023-03-31	PI-004	Scarf	3	0.2
2013	999	2023-03-31	PI-008	Mug	1	0.0
2014	1000	2023-03-31	PI-005	Gloves	1	0.1
2015	1000	2023-03-31	PI-016	Handbag	2	0.0

	Cost	List Price	Extension - Discounted	Margin	Quantity in Stock \
2011	4.21	7.02	7.020	2.810	14
2012	6.79	11.32	27.168	6.798	39
2013	27.29	45.48	45.480	18.190	38
2014	13.32	22.20	19.980	6.660	17
2015	10.75	17.91	35.820	14.320	16

	Emp ID	Name	Start Date	Weekly Payment	Store ID \
2011	EMP-008	Nathaniel Marquez	2022-09-07	1072	ST-004
2012	EMP-007	Carol Parker	2022-04-03	1175	ST-003
2013	EMP-007	Carol Parker	2022-04-03	1175	ST-003
2014	EMP-001	Bradley Marshall	2022-09-27	1084	ST-001
2015	EMP-001	Bradley Marshall	2022-09-27	1084	ST-001

	Store Name	Address
2011	South	2320 Saunders Square Suite 940, Los Angeles, C...
2012	North	078 Cindy Shore, Los Angeles, CA 96017
2013	North	078 Cindy Shore, Los Angeles, CA 96017
2014	East	98982 Adam Ports Suite 231, Los Angeles, CA 91696
2015	East	98982 Adam Ports Suite 231, Los Angeles, CA 91696

Q2: Generate a monthly report showing the total and average sales.
To tackle Q2, we start by using the `.dt` accessor and `strftime()` format codes to extract month names:

```
In[#]:

sales["Date"].dt.strftime("%B")

Out[#]:

0          January
1          January
2          January
3          January
4          January
            ...
2011        March
2012        March
2013        March
2014        March
2015        March
Name: Date, Length: 2016, dtype: object
```

Next, create a pivot table using the extracted month names to generate a monthly summary report as below:

```
In[#]:

q2 = pd.pivot_table(sales, values="Extension - Discounted", index=
sales["Date"].dt.strftime("%B"), aggfunc=["sum", "mean"])
q2

Out[#]:
```

	sum	mean
	Extension - Discounted	Extension - Discounted
Date		
February	29128.5940	44.882271
January	30682.0385	45.454872
March	32612.6595	47.128121

Although concise, using the "Date" and "Extension - Discounted" columns for two aggregation functions introduces three minor issues: 1) the index name remains "Date" instead of "Month"; 2) an undesired hierarchical index (`MultiIndex`) is created in the columns of q2; 3) the rows are not in the ordinary order.

To address the first issue, we rename the index by assigning "Month" to q2.index.name:

```
In[#]:
q2.index.name = "Month"
q2
Out[#]:
```

	sum	mean
	Extension – Discounted	Extension – Discounted
Month		
February	29128.5940	44.882271
January	30682.0385	45.454872
March	32612.6595	47.128121

Next, we follow the steps outlined in Chapter 4, Q2 to remove the MultiIndex from the columns:

```
In[#]:
q2.columns = q2.columns.droplevel(0) # Remove the level 0 indices
q2
Out[#]:
```

	Extension – Discounted	Extension – Discounted
Month		
February	29128.5940	44.882271
January	30682.0385	45.454872
March	32612.6595	47.128121

You can also rename the column labels to eliminate duplicates and enhance clarity:

```
In[#]:

q2.columns = ["Sales Totals", "Daily Average"]
q2

Out[#]:
```

	Sales Totals	Daily Average
Month		
February	29128.5940	44.882271
January	30682.0385	45.454872
March	32612.6595	47.128121

In Pandas, you can use `loc[]` to reorder specific rows:

```
In[#]:

# Reorder rows using loc[] with row labels
q2 = q2.loc[["January", "February", "March"]]
q2

Out[#]:
```

	Sales Totals	Daily Average
Month		
January	30682.0385	45.454872
February	29128.5940	44.882271
March	32612.6595	47.128121

Q3: Create a line chart to depict the weekly sales trend and identify the top three weeks with the highest sales amounts.

Similar to Q2, we first create a pivot table using the week numbers to generate a weekly summary report as below:

```
In[#]:

q3 = pd.pivot_table(sales, values="Extension - Discounted", index=
sales["Date"].dt.strftime("%U"), aggfunc="sum")
q3
```

Out[#]:

	Extension - Discounted
Date	
01	8346.5425
02	6202.4730
03	7021.0645
04	6591.0520
05	5927.2600
06	7927.3525
07	7143.1990
08	7392.4025
09	6664.9965
10	8131.4195
11	9262.9400
12	6780.4990
13	5032.0910

Then we rename the index by assigning "Week" to q3.index.name:

In[#]:

```
q3.index.name = "Week"
q3
```

Out[#]:

	Extension - Discounted
Week	
01	8346.5425
02	6202.4730
03	7021.0645
04	6591.0520
05	5927.2600
06	7927.3525
07	7143.1990
08	7392.4025
09	6664.9965
10	8131.4195
11	9262.9400
12	6780.4990
13	5032.0910

We further rename the column labels for clarity:

```
In[#]:

q3.columns = ["Sales Totals"]
q3
```

Out[#]:

	Sales Totals
Week	
01	8346.5425
02	6202.4730
03	7021.0645
04	6591.0520
05	5927.2600
06	7927.3525
07	7143.1990
08	7392.4025
09	6664.9965
10	8131.4195
11	9262.9400
12	6780.4990
13	5032.0910

Now, with the modified q3, we can call plot() to quickly create a line chart as below:

```
In[#]:

q3.plot(kind = "line", title="Weekly Sales",  marker="o")
```

Out[#]:

```
<Axes: title={"center": "Weekly Sales"}, xlabel="Week">
```

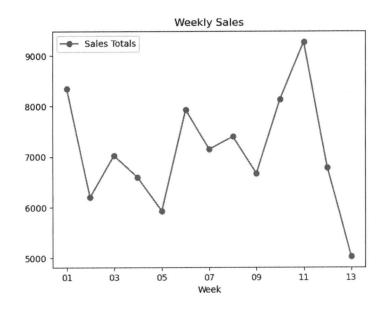

To retrieve the top 3 weeks with the highest values in a Pandas DataFrame, you can use the `nlargest()` function, as introduced in Chapter 4, Q1. This method allows you to get the rows with the largest values (and sorted in the descending order) from a specified numerical column.

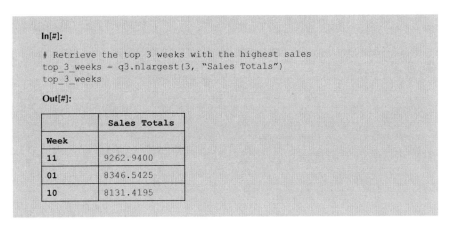

Q4: Find the busiest weekdays using the number of line items in a transaction as the measure of activity.

For Q4, we create a pivot table using the weekday names to generate a items-by-weekday report as follows:

In[#]:

```
q4 = pd.pivot_table(sales, values="Invoice Number", index=
sales["Date"].dt.strftime("%A"), aggfunc="count")
q4
```

Out[#]:

	Invoice Number
Date	
Friday	324
Monday	300
Saturday	250
Sunday	274
Thursday	299
Tuesday	251
Wednesday	318

Then we rename the index name and the column name:

In[#]:

```
q4.index.name = "Weekday"
q4.columns = ["Count"]
q4
```

Out[#]:

	Count
Weekday	
Friday	324
Monday	300
Saturday	250
Sunday	274
Thursday	299
Tuesday	251
Wednesday	318

In[#]:

```
# Retrieve the busiest weekday with the largest count
busiest_weekday = q4.nlargest(1, "Count")
busiest_weekday
```

Out[#]:

	Count
Weekday	
Friday	324

8.4 DISCUSSIONS

The table below provides a side-by-side comparison of Excel's Date Functions, Python's datetime Module, and Pandas' .dt Accessor:

Feature	Excel's Date Functions	Python's datetime Module	Pandas' .dt Accessor
Data Structure	Cell-based (row by row)	Individual date/time objects	Column/Series-based (vectorized)
Operations	Basic date functions (`YEAR()`, `MONTH()`, `DAY()`, `WEEKDAY()`, `WORKDAY()`)	Date extraction, date arithmetic (`timedelta`), parsing, formatting	More date extraction, flexible time arithmetic, resampling
Time-Series Support	Limited (manual functions)	No built-in time-series features	Built-in time-series tools (`resample()`, `date_range()`)
Scalability	Manual; slow for large datasets	Not designed for bulk operations	Scales well for large datasets
Vectorized Operations	No (formula-driven, row-by-row)	No (works with individual objects)	Yes (operates on entire columns)
Aggregation & Grouping	Limited with pivot tables	Requires manual implementation	Built-in aggregation with pivot tables and `groupby()`
Ease of Use	Easy for simple tasks; UI-driven	Requires programming knowledge	Requires basic programming with Pandas
Customization	Limited to Excel formulas	Highly customizable with Python	Extensive options using DataFrame methods

Key Takeaways

1. Excel's Date Functions:
   1) Easy to use but formula-driven and not scalable for large datasets.
   2) Suitable for manual data analysis but lacks advanced automation.
2. Python's datetime Module:
   1) Great for date/time manipulation, parsing, and formatting.
   2) Limited scalability due to its focus on individual objects.
3. Pandas' .dt Accessor:
   1) Best for large datasets with powerful time-series processing capabilities.
   2) Supports vectorized operations, making it faster and more efficient for time-based analysis.

While Excel's date functions are user-friendly, they are limited in scalability and automation. Python's datetime module provides robust date manipulation but lacks native support for time-series aggregation. Pandas' `.dt` accessor combines the strengths of both, enabling powerful, scalable, and efficient time-based analysis for large datasets.

8.5 EXERCISES

Using the concepts covered in this chapter, complete the following exercises using "Exercise-Ch08.xlsx" as your dataset.

E1: Create a monthly report using the "**Purchase Order**" dataset to show the total and average amounts of purchase.

E2: Create a line chart to depict the weekly purchase trend and identify the top three weeks with the highest purchase amounts.

E3: Find the weekday with the highest purchase quantity for coffee beans.

## CHAPTER 9

Table Join and Merge

IN DATA MANAGEMENT AND analysis, information is rarely stored in a single, all-encompassing table. For example, in previous chapters using the "**Invoice**" sheet, we combined invoice data with product items, employees, and stores. While this simplified approach may seem convenient, it introduces **data redundancy** and risks of **data inconsistency**. Consider the addresses of four stores appearing repeatedly across 2,016 rows of transactional data. Every transaction entry requires filling in the store address, increasing the risk of clerical errors and inconsistent records. Additionally, if a store changes its address in April, every related entry in the "**Invoice**" sheet must be updated to reflect the change. Failing to do so could create multiple conflicting versions of the same store's address. Similar redundancy issues could arise with other repeating data fields, such as product names, employee start dates, and other frequently referenced information.

In **database theory**, **normalization** ensures that data is stored efficiently by minimizing redundancy and organizing it into multiple related tables. This process reduces data duplication, improves **data integrity**, and optimizes **storage management**. Following the principles of **relational database design**, related data is stored in separate tables linked by common

DOI: 10.1201/9781003567103-10

keys to maintain consistency and prevent anomalies such as data inconsistency, insertion errors, and update conflicts.

While normalization improves database reliability, it also means that no single table contains all the necessary information for comprehensive analysis. For example, a business database might store customer details, product information, and order transactions in separate tables. Generating a complete sales report would require joining these tables using shared fields like CustomerID or ProductID. This process of **table joining** allows data analysts to reconstruct meaningful datasets from normalized structures, enabling detailed reporting, advanced analytics, and business insights while preserving the underlying database's efficiency and consistency.

In this chapter, we will explore the concepts of **table joins and merges**, comparing how they work in two powerful tools: Pandas' **join** and **merge** methods in Python and **Power Pivot** in Excel. While Pandas is a code-based library widely used in data science, Excel's Power Pivot offers a graphical interface for business professionals. Through step-by-step guides, this chapter will illustrate how mastering table joins and merges can significantly improve your data analysis workflow. Whether you're working in a programming environment or a spreadsheet application, understanding how to perform table joins is fundamental to unlock enterprise-level relational databases, supporting tasks from daily queries to advanced data modeling and analytics.

9.1 COMMON TYPES OF TABLE JOINS

Table joins are essential because they allow you to bring related records together based on shared fields, known as **keys**. By establishing connections between tables using shared keys, joins enable more comprehensive and meaningful analysis. Without the table join mechanism, working with a normalized database would require tedious manual lookups, making analysis inefficient and prone to errors.

In relational databases, join operations are used to combine rows from two or more tables based on a related column or key. The four primary types of join operations defined in **SQL (Structured Query Language)** – the query language developed in the relational database, are **inner join**, **outer join** (also known as **full outer join**), **left join**, and **right join**. Each join type returns a different set of rows based on how the keys from the tables match. The diagram below illustrates the varying effects of the four different join types:

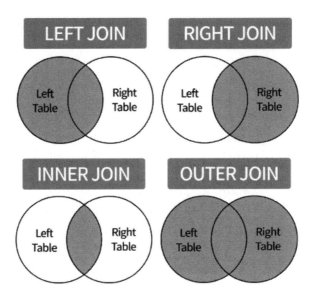

1. **Inner join:**

   An inner join returns only the rows that have matching keys in both tables. If a key is present in one table but not in the other, the row will not be included in the result. You may consider an inner join as an "**intersection**" between two data tables.

2. **Outer join (Full Outer Join):**

   An outer join returns all rows from both tables. If a key is present in one table but not in the other, the result will include the row with missing values filled with nulls (or another specified value). You may consider an outer join as a "**union**" between two data tables.

3. **Left join:**

   A left join returns all rows from the left table and any matching rows from the right table. If a key is present in the left table but not in the right table, the result will include the row with missing values filled with nulls (or another specified value).

4. **Right join:**

   A right join returns all rows from the right table and any matching rows from the left table. If a key is present in the right table but not in the left table, the result will include the row with missing values filled with nulls (or another specified value). Basically, a right join can be replaced by a left join by switching the tables on both sides.

Consider a business database where customer information and order records are stored separately. A **Customer** table for customers contains fields such as **CustomerID** and Name, while another **Order** table records sales with fields like OrderID, **CustomerID**, and Amount. If we need to see customers who have placed orders, an **inner join** using the shared **CustomerID** retrieves only matching records. However, if we want to see **all customers**, regardless of whether they have made an order, a **left join** from **Customer** to **Order** would be more appropriate. This approach ensures that even customers without orders are included, though with empty values in the **Amount** field. The simple examples showcase that with different table joins, we can link the customer information to the sales records and create varying views of customer transactions.

• **Table Joins with Bookstore Dataset**
We will use the "**Bookstore-Ch09.xlsx**" file to explore **table join tools** in both **Excel** and **Python**. The workbook includes a consolidated "**Invoice**" sheet, serving as a reference for table joins, along with five **normalized tables**: "**Invoice Head**", "**Invoice Items**", "**Item**", "**Employee**", and "**Store**". These tables are structured to demonstrate table join functionalities across the two platforms. Before diving into the exercises, take a moment to review the contents of these sheets to better understand how they relate to one another.

Q1: Combine the tables "**Invoice Head**", "**Invoice Items**", "**Item**", "**Employee**", and "**Store**" through merging or joining to create a unified table identical to "**Invoice**".

Q2: Compute the total and average amounts of extension and margin by store using the "**Invoice**" dataset and the newly-joined dataset.

9.2 EXCEL

To solve the two questions in Excel, we need to utilize Excel's "**Power Pivot**" tool. **Power Pivot** is a built-in feature in Excel 2013 and newer versions. It is an Excel add-in that enables you to analyze large datasets, build complex data models, and create advanced Pivot Tables using data from various sources. It supports relational data models and **DAX** (Data Analysis Expressions) formulas for calculated columns and measures for powerful data analysis. Follow the steps below to get started with **Power Pivot**:

1. Before using Power Pivot, please check your Excel version to ensure you have Microsoft 365, Excel Professional Plus, or Excel Standalone newer than Excel 2013. It is currently only available on Windows versions of Excel, not supported on Excel for Mac.

2. To enable the "**Power Pivot**" add-in, go to File → Options → Add-ins to open the Office Add-ins management. Then, select "**COM Add-ins**" from the dropdown and click **Go**, as shown below:

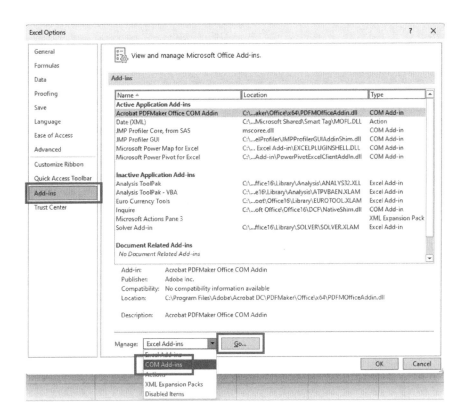

3. Now, check "Microsoft Power Pivot for Excel" and click OK.

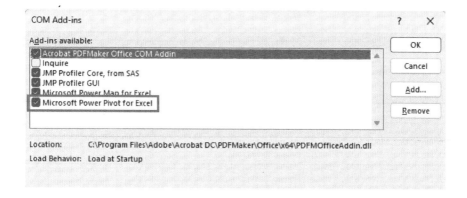

4. On the "Data" tab, under the "Data Tools", you will have the "Manage Data Model" button on the ribbon, as shown below:

Q1: Combine the tables "**Invoice Head**", "**Invoice Items**", "**Item**", "**Employee**", and "**Store**" through merging or joining to create a unified table.

1. First, convert all sheets to Excel tables and rename them as "**head**", "**lines**", "**item**", "**emp**", and "**store**", respectively. Below is the example of "head":

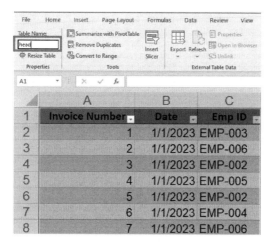

2. In the "Data" tab, under the "Data Tools", click the "Manage Data Model" button to open the "**Power Pivot**" environment, as illustrated below:

3. In the **Power Pivot** window, click **Diagram View** on the ribbon to access the visual tool for creating relationships among the defined tables:

4. To create a relationship between the "**head**" and "**lines**" tables using their shared column "**Invoice Number**", simply drag the "Invoice Number" field from the "**head**" table to the corresponding column in the "**lines**" table. This action establishes the relationship, as illustrated in the screenshot below:

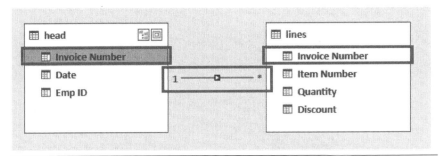

You may click the line connecting "**head**" and "**lines**" to verify that the relationship has been established correctly, as shown in the screenshot below:

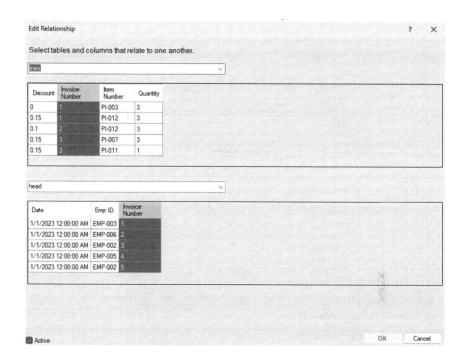

5. Follow the same steps to create additional relationships:

- Use the shared "**Item Number**" column to relate "**lines**" and "**item**":

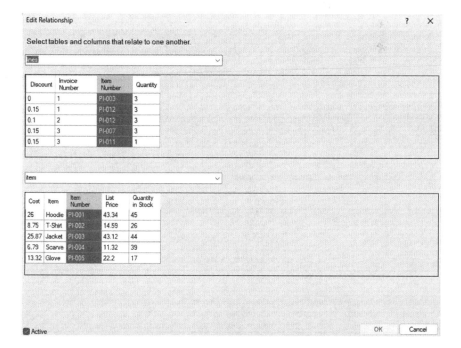

- Use the shared "**Emp ID**" column to relate "**head**" and "**emp**":

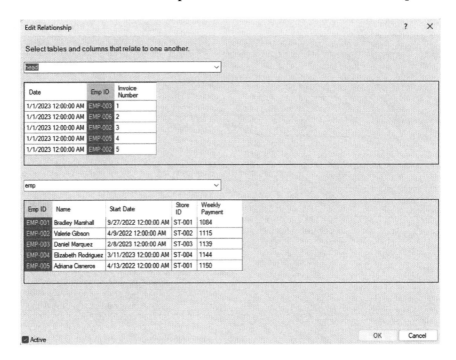

- Use the shared "**Store ID**" column between "**emp**" and "**store**":

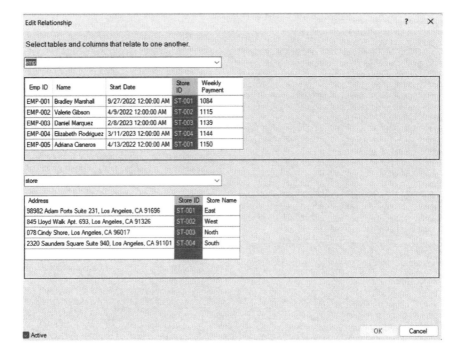

The completed data model, containing five related tables, will be displayed in Diagram View, as illustrated in the screenshot below. This visual representation confirms that all necessary relationships have been successfully established.

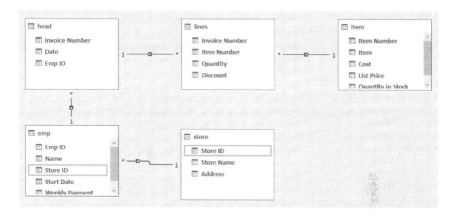

Q2: Compute the total and average amounts of extension and margin by store using the newly-joined dataset and compare the results with the "**Invoice**" sheet.

To solve **Q2**, we'll use **Power Pivot's Calculated Field** feature to calculate "**Extension – Discounted**" and "**Margin**", followed by creating a **Pivot Table** based on the data model. These tasks involve related columns from different tables, making table joins essential. For instance, calculating extensions in the "**lines**" table requires the "**List Price**" from the "**item**" table, matched through the shared "**Item Number**" field. Without this relationship, such calculations wouldn't be possible, demonstrating the critical role of table joins or merges in data modeling.

1. In the Power Pivot window, click **Data View** on the ribbon to switch from Diagram View to the Table View, where you can see and work with the data from individual tables:

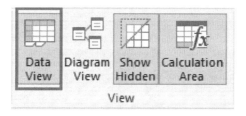

Then, at the bottom table tabs, select the "lines" table to work with its data:

2. To add a calculated column, click the "**Add Column**" cell on the far right of the table. Enter "**Extension – Discounted**" as the label for the new column, as shown in the screenshot below:

3. In the formula bar of the "**Extension – Discounted**" column, enter "**RELATED(**" and select **"item"[List Price]** from the field list. The field list will display all available fields from related tables, enabling seamless development of DAX formulas by referencing related data across tables.

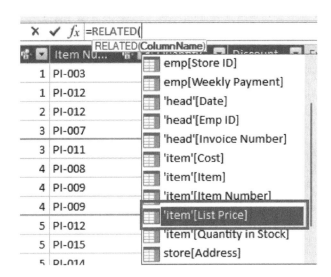

4. Now, complete the following DAX formula to calculate the "**Extension – Discounted**":

```
✕  ✓  fx  =RELATED('item'[List Price]) * lines[Quantity] * (1 - lines[Discount])
```

Check the first few rows of the table to ensure the values are calculated correctly:

Extension - Discounted ▾
129.36
106.5645
112.833
17.901
2.2015
115.974
47.2515
33.354

5. Follow the same steps to add a new "**Margin**" column by creating the formula below:

```
fx  =lines[Extension - Discounted] - lines[Quantity] * RELATED('item'[Cost])
```

Check your answers for the first few rows:

Margin ▾
51.75
31.3545
37.623
5.271
0.6515
34.104
13.8915
11.114

6. On the Power Pivot ribbon, click the **PivotTable** dropdown menu and select PivotTable, as shown below:

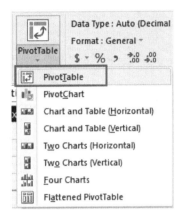

In the **Create PivotTable** dialog box, choose **New Worksheet** to place the Pivot Table on a new worksheet.

7. You will be directed to the Pivot Table Analyze Canvas, where you can see fields from all five tables in the data model. Unlike traditional pivot tables, this interface allows you to access fields across related tables, offering a comprehensive view of the data.

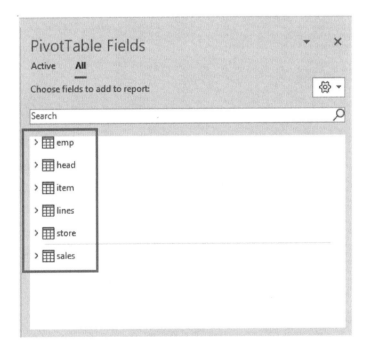

8. Expand the "lines" and "store" tables from the Pivot Table Fields pane, drag "**Store Name**" from the "**store**" table into the Rows section and drag both "**Extension – Discounted**" and "**Margin**" from the "**lines**" table into the Values section twice. Then change the last two aggregation functions to "**Average**", as shown in the screenshot below:

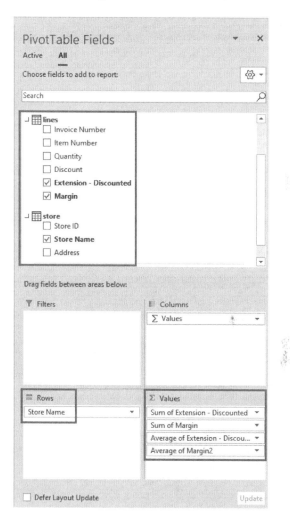

9. Your pivot table will now display the total and average sales and margin amounts for each store. You may verify your answers with the screenshot below:

Store	Sum of Extension - Discounted	Sum of Margin	Average of Extension - Discounted2	Average of Margin2
East	$23,126.82	$7,599.37	$45.44	$14.93
North	$21,546.23	$6,943.70	$44.15	$14.23
South	$24,775.27	$8,043.55	$48.39	$15.71
West	$22,974.97	$7,475.41	$45.32	$14.74
Grand Total	$92,423.29	$30,062.03	$45.84	$14.91

The pivot table above leverages fields from all related tables, enabling advanced data analysis beyond Excel's standard capabilities. This process demonstrates how table joins in **Power Pivot** simplify complex data modeling and support dynamic reporting through calculated fields and aggregated metrics.

9.3 PYTHON

Please refer to the Jupyter notebook file "Bookstore-Ch09.ipynb" to access the code, or view the "Bookstore-Ch09.html" file to see the outputs of all code.

9.3.1 Pandas' Merge, Join, and Concat

In many real-world scenarios, data is spread across multiple tables, with each table containing a specific aspect or entity of the data. Table joins (or merges) play a crucial role in data processing and analysis by combining related data, reducing redundancy, ensuring data integrity, enabling complex analysis, and improving performance. They are an indispensable tool for working with relational databases and structured, tabular data.

In Pandas, `merge` and `join` are two methods used to combine DataFrames based on specific key columns or indices. While both methods achieve similar goals, they have different use cases and syntax. `merge` is used to combine DataFrames based on columns, while `join` is used to combine DataFrames based on indices. Both methods provide options to control the type of join and the keys or indices to join on. On the other hand, `concat` is a powerful tool for directly concatenating datasets while preserving their indexes and column/row labels without considering dataset relationships. You may use the method that best fits your specific use case when combining DataFrames in Pandas.

• **Merge**

Merge is a function that combines DataFrames based on one or more common columns (keys). It is similar to a SQL join operation. The merge function provides various options to control the type of join (inner, outer, left, or right) and the columns to join on.

Syntax:

left_df.merge(right_df, how="inner", on=None, left_on=None, right_on=None, suffixes=[]...), or

pd.merge(left_df, right_df, how="inner", on=None, left_on=None, right_on=None, suffixes=[]...)

- left_df and right_df: The DataFrames to be merged.
- how: The type of join ("inner", "outer", "left", or "right"). Defaults to "inner".
- on: Column(s) to join on. Must be found in both DataFrames.
- left_on: Column(s) from the left DataFrame to use as keys.
- right_on: Column(s) from the right DataFrame to use as keys.

Join Types

As discussed in the beginning of this chapter, when combining tables, different types of joins are used depending on the analytical goal. Inner joins extract only matching records from both tables, providing a focused view of relevant data. In contrast, left joins return all records from the first table while including matches from the second, ensuring that no critical data is lost. Right joins work similarly but prioritize the second table, while full outer joins combine all records from both tables, filling in missing values where necessary.

The example below demonstrates an inner join of two data frames, where both data frames share a common column named key. We start by using the more Pythonic df.merge syntax:

```
In[#]:

import pandas as pd

data1 = {"key": ["A", "B", "C", "D"], "value": [1, 2, 3, 4]}
data2 = {"key": ["B", "D", "E", "F"], "value": [5, 6, 7, 8]}

df1 = pd.DataFrame(data1)
df2 = pd.DataFrame(data2)

merged_df = df1.merge(df2, on="key", how="inner") # Create an inner
join on the same "key" column using df1.merge
print(df1,"\n", df2,"\n", merged_df)
```

Out[#]:

```
   key  value
0   A      1
1   B      2
2   C      3
3   D      4
   key  value
0   B      5
1   D      6
2   E      7
3   F      8
   key  value_x  value_y
0   B      2        5
1   D      4        6
```

As shown above, the inner join returns only the rows with matching keys in both df1 and df2, specifically keys B and D. These represent the intersection of df1 and df2. Additionally, a suffix of x is added to the overlapping value column from df1, while y is added to the value column from df2. This helps distinguish columns with the same name after the merge. You may also use the suffixes parameter to define customized suffixes.

The example below demonstrates an inner join where the two data frames use different column names as keys. This time we use the syntax of pd.merge:

In[#]:

```python
data1 = {"k1": ["A", "B", "C", "D"], "value": [1, 2, 3, 4]}
data2 = {"k2": ["B", "D", "E", "F"], "value": [5, 6, 7, 8]}

df1 = pd.DataFrame(data1)
df2 = pd.DataFrame(data2)

merged_df = pd.merge(df1, df2, left_on="k1", right_on="k2", how=
"inner") # An inner join on two different key columns
print(df1,"\n", df2,"\n", merged_df)
```

Out[#]:

```
   k1  value
0   A      1
1   B      2
2   C      3
3   D      4
   k2  value
0   B      5
1   D      6
2   E      7
3   F      8
   k1  value_x k2  value_y
0   B      2    B      5
1   D      4    D      6
```

In the example below, we demonstrate how to perform an `outer` join on three data frames at once using Python's `method chaining`:

```
In[#]:
# create first data frame
df1 = pd.DataFrame({"key": ["A", "B", "C", "D"],
                    "value1": [1, 2, 3, 4]})
# create second data frame
df2 = pd.DataFrame({"key": ["B", "D", "E", "F"],
                    "value2": [5, 6, 7, 8]})
# create third data frame
df3 = pd.DataFrame({"key": ["A", "C", "E", "G"],
                    "value3": [9, 10, 11, 12]})
# join the data frames on the "key" column
merged_df = pd.merge(pd.merge(df1, df2, on="key", how="outer"), df3,
on="key", how="outer")

print(merged_df)

Out[#]:
  key  value1  value2  value3
0   A     1.0     NaN     9.0
1   B     2.0     5.0     NaN
2   C     3.0     NaN    10.0
3   D     4.0     6.0     NaN
4   E     NaN     7.0    11.0
5   F     NaN     8.0     NaN
6   G     NaN     NaN    12.0
```

In this example we create three data frames – df1, df2, and df3 – each containing a key column and a different value column. Using the `pd.merge()` function, we perform an `outer` join on the `key` column to combine all three data frames. The resulting merged_df contains all rows from the original data frames, with missing values (represented as `NaN`) added where data is unavailable.

Note: NaN stands for "Not a Number" and is a special floating-point value used in many programming languages and libraries, including Python and its popular libraries like NumPy and Pandas. It represents missing, undefined, or unrepresentable values in datasets or computations.

• **Join**

In addition to `merge`, there is a `join` method that can be used to combine DataFrames based on their index. Unlike `merge`, which joins data frames based on key columns, to use the `join` method, you need to set the index to the key columns in each data frame.

Syntax:

   left_df.join(right_df, how="left", on=None, lsuffix="", rsuffix="", ...)

- right_df: The DataFrame to be joined with the calling DataFrame (left_df).
- how: The type of join ("left", "right", "outer", or "inner"). Defaults to "left".
- on: Column(s) to join on. The default is None (join on index).
- lsuffix: Suffix to add to the overlapping columns from the left_df.
- rsuffix: Suffix to add to the overlapping columns from the right_df.

The example below shows how to join two data frames using the set_ index function to set the index to the key columns in each data frame. Since both datasets have the same column name of "Value", it is *necessary* to assign different suffixes to lsuffix and rsuffix (or at least one of them):

```
In[#]:

# Create two DataFrames
data1 = {"ID1": [1, 2, 3, 4], "Value": [10, 20, 30, 40]}
data2 = {"ID2": [2, 4, 5, 6], "Value": [50, 60, 70, 80]}

df1 = pd.DataFrame(data1)
df2 = pd.DataFrame(data2)

# Set the "ID" column as the index for both DataFrames
df1 = df1.set_index("ID1")
df2 = df2.set_index("ID2")

# Join the DataFrames on the "ID1" and "ID2" columns since they are
indexes (inner join)
joined_df = df1.join(df2, how="inner", lsuffix = "_A", rsuffix = "_B")

print(joined_df)

Out[#]:

    Value_A  Value_B
2        20       50
4        40       60
```

Note that if you execute df1.set_index("ID") without assigning the result back to df1, the "ID1" column will not be set as the index in df1. Alternatively, you can use the inplace=True parameter in the set_ index() method to modify the original DataFrame in place.

• Concat

Panda's concat() is used to concatenate multiple DataFrames or Series objects along a particular axis (either rows or columns). Below are some key features and examples of using pd.concat():

1. Basic concatenation of DataFrames along rows (`axis=0`):

```
In[#]:

df1 = pd.DataFrame({"A": [1, 2], "B": [3, 4]})
df2 = pd.DataFrame({"A": [5, 6], "B": [7, 8]})

result = pd.concat([df1, df2], axis=0)
print(result)

Out[#]:

   A  B
0  1  3
1  2  4
0  5  7
1  6  8
```

2. Concatenation of DataFrames along columns (`axis=1`):

```
In[#]:

result = pd.concat([df1, df2], axis=1)
print(result)

Out[#]:

   A  B  A  B
0  1  3  5  7
1  2  4  6  8
```

Note that the column labels from the original DataFrames are preserved. You can use the keys parameter to create a `MultiIndex` on the columns and distinguish between the original DataFrames:

```
In[#]:

result = pd.concat([df1, df2], axis=1, keys=["df1", "df2"])
print(result)

Out[#]:

  df1     df2
   A  B    A  B
0  1  3    5  7
1  2  4    6  8

In[#]:

print(result.columns)
```

```
Out[#]:

MultiIndex([("df1", "A"),
            ("df1", "B"),
            ("df2", "A"),
            ("df2", "B")],
           )
```

3. Handling index duplication with ignore_index parameter:

```
In[#]:

result = pd.concat([df1, df2], axis=0, ignore_index=True)
print(result)
```

```
Out[#]:

   A  B
0  1  3
1  2  4
2  5  7
3  6  8
```

```
In[#]:

result.loc[1,["A","B"]]
```

```
Out[#]:

A    2
B    4
Name: 1, dtype: int64
```

4. Concatenating DataFrames with different columns:

```
In[#]:

df3 = pd.DataFrame({"C": [1, 2], "D": [3, 4]})
result = pd.concat([df1, df3], axis=0)
print(result)
```

```
Out[#]:

     A    B    C    D
0  1.0  3.0  NaN  NaN
1  2.0  4.0  NaN  NaN
0  NaN  NaN  1.0  3.0
1  NaN  NaN  2.0  4.0
```

In this case, the resulting DataFrame will have all columns from both original DataFrames, and NaN values will be filled for missing data.

9.3.2 Data Import

As in Chapter 5, we use the read_excel() method to import all sheets from the "Bookstore-Ch09.xlsx" at once:

```
In[#]:

import pandas as pd

filepath = "/Users/chi2019/Desktop/Book/Excel Files/Bookstore-Ch09.
xlsx" # Change the path according to your file location

# For Windows users, prefix r is added:
# filepath = r"C:\Users\chi2019\Desktop\Book\Excel Files\Bookstore-
Ch09.xlsx"

df = pd.read_excel(filepath, sheet_name = None)
# print(df) # You may print all dfs yourself.

In[#]:

df.keys() # Use keys to outline the dictionary entries

Out[#]:

dict_keys(["Invoice", "Invoice Head", "Invoice Items", "Item",
"Employee", "Store"])
```

For convenience, we then assign more descriptive DataFrame names to the six dictionary entries:

```
In[#]:

invoice = df["Invoice"]
head = df["Invoice Head"]
lines = df["Invoice Items"]
item = df["Item"]
emp = df["Employee"]
store = df["Store"]
```

9.3.3 Table Join and Merge Exercises Using Pandas

In the following questions, we will use `merge()` to demonstrate how to join Pandas DataFrames using shared key columns. While `join()` offers similar functionality, it primarily works with DataFrame indexes. Keep in mind, in many cases, you can use `join()` as an alternative to `merge()`, depending on how your DataFrames are structured.

Q1: Combine the tables "Invoice Head", "Invoice Items", "Item", "Employee", and "Store" through merging or joining to create a unified table.

To streamline the process of joining the five DataFrames, we will use a `for-loop` to merge them all at once. First, we create a list of DataFrame names and initialize `joined` with `head` as the host table. Next, we define a list of shared keys corresponding to the columns used for joining. Using a `for-loop`, we iterate through the list of DataFrames (excluding the host table) and merge each one with the `joined` DataFrame based on its respective key using `merge()`. This approach automates the merging process and simplifies the code.

```
In[#]:

data_frames = [head, lines, item, emp, store] # Create a list of
DataFrame names
joined = data_frames[0] # Initialize `joined` with `head` as the
host table
keys = ["Invoice Number", "Item Number", "Emp ID", "Store ID"] #
Define a list of shared keys
i=0 # The counter to access keys in the for-loop

for df in data_frames[1:]:
    joined = joined.merge(df, on=keys[i], how="inner") # Merge each
table with the `joined` DataFrame based on keys
    i+=1
print(joined)

Out[#]:
```

	Invoice Number	Date	Emp ID	Item Number	Quantity	Discount	\
0	1	2023-01-01	EMP-003	PI-003	3	0.00	
1	1	2023-01-01	EMP-003	PI-012	3	0.15	
2	2	2023-01-01	EMP-006	PI-012	3	0.10	
3	3	2023-01-01	EMP-002	PI-007	3	0.15	
4	3	2023-01-01	EMP-002	PI-011	1	0.15	
...	...	...	...	...	...	...	
2011	998	2023-03-31	EMP-008	PI-001	2	0.15	
2012	999	2023-03-31	EMP-007	PI-008	1	0.00	
2013	999	2023-03-31	EMP-007	PI-004	3	0.20	
2014	1000	2023-03-31	EMP-001	PI-005	1	0.10	
2015	1000	2023-03-31	EMP-001	PI-016	2	0.00	

	Item	Cost	List Price	Quantity in Stock	Name	\
0	Jacket	25.87	43.12	44	Daniel Marquez	
1	Pen	25.07	41.79	32	Daniel Marquez	
2	Pen	25.07	41.79	32	Kristin Lee	
3	Baseball Cap	4.21	7.02	14	Valerie Gibson	
4	Stuffed Mascot	1.55	2.59	22	Valerie Gibson	
...	...	...	...	...	...	
2011	Hoodie	26.00	43.34	45	Nathaniel Marquez	
2012	Mug	27.29	45.48	38	Carol Parker	
2013	Scarf	6.79	11.32	39	Carol Parker	
2014	Gloves	13.32	22.20	17	Bradley Marshall	
2015	Handbag	10.75	17.91	16	Bradley Marshall	

	Store ID	Start Date	Weekly Payment	Store Name	\
0	ST-003	2023-02-08	1139	North	
1	ST-003	2023-02-08	1139	North	
2	ST-002	2022-01-05	1013	West	
3	ST-002	2022-04-09	1115	West	
4	ST-002	2022-04-09	1115	West	
...	...	...	...	...	
2011	ST-004	2022-09-07	1072	South	
2012	ST-003	2022-04-03	1175	North	

```
2013   ST-003 2022-04-03           1175        North
2014   ST-001 2022-09-27           1084        East
2015   ST-001 2022-09-27           1084        East

                                               Address
0              078 Cindy Shore, Los Angeles, CA 96017
1              078 Cindy Shore, Los Angeles, CA 96017
2         845 Lloyd Walk Apt. 693, Los Angeles, CA 91326
3         845 Lloyd Walk Apt. 693, Los Angeles, CA 91326
4         845 Lloyd Walk Apt. 693, Los Angeles, CA 91326
...                                               ...
2011   2320 Saunders Square Suite 940, Los Angeles, C...
2012            078 Cindy Shore, Los Angeles, CA 96017
2013            078 Cindy Shore, Los Angeles, CA 96017
2014   98982 Adam Ports Suite 231, Los Angeles, CA 91696
2015   98982 Adam Ports Suite 231, Los Angeles, CA 91696

[2016 rows x 16 columns]
```

While the for-loop above is efficient and concise, even when compared to Excel's Power Pivot, it can be made more Pythonic. The refined code snippet below uses Python's zip() function to pair elements from the "data_frames" and "keys" lists, eliminating the need for a separate index counter:

In[#]:

```
joined_zip = data_frames[0] # Initialize a new `joined_zip` with
`head` as the host table

# Merge using zip(), no idex counter is used
for df, key in zip(data_frames[1:], keys):
    joined_zip = joined_zip.merge(df, on=key, how="inner")

print(joined_zip)
```

Out[#]:

```
       Invoice Number       Date   Emp ID Item Number  Quantity  Discount \
0                   1 2023-01-01  EMP-003      PI-003         3      0.00
1                   1 2023-01-01  EMP-003      PI-012         3      0.15
2                   2 2023-01-01  EMP-006      PI-012         3      0.10
3                   3 2023-01-01  EMP-002      PI-007         3      0.15
4                   3 2023-01-01  EMP-002      PI-011         1      0.15
...               ...        ...      ...         ...       ...       ...
2011              998 2023-03-31  EMP-008      PI-001         2      0.15
2012              999 2023-03-31  EMP-007      PI-008         1      0.00
2013              999 2023-03-31  EMP-007      PI-004         3      0.20
2014             1000 2023-03-31  EMP-001      PI-005         1      0.10
2015             1000 2023-03-31  EMP-001      PI-016         2      0.00

         Item   Cost  List Price  Quantity             Name \
                                  in Stock
0      Jacket  25.87       43.12        44   Daniel Marquez
1         Pen  25.07       41.79        32   Daniel Marquez
2         Pen  25.07       41.79        32      Kristin Lee
```

```
   3   Baseball Cap   4.21        7.02       14      Valerie Gibson
   4 Stuffed Mascot   1.55        2.59       22      Valerie Gibson
 ...           ...     ...         ...      ...               ...
2011         Hoodie  26.00       43.34       45  Nathaniel Marquez
2012            Mug  27.29       45.48       38        Carol Parker
2013          Scarf   6.79       11.32       39        Carol Parker
2014         Gloves  13.32       22.20       17    Bradley Marshall
2015        Handbag  10.75       17.91       16    Bradley Marshall

      Store ID Start Date  Weekly Payment Store Name  \
0      ST-003 2023-02-08            1139      North
1      ST-003 2023-02-08            1139      North
2      ST-002 2022-01-05            1013       West
3      ST-002 2022-04-09            1115       West
4      ST-002 2022-04-09            1115       West
 ...      ...        ...             ...        ...
2011   ST-004 2022-09-07            1072      South
2012   ST-003 2022-04-03            1175      North
2013   ST-003 2022-04-03            1175      North
2014   ST-001 2022-09-27            1084       East
2015   ST-001 2022-09-27            1084       East

                                            Address
0               078 Cindy Shore, Los Angeles, CA 96017
1               078 Cindy Shore, Los Angeles, CA 96017
2         845 Lloyd Walk Apt. 693, Los Angeles, CA 91326
3         845 Lloyd Walk Apt. 693, Los Angeles, CA 91326
4         845 Lloyd Walk Apt. 693, Los Angeles, CA 91326
 ...                                             ...
2011  2320 Saunders Square Suite 940, Los Angeles, C...
2012            078 Cindy Shore, Los Angeles, CA 96017
2013            078 Cindy Shore, Los Angeles, CA 96017
2014  98982 Adam Ports Suite 231, Los Angeles, CA 91696
2015  98982 Adam Ports Suite 231, Los Angeles, CA 91696

[2016 rows x 16 columns]
```

• Complementary Note – The `zip()` Function

The `zip()` function is a built-in Python function that takes iterables (like lists, tuples, etc.), aggregates them into pairs, and returns an `iterator` of tuples. Then you may use it in a for loop or convert the zipped object to a list or a tuple.

Below is an example of using `zip()` to pair three lists:

```
In[#]:

a = [[1, 2], [3, 4], [5, 6]]
b = ["rock", "paper", "scissors"]
c = ["x", "y", "z"]

zipped = zip(a, b, c)

for num, word, var in zipped: # unpacking zipped
    print(f"List a are {num}, list b are {word}, and list c are
    {var}")
```

Out[#]:

```
List a are [1, 2], list b are rock, and list c are x
List a are [3, 4], list b are paper, and list c are y
List a are [5, 6], list b are scissors, and list c are z
```

Key Things to Know About zip()

1. zip object can only be iterated for once

Please note that zip() returns a zip object. In Python, a zip object is an iterator, and unlike iterables (such as list and tuple), iterators do not store data elements. Therefore, it can only be iterated for once. That is why, the second call of "zipped" below prints nothing since it has been exhausted by the first call (the first for-loop):

In[#]:

```
for num, word, var in zipped: # The second call of "zipped" prints
nothing
        print(f"List a are {num}, list b are {word}, and list c are
{var}")
type(zipped)
```

Out[#]:

```
zip
```

If you want to store the iterable data elements for later reuse, you may convert the zip object into a list (or a tuple) and iterate through the list as many times as you want:

In[#]:

```
zipped = zip(a, b, c)

list_of_zips = list(zipped) # Convert the zip object to a list using
the list() method

for num, word, var in list_of_zips: # Using the list to loop
print(f"List a are {num}, list b are {word}, and list c are {var}")

print(list_of_zips) # The list still exists
```

Out[#]:

```
List a are [1, 2], list b are rock, and list c are x
List a are [3, 4], list b are paper, and list c are y
List a are [5, 6], list b are scissors, and list c are z
[([1, 2], "rock", "x"), ([3, 4], "paper", "y"), ([5, 6],
"scissors", "z")]
```

2. The `shortest length` rule

By default, `zip()` uses the shortest length of all the iterables (like lists) being zipped. It pairs elements from the input lists until the shortest list is exhausted, discarding extra elements from longer lists.

```
In[#]:
a = [[1, 2], [3, 4]] # a has the shortest length
b = ["rock", "paper", "scissors"]
c = ["x", "y", "z", "test", 1, 2, 3]

zipped = zip(a, b, c)

for num, word, var in zipped: # Stops at the shortest list because
zip pairs elements one by one
print(f"List a are {num}, list b are {word}, and list c are {var}")

Out[#]:

List a are [1, 2], list b are rock, and list c are x
List a are [3, 4], list b are paper, and list c are y
```

The `zip()` function is particularly useful in linear modeling, where it pairs the dependent variable (target) with the independent variables (features), streamlining data preparation. This makes passing paired inputs into functions or models more straightforward. It is commonly used in machine learning and statistical modeling.

Q2: Compute the total and average amounts of extension and margin by store using the newly-joined dataset.
With all necessary columns present in the `joined` DataFrame, we can easily create the `Extension - Discounted` and `Margin` columns using the following code:

```
In[#]:
joined["Extension - Discounted"] = joined["List Price"] *
joined["Quantity"] * (1 - joined["Discount"])
joined["Margin"] = joined["Extension - Discounted"] -
joined["Quantity"] * joined["Cost"]
print(joined)
```

Out[#]:

	Invoice Number	Date	Emp ID	Item Number	Quantity	Discount	\
0	1	2023-01-01	EMP-003	PI-003	3	0.00	
1	1	2023-01-01	EMP-003	PI-012	3	0.15	
2	2	2023-01-01	EMP-006	PI-012	3	0.10	
3	3	2023-01-01	EMP-002	PI-007	3	0.15	
4	3	2023-01-01	EMP-002	PI-011	1	0.15	
...	...	...	...	...	...	...	
2011	998	2023-03-31	EMP-008	PI-001	2	0.15	
2012	999	2023-03-31	EMP-007	PI-008	1	0.00	
2013	999	2023-03-31	EMP-007	PI-004	3	0.20	
2014	1000	2023-03-31	EMP-001	PI-005	1	0.10	
2015	1000	2023-03-31	EMP-001	PI-016	2	0.00	

	Item	Cost	List Price	Quantity in Stock	Name	\
0	Jacket	25.87	43.12	44	Daniel Marquez	
1	Pen	25.07	41.79	32	Daniel Marquez	
2	Pen	25.07	41.79	32	Kristin Lee	
3	Baseball Cap	4.21	7.02	14	Valerie Gibson	
4	Stuffed Mascot	1.55	2.59	22	Valerie Gibson	
...	...	...	...	...	...	
2011	Hoodie	26.00	43.34	45	Nathaniel Marquez	
2012	Mug	27.29	45.48	38	Carol Parker	
2013	Scarf	6.79	11.32	39	Carol Parker	
2014	Gloves	13.32	22.20	17	Bradley Marshall	
2015	Handbag	10.75	17.91	16	Bradley Marshall	

	Store ID	Start Date	Weekly Payment	Store Name	\
0	ST-003	2023-02-08	1139	North	
1	ST-003	2023-02-08	1139	North	
2	ST-002	2022-01-05	1013	West	
3	ST-002	2022-04-09	1115	West	
4	ST-002	2022-04-09	1115	West	
...	...	...	...	...	
2011	ST-004	2022-09-07	1072	South	
2012	ST-003	2022-04-03	1175	North	
2013	ST-003	2022-04-03	1175	North	
2014	ST-001	2022-09-27	1084	East	
2015	ST-001	2022-09-27	1084	East	

	Address	\
0	078 Cindy Shore, Los Angeles, CA 96017	
1	078 Cindy Shore, Los Angeles, CA 96017	
2	845 Lloyd Walk Apt. 693, Los Angeles, CA 91326	
3	845 Lloyd Walk Apt. 693, Los Angeles, CA 91326	
4	845 Lloyd Walk Apt. 693, Los Angeles, CA 91326	
...	...	
2011	2320 Saunders Square Suite 940, Los Angeles, C...	
2012	078 Cindy Shore, Los Angeles, CA 96017	
2013	078 Cindy Shore, Los Angeles, CA 96017	
2014	98982 Adam Ports Suite 231, Los Angeles, CA 91696	
2015	98982 Adam Ports Suite 231, Los Angeles, CA 91696	

	Extension - Discounted	Margin
0	129.3600	51.7500
1	106.5645	31.3545
2	112.8330	37.6230

```
3                      17.9010    5.2710
4                       2.2015    0.6515
...                        ...       ...
2011                   73.6780   21.6780
2012                   45.4800   18.1900
2013                   27.1680    6.7980
2014                   19.9800    6.6600
2015                   35.8200   14.3200

[2016 rows x 18 columns]
```

To match the column order of the "invoice" table structure, follow the steps below to reorganize the `joined` DataFrame and save the result as a new DataFrame called `new_invoice`.

In[#]:

```python
cols = invoice.columns
cols
```

Out[#]:

```
Index(["Invoice Number", "Date", "Item Number", "Item", "Quantity",
"Discount",
       "Cost", "List Price", "Extension - Discounted", "Margin",
       "Quantity in Stock", "Emp ID", "Name", "Start Date", "Weekly
       Payment",
       "Store ID", "Store Name", "Address"],
        dtype="object")
```

In[#]:

```python
new_invoice = joined[cols] # Use invoice's column order to reorganize
the "joined" data frame
print(new_invoice)
```

Out[#]:

```
      Invoice Number        Date Item Number            Item  Quantity  \
0                  1  2023-01-01      PI-003          Jacket         3
1                  1  2023-01-01      PI-012             Pen         3
2                  2  2023-01-01      PI-012             Pen         3
3                  3  2023-01-01      PI-007    Baseball Cap         3
4                  3  2023-01-01      PI-011  Stuffed Mascot         1
...              ...         ...         ...             ...       ...
2011             998  2023-03-31      PI-001          Hoodie         2
2012             999  2023-03-31      PI-008             Mug         1
2013             999  2023-03-31      PI-004           Scarf         3
2014            1000  2023-03-31      PI-005          Gloves         1
2015            1000  2023-03-31      PI-016         Handbag         2

      Discount   Cost  List Price  Extension - Discounted    Margin  \
0         0.00  25.87       43.12                129.3600   51.7500
1         0.15  25.07       41.79                106.5645   31.3545
2         0.10  25.07       41.79                112.8330   37.6230
3         0.15   4.21        7.02                 17.9010    5.2710
4         0.15   1.55        2.59                  2.2015    0.6515
...        ...    ...         ...                     ...       ...
```

```
2011    0.15  26.00       43.34                  73.6780  21.6780
2012    0.00  27.29       45.48                  45.4800  18.1900
2013    0.20   6.79       11.32                  27.1680   6.7980
2014    0.10  13.32       22.20                  19.9800   6.6600
2015    0.00  10.75       17.91                  35.8200  14.3200

      Quantity in Stock    Emp ID               Name Start Date \
0                    44  EMP-003     Daniel Marquez 2023-02-08
1                    32  EMP-003     Daniel Marquez 2023-02-08
2                    32  EMP-006       Kristin Lee 2022-01-05
3                    14  EMP-002     Valerie Gibson 2022-04-09
4                    22  EMP-002     Valerie Gibson 2022-04-09
...                 ...      ...                ...        ...
2011                 45  EMP-008  Nathaniel Marquez 2022-09-07
2012                 38  EMP-007       Carol Parker 2022-04-03
2013                 39  EMP-007       Carol Parker 2022-04-03
2014                 17  EMP-001  Bradley Marshall 2022-09-27
2015                 16  EMP-001  Bradley Marshall 2022-09-27

      Weekly Payment Store ID Store Name \
0               1139   ST-003      North
1               1139   ST-003      North
2               1013   ST-002       West
3               1115   ST-002       West
4               1115   ST-002       West
...              ...      ...        ...
2011            1072   ST-004      South
2012            1175   ST-003      North
2013            1175   ST-003      North
2014            1084   ST-001       East
2015            1084   ST-001       East

                                              Address
0               078 Cindy Shore, Los Angeles, CA 96017
1               078 Cindy Shore, Los Angeles, CA 96017
2        845 Lloyd Walk Apt. 693, Los Angeles, CA 91326
3        845 Lloyd Walk Apt. 693, Los Angeles, CA 91326
4        845 Lloyd Walk Apt. 693, Los Angeles, CA 91326
...                                               ...
2011  2320 Saunders Square Suite 940, Los Angeles, C...
2012            078 Cindy Shore, Los Angeles, CA 96017
2013            078 Cindy Shore, Los Angeles, CA 96017
2014  98982 Adam Ports Suite 231, Los Angeles, CA 91696
2015  98982 Adam Ports Suite 231, Los Angeles, CA 91696

[2016 rows x 18 columns]
```

Now, we can create a pivot table using the new_invoice DataFrame:

In[#]:

```
pivot_new_invoice = pd.pivot_table(new_invoice, values=["Extension -
Discounted", "Margin"],
                    index="Store Name", aggfunc=["sum", "mean"])
pivot_new_invoice
```

Out[#]:

	sum		mean	
	Extension – Discounted	Margin	Extension – Discounted	Margin
Store Name				
East	23126.8215	7599.3715	45.435799	14.930003
North	21546.2335	6943.7035	44.152118	14.228901
South	24775.2655	8043.5455	48.389190	15.710050
West	22974.9715	7475.4115	45.315526	14.744401

9.4 DISCUSSIONS

Both Excel's `Power Pivot` and Pandas' `merge()` and `join()` functions offer powerful solutions for combining data from multiple tables. However, their design, use cases, and workflows differ significantly, making each tool suitable for specific tasks depending on the user's goals and technical background.

1. Excel's `Power Pivot`: Business-Focused Data Integration

`Power Pivot` is a GUI-based tool designed for business analysts and non-programmers. It simplifies data integration by enabling users to visually create relationships between tables using a drag-and-drop interface. It also supports DAX formulas, allowing for advanced calculations directly within Excel, making it ideal for building interactive reports, dashboards, and summaries. Its seamless integration with Excel's Pivot Tables and data import features makes Power Pivot a highly accessible tool for business reporting. However, `Power Pivot` is limited by Excel's memory constraints and lacks support for dynamic, query-based joins. For example, it does not explicitly provide left, right, or outer joins like SQL or Pandas.

2. Pandas' Merge and Join: Data Science and Automation

Pandas in Python provides `merge()` and `join()`, offering code-driven and highly flexible table joining capabilities. With Pandas, users can perform varying SQL-like joins, including inner, left, right, outer, and cross joins. You can also automate joins using loops, making the process highly efficient when working with larger datasets. Those features make Pandas `merge()`

and `join()` methods suitable for data scientists, engineers, and anyone dealing with large-scale data processing. Additionally, Pandas' extensibility through libraries like `SQLAlchemy` (refer to the Complementary Note below) enhances its ability to handle database operations like SQL executions. However, Pandas requires coding knowledge and lacks the intuitive, visual interface provided by Excel's `Power Pivot`.

Both tools excel at table joins, with Pandas offering greater flexibility through coding, while Power Pivot provides an accessible, no-code solution for business users. Understanding when to use each can significantly enhance your data analysis capabilities. As a business user, we recommend you use Excel's Power Pivot if you prefer a visual interface, need interactive reports, and are working with moderate-sized datasets. On the other hand, if you need advanced automation, scalable data processing, and the ability to handle large datasets, Pandas is definitely a more powerful solution.

• Complementary Note – SQLAlchemy

Pandas' integration with `SQLAlchemy` expands its capabilities from dataframe processing to enterprise-level databases. This makes it a valuable tool for data scientists working on projects that require complex data extraction, transformation, and storage. Technically, `SQLAlchemy` acts as a database abstraction layer, enabling Pandas to connect to a wide range of SQL-based databases such as PostgreSQL, MySQL, SQLite, and more.

To use `SQLAlchemy`, first install it and restart the kernel:

```
In[#]:

pip install sqlalchemy
Requirement already satisfied: sqlalchemy in /opt/anaconda3/lib/
python3.12/site-packages (2.0.34)
Requirement already satisfied: typing-extensions>=4.6.0 in /opt/
anaconda3/lib/python3.12/site-packages (from sqlalchemy) (4.11.0)
Requirement already satisfied: greenlet!=0.4.17 in /opt/anaconda3/lib/
python3.12/site-packages (from sqlalchemy) (3.0.1)
Note: you may need to restart the kernel to use updated packages.
```

In the following example, we first establish a connection to the `SQLite` database engine and write two DataFrames, df_customers and df_orders, to the database using Pandas' `to_sql()` method. Next, we define a SQL query to dynamically join the two tables, applying a simple condition for execution:

```
In[#]:

import pandas as pd
from sqlalchemy import create_engine

# Create SQLite In-Memory Database
engine = create_engine("sqlite://", echo=False)

# Sample DataFrames
df_customers = pd.DataFrame({
    "CustomerID": [1, 2, 3],
    "Name": ["Alice", "Bob", "Charlie"]
})

df_orders = pd.DataFrame({
    "OrderID": [101, 102, 103],
    "CustomerID": [1, 2, 2],
    "Product": ["Laptop", "Phone", "Tablet"]
})

# Write DataFrames to SQL Tables
df_customers.to_sql("customers", con=engine, index=False, if_exists=
"replace")
df_orders.to_sql("orders", con=engine, index=False, if_exists=
"replace")

# Execute SQL JOIN Query
query = """
SELECT customers.Name, orders.Product
FROM customers
JOIN orders ON customers.CustomerID = orders.CustomerID
WHERE customers.Name = "Bob"
"""
result = pd.read_sql_query(query, con=engine)

# Display the result
print(result)

Out[#]:

   Name Product
0  Bob    Phone
1  Bob   Tablet
```

As the example above demonstrates, Pandas' extensibility through SQLAlchemy enhances its capability to execute a variety of database operations seamlessly. This integration is particularly useful when working with large datasets, complex queries, and data pipelines that go beyond in-memory DataFrame processing.

9.5 EXERCISES

Using the concepts covered in this chapter, complete the following exercises using "Exercise-Ch09.xlsx" as your dataset.

E1: Combine the tables "**Purchase Order Head**", "**Purchase Order Items**", "**Item**", "**Supplier**", and "**Store**" through merging or joining to create a unified table "**PO**" identical to "**Purchase Order**".

E2: Compute the total and average amounts of extension by store using the newly-joined "**PO**" dataset.

Index

Printed in the United States
by Baker & Taylor Publisher Services